Live! from Marilyn's Kitchen

Live! from Marilyn's Kitchen

By Marilyn Harris

PELICAN PUBLISHING COMPANY

Gretna 2003

The word "Pelican" and the depiction of a pelican are trademarks
of Pelican Publishing Company, Inc., and are registered
in the U.S. Patent and Trademark Office.

Library of Congress Cataloging-in-Publication Data

Harris, Marilyn (Marilyn Marion)
 Live! from Marilyn's kitchen / Marilyn Harris.
   p. cm.
 ISBN 1-58980-165-2 (hardcover : alk. paper)
 1. Cookery, American. I. Title.
 TX715 .H2999 2003
 641.5973—dc21

2003011254

Printed in the United States of America

Published by Pelican Publishing Company, Inc.
1000 Burmaster Street, Gretna, Louisiana 70053

Contents

Preface

Welcome to "Cooking with Marilyn!" and welcome to my kitchen!

In 1988, someone, and I really don't remember who it was, told me that they needed a new "cooking lady" on the local talk-radio station and suggested that I go over and interview for the job. At that time the radio station was literally two blocks away from my office at a downtown-Cincinnati department store and, since a good part of my job at that time was public relations, my boss thought it sounded like a good idea. So I called to say that I would be interested in the vacancy and was invited to come around at 9 o'clock the next morning. When I reached the old WCKY building, they ushered me into a studio, put a headset on me, and stuck a microphone in my face. The "audition" was live. "Where are your books?" my co-host, Mike McMurray, asked me. Apparently, the others who had come in to audition had brought stacks of reference books. "What books?" I asked. "Do you really want me to look things up on live radio? If they ask me something I don't know, I'll just fake it." Mike grinned and said, "Okay. It's up to you." And away we went. The hour flew by. We had lots of callers, all of them as nice as could be, and I was able to answer all their questions. The station manager came by and told me to come back on Thursday. And that's how "Cooking with Marilyn!" was born. I went home and told my husband that I would be talking to people on the phone about cooking twice a week for an hour and he was astonished that someone would want to pay me to do that, since that's pretty much what I always did anyway. Mike and I worked together for a year or so and to this day I don't think he has ever figured out whether I was actually answering all those questions or just making stuff up. Well, maybe I have made up some stuff now and then, but for the most part I am lucky to have a good, solid culinary foundation and I keep learning as I go along. All my listeners have heard me say that I learn more than anyone on my show. But just so you know how I came to know those answers, I think it might be good to insert a little autobiography here.

After being nurtured on good Southern cooking and watching,

and sometimes helping, my mother turn out good, satisfying meals, I was trained in college—at Mississippi State College for Women, now Mississippi Women's University—in home economics with a specialty in food and nutrition. In New Orleans, while my husband was in graduate school at Tulane University, I worked in the public-relations area of the gas and electric utilities in the days when they encouraged us to use more energy rather than less. For the most part my job was to teach people about their kitchen appliances. It also included a lot of cooking and recipe writing and my wonderful supervisor taught me a lot about New Orleans cooking. I've had the rare opportunity to travel a good deal and to spend extended periods of time in Europe. It was there that I did my real apprenticeship: taking advanced courses in London and Paris and cooking and observing in the restaurants of some of the best chefs in the world in Lyon. Back in Cincinnati, I taught cooking classes at a shop called Hurrah! and was, in my husband's words, a "culinary circuit rider" teaching cooking in Dayton, Ohio, Lexington, Kentucky, and Bloomington, Indiana. I had a great time meeting all kinds of wonderful people and putting my love of cooking to the best possible use. A big challenge and great adventure for me was taking on the job of creating and directing "The Fourth Street Market Cooking School" in a downtown department store, Cincinnati's beloved Pogue's. I was there for eight years until it was plundered by merger-happy executives. After its demise I found the time to write my first cookbook and begin a regular column in the *Cincinnati Enquirer*, continued teaching in some great area cooking schools, and consulted on some fascinating projects in the food industry. I'm still doing all of those things and more and enjoying it.

So you see, all those years of experience were incredibly valuable to me when it came time to answer all the questions that have been put to me on the air since the 1980s. After many changes of call letters and broadcast times, and after several co-hosts, including my good friend Jan Mickelson, now at WHO in Des Moines, I have settled into a three-hour slot on Saturday afternoons on WKRC 550 AM.

I don't actually broadcast from my kitchen, which is located on the second floor of my weird old house, originally built as an artist's studio, in Clifton, the gaslight section of Cincinnati. But for this book I am inviting you into my "kitchen on the air." You will find here many of the recipes I have shared with my wonderful, loyal listeners, as well as a number they have contributed from their own kitchens. I am always telling them they are the most important ingredient on my call-in talk show. It is a cooking class of sorts, as well as the great community recipe exchange for this area.

If you are out of our broadcasting range, you can still join us on the air via the Internet on Saturday afternoons between 1:00 and 4:00 P.M. EST. Just go to www.55krc.com and click on "listen." In any case, I hope you will have fun trying some of our recipes from this book in your own kitchen.

So, welcome to the "Cooking with Marilyn!" show and to my kitchen!

P.S. Some of these recipes appeared in *More Cooking with Marilyn*. That book is long since out of print and the recipes have been updated for this publication.

Acknowledgments

This book is dedicated to the memory of Russ Wiles (February 27, 1939-March 31, 2003).

I am blessed with a host of wonderful friends. I wish I could name them all here. They are special people in my life and I can count on them to encourage me, cook, eat, and drink wine with me, and just generally make life more pleasant, whether they are sitting in my kitchen or calling me from a distant place. I would like to extend special thanks to those who contributed their recipes to the book. Their names appear with their recipes. Others who should be mentioned are: Marj Valvano, Connie Wiles, Sandy Cohan, Alice Fixx, Dave Patania, Renate and Jerry Glenn, Lana Santavicca, Sara and Hardy Friedrichsmeyer, Tori Houlihan and Dave Henry, Barbara and Klaus Jeziorkowski, Nancy Pigg, Faye Volkman, Mary and Paul Fricke, Carol and Rex Stockwell, Chris Hassall, John Mocker, Sue and Bob Dyrenforth, Sylvia and Olin Gentry, all my pals at the radio stations, Nathalie Dupree, Julia della Croce, Joyce Hendley, Shirley O. Corriher, Lila Gault, Doralece Dullaghan, Denise Fredrick, Chuck Martin, Jane Miller, Penny Peoples, Betty and Dan Hise, Laura Dickhaut, my many cooking students, all the great ladies from my "foodie" travel groups ("Marilyn and the Gastronauts"), and the whole crowd of local chef and restaurant buddies I'm proud to call my friends.

A very special word of thanks goes to Diane Bowman, who designed the jacket of this book as well as that of *The Marilyn Harris Cooking School Cookbook*.

Finally, much loving gratitude to my wonderfully helpful and patient husband. He is my writing mentor and in-house computer guru. Without him none of my books would ever have been written.

ABBREVIATIONS

Standard

tsp. = teaspoon
tbsp. = tablespoon
oz. = ounce
qt. = quart
lb. = pound

Metric

ml. = milliliter
l. = liter
g. = gram
kg. = kilogram
mg. = milligram

STANDARD-METRIC APPROXIMATIONS

$\frac{1}{8}$ teaspoon	=	.6 milliliter		
$\frac{1}{4}$ teaspoon	=	1.2 milliliters		
$\frac{1}{2}$ teaspoon	=	2.5 milliliters		
1 teaspoon	=	5 milliliters		
1 tablespoon	=	15 milliliters		
4 tablespoons	=	$\frac{1}{4}$ cup	=	60 milliliters
8 tablespoons	=	$\frac{1}{2}$ cup	=	118 milliliters
16 tablespoons	=	1 cup	=	236 milliliters
2 cups	=	473 milliliters		
$2\frac{1}{2}$ cups	=	563 milliliters		
4 cups	=	946 milliliters		
1 quart	=	4 cups	=	.94 liter

SOLID MEASUREMENTS

$\frac{1}{2}$ ounce	=	15 grams		
1 ounce	=	25 grams		
4 ounces	=	110 grams		
16 ounces	=	1 pound	=	454 grams

Substitutions

Nothing is more aggravating than to start a recipe and then discover that your pantry lacks a key ingredient. I hope that this little list will be helpful to you.

Arrowroot: for 1½ tsp. substitute ½ tsp. flour
Baking powder: for 1 tsp. substitute ¼ tsp. baking soda and ⅝ tsp. cream of tartar
Buttermilk: substitute plain yogurt or 1 tbsp. lemon juice or white vinegar mixed with milk to equal 1 cup
Chocolate, semisweet: for 1 oz. substitute ½ oz. unsweetened chocolate plus 1 tbsp. sugar
Chocolate, unsweetened: for 1 oz. substitute 3 tbsp. cocoa powder plus 1 tbsp. butter
Cornstarch for thickening: for 1 tbsp. substitute 2 tbsp. all-purpose flour
Fresh herbs: for 1 tbsp. minced substitute 1 tsp. dried
Graham-cracker crumbs: for 1 cup substitute 15 graham crackers, ground in the food processor, or 1 cup vanilla-wafer crumbs
Half and half: for 1 cup substitute ⅞ cup whole milk plus 1½ tbsp. butter
Light brown sugar: for 1 cup substitute ½ cup dark brown sugar and ½ cup granulated sugar or 1 cup granulated sugar and 1 tbsp. molasses
Mustard, prepared: for 1 tsp. substitute 1 tsp. dry mustard mixed with 2 tsp. wine vinegar, white wine, or water
Self-rising flour: for 1 cup substitute 1 cup all-purpose flour plus 1 tsp. baking powder and ⅛ tsp. salt
Sifted cake flour: for 1 cup substitute ¾ cup plus 2 tbsp. sifted all-purpose flour
Superfine sugar: substitute granulated sugar mixed in the food processor until it is powdery
White wine: for cooking, substitute dry vermouth

Live! from Marilyn's Kitchen

Breakfast and Brunch Favorites

Whether cooking up a hearty breakfast for one's own family or inviting a houseful of friends for a weekend brunch, everybody seems to love this kind of food. This chapter certainly reflects my Southern heritage. Down in Dixie, the morning meal has always been given a lot of special, loving attention. Such comforting dishes as fluffy buttermilk biscuits napped with spicy sausage gravy are likely to be more appreciated today than when I ate them at my grandmother's table. That's because we now tend to reserve them as special and somewhat indulgent treats for special occasions such as a Sunday brunch with invited guests, which is one of my favorite ways to entertain.

Not all of these recipes reflect my Southern roots. My love for the Southwest and its cuisine as well as my classic French cooking training are present too. I've selected recipes that are practical as well as yummy. Some can be made the day before while others can be whipped up on the spur of the moment. So, in the hope that more than one of your days will get off to a pleasant start because of good things to eat, I submit some of my tried and true favorites for the morning hours.

Make-Ahead Poached Eggs

A friend once returned from vacationing in a posh resort and told me about the "fancy" eggs they had for breakfast. He said they must have cooked their poached eggs in a special mold because they were all egg shaped. I smiled and told him they simply had a good breakfast chef who had learned the proper technique for poaching eggs. You don't have to be a trained chef to do it. Simply follow my directions and practice a few times before you serve poached eggs to company.

As directed in this recipe, it is okay to poach eggs hours before you serve them. Submerge them, cooked, in room-temperature water and hold them for several hours or overnight in a cool kitchen. Longer holding times should take place in the refrigerator, but then reheating is not as quick or easy.

Eggs
Water
1 tbsp. white vinegar per qt. water

- Break the eggs, one at a time, into a small bowl or custard cup.

- Pour enough water in a nonstick skillet or saucepan to cover the eggs completely. Bring to a boil and stir in the vinegar. Bring the water back to a rolling boil and reduce to a simmer.

- With a large slotted spoon, stir the water to make a small whirlpool. With the side of the bowl actually touching the water, gently slide one egg into the center of the whirlpool. Repeat quickly with remaining eggs (best not to try to do too many at a time). Keep the water below the boiling point and cook until the white is completely cooked and opaque. Cooking time depends on desired doneness. For runny yolks, remove the eggs as soon as the white is opaque and firm and covers the yolk. For firmer yolks, allow the eggs to remain in the water 3 to 4 minutes longer.

- Remove the poached eggs to a dish filled with enough room-temperature water to cover.

- Cover the dish with plastic wrap and allow to sit at room temperature until ready to serve. Just before serving, lift the eggs with a slotted spoon and slide them into a pan of hot (not boiling) water for 1 or 2 minutes to warm them. Remove with the slotted spoon. Pat quickly with a paper towel to remove excess water and serve.

Poached Egg with Quick Tomato-Hollandaise Sauce

1 slice warm ham or Canadian bacon
½ English muffin, buttered and toasted
1 poached egg
3 egg yolks
2 tbsp. fresh lemon juice
½ tsp. salt
¼ tsp. hot pepper sauce
1 stick unsalted butter, melted and very hot
1 ripe medium to large tomato, peeled, seeded, and finely chopped
1 tsp. finely shredded fresh basil leaves

- Place the ham or Canadian bacon on the English muffin. Top with the poached egg.

- Place the yolks in a food processor with steel cutting blade. Add the lemon juice, salt, and hot pepper sauce. Process until the mixture is light and fluffy. With machine running, pour in the hot butter in a steady stream. Process until mixture is thickened and fluffy. Remove to a bowl and quickly fold in the tomato and basil. Spoon some of this sauce over the poached egg.

Use your freshest eggs for poached eggs. The white is thicker and gathers around the yolk better. Eggs that have been in the refrigerator longer are best for boiling, since they are easier to peel. Always note the date on the egg carton and use within a few days after the date is expired.

Poached Egg with Dilly-Cheese Sauce

1 slice smoked salmon
½ English muffin, buttered and toasted
1 poached egg
3 tbsp. butter
¼ cup finely chopped onion
2 tbsp. flour
1 cup milk (or light cream), heated
1 tbsp. chopped fresh dill (or 1 tsp. dried)
1 cup freshly grated Parmigiano-Reggiano
Salt and freshly ground black pepper, to taste

- Place the salmon on the English muffin. Top with the poached egg.

- Melt the butter in a small, heavy saucepan. Add the onion and cook over medium heat, stirring, for 2 to 3 minutes. Stir in the flour and cook, without browning, stirring constantly for 2 minutes more.

Parmigiano-Reggiano has much more flavor when it is purchased in a piece and grated as it is needed. Wrap the cheese securely in plastic wrap and store in the refrigerator cheese drawer. A small amount can be easily grated with a hand grater, but a food processor is the quickest and most efficient way to grate larger amounts.

- Whisk in the heated milk, stirring until the mixture thickens.
- Remove from heat and stir in the dill and cheese.
- Season to taste with salt and pepper.
- Spoon some of this sauce over the poached egg.

French Pan Omelets

I don't know how many times I have demonstrated this procedure for my cooking students. I have also cooked individual pan omelets for as many as 150 people for a fund-raising brunch (with some good help, of course!). There are many times when a properly cooked omelet, some crunchy toast, and a cheerful beverage is the perfect simple brunch menu. If you want to master the omelet-making technique, you will need a good omelet pan. I prefer one with a nonstick finish. With the right pan and a little practice you should be able to turn out perfect omelets in no time. Allow me to recommend starting with small groups.

1 7- to 9-in. pan
2 large eggs
Salt and freshly ground black pepper, to taste
1 generous tbsp. butter

- Season the eggs with salt and pepper.
- Beat the eggs about 25 times with a fork.
- Place the butter in the pan.
- Over high heat, heat the butter until melted and bubbly—it should not brown.
- Let the bubbles start to subside and immediately pour in the eggs.
- Stir gently with the fork at right angles to the pan 8 or 9 times.
- Shake the pan over the heat until the eggs puff and the center is partially set.
- Place the filling across middle—at a right angle to the handle of the pan.
- With the back of a fork, fold one-third of the omelet away from you toward the center of the pan.
- Tilt the pan and let the omelet roll out, making a triple fold.
- Serve immediately on heated plates.

Mexican Omelet

Tomatoes, chopped, peeled, and seeded
Extra-virgin olive oil
Jalapeño peppers, sautéed
Onions, chopped
Sour cream
Fresh cilantro, chopped

- Lightly cook the tomatoes in oil.
- Remove the tomatoes and mix in the peppers and onions.
- Fill the omelet with the mixture. Top the finished omelet with sour cream and cilantro.

Avocado and Bacon Omelet

Avocado slices
Crisp bacon pieces
Sour cream
Fresh dill, chopped

- Fill the omelet with avocado and bacon. Top the omelet with sour cream and dill.

Mushroom and Brie Omelet

Mushrooms, sliced
Shallots, finely chopped
Parsley, chopped
Butter
1 small slice Brie (rind removed)

- Sauté mushrooms, shallots, and parsley in butter. Add the Brie.
- Fill omelet with the mixture. Top the finished omelet with parsley.

Southwestern Brunch Eggs

For those brunches that are really more lunch than breakfast, try this egg dish with a Mexican flavor. If it looks like a lot of trouble to make in the morning, simply plan ahead and make the onion-tomato sauce the day before. You only have to reheat the sauce and proceed with the egg-cooking step.

Store garlic and onions in a cool, dry place and in a basket or other container that "breathes."

8 strips bacon, diced
2 tbsp. olive or vegetable oil
2 large red Spanish onions, coarsely chopped
2 cloves garlic, finely chopped
2 fresh jalapeño peppers, seeded and finely chopped
1 4-oz. can chopped mild green chiles
1 28-oz. can diced plum tomatoes, drained
½ tsp. salt, or to taste
Hot pepper sauce, to taste
¼ cup chopped fresh cilantro
8 large eggs
1 cup shredded jack cheese
Extra chopped cilantro, for garnish
Vegetable oil, for frying tortillas
8 corn tortillas

• Fry the bacon in a large heavy skillet until crisp. Remove with a slotted spoon to drain on paper towels. Pour the bacon fat from the skillet.

• Heat the oil in the skillet. Sauté the onions, garlic, and jalapeño peppers over medium heat, stirring often, until the onions are tender.

• Stir in the canned chiles and the tomatoes. Season with salt and hot pepper sauce and return the bacon pieces. Cook, stirring often, over medium-high heat for 15 minutes.

• Stir in the fresh cilantro.

• Break the eggs, one at a time, into a small bowl. Carefully place them on top of the onion mixture, spacing them so they will cover the top of the sauce when done. Cover the skillet and cook for 5 to 8 minutes or until the yolks are set but not hard.

• Sprinkle the top of each egg with cheese and return the lid just until the cheese is melted.

- Sprinkle with the extra chopped cilantro.
- In about 1 in. vegetable oil in a small, heavy skillet, fry the tortillas until they are crisp. Drain on paper towels and place on a paper-towel-lined baking sheet in a warm oven until ready to serve.
- With a large cooking spoon, remove 1 egg with some of the onion mixture under it and place on 1 crisp tortilla. Repeat with remaining eggs. Spoon any extra sauce around the tortillas.
- Serves 4 to 8.

Eggs Mexicana

For a brunch on a warm, sunny morning, a chilled dish can be special and fun. I love to serve this one outdoors. It is practical, too, because almost all of the preparation can be done hours ahead. Hold everything in the refrigerator: the sauce, the eggs, and the washed and dried lettuce leaves. Wait until shortly before serving time to slice the avocados and assemble this colorful and tasty dish. It looks beautiful arranged on a large cheerful platter. Serve it with some warm corn tortillas and fresh fruit, and your guests will love it.

2 tbsp. extra-virgin olive oil
½ cup chopped yellow onion
2 cloves garlic, finely chopped
2 roasted mild green chiles, peeled, seeded, and chopped
2-3 jalapeño peppers, seeded and finely chopped
4 medium tomatoes, peeled and coarsely diced
2 tbsp. red-wine vinegar
2 tbsp. chopped cilantro
½ tsp. salt
1 tsp. sugar
1 cup mayonnaise
1 cup sour cream
2 ripe avocados
Fresh lemon juice
8 hard-cooked eggs
Crisp lettuce leaves
Cilantro, for garnish

Roasting mild green chiles such as anaheim or poblano brings out their best flavors. To roast peppers, preheat oven to 400 degrees. Place a baking sheet on bottom rack to catch any drips. Place the peppers directly on the rack and roast until skin is puffed and brown and peppers are tender. Remove with tongs or a long-handled fork to a plastic bag with a resealable top. Close the bag immediately and allow the peppers to cool sealed in the bag. They sweat as they cool, softening the skin and making peeling much easier. Peel, remove the stems, and scrape out the seeds. The stringy veins on the insides should be removed.

- Heat the oil in a skillet. Sauté the onion and garlic for 3 to 4 minutes. Stir in the mild chiles and jalapeños, remove from the heat, and let cool. Put into a bowl and mix with the tomatoes, vinegar, cilantro, salt, and sugar.
- Gently stir the tomato mixture into the mayonnaise and sour cream. Chill until serving time.
- At serving time, peel and slice the avocados. Acidulate with lemon juice. Place the whole, peeled eggs on a bed of crisp lettuce and spoon over the sauce to cover well. Surround with the avocado slices and garnish with cilantro.
- Serves 8.

Sausage-Mushroom Frittata

An egg dish with Italian origins, a frittata can have as many flavors as you have ingredients in the refrigerator. In fact, it's a good way to use up leftovers. Another favorite flavor combination is cubed boiled potatoes and ham with a flavorful cheese such as Gruyere. Tomatoes, onion, and just enough garlic and fresh basil to flavor it make a glorious frittata for a summer morning. I also often grate in a bit of Parmigiano-Reggiano, my favorite cheese.

> 1 lb. spicy pork sausage, crumbled
> 2 tbsp. butter
> 1 large sweet salad onion, halved and thinly sliced
> 8 oz. mushrooms, washed and thinly sliced
> 2 tbsp. chopped flat-leaf parsley
> ½ tsp. salt, or to taste
> 10 large eggs
> Dash hot pepper sauce
> 6 oz. (1½ cups) shredded Swiss or Gruyere cheese

- Cook the sausage in a heavy skillet, stirring occasionally, until all the red is gone. Remove with a slotted spoon to a paper-towel-lined dish.
- Heat the butter in a 10-in. nonstick skillet.

When a recipe calls for "sweet salad onion," you may choose from Red Spanish Onions, which are generally available year round; Vidalia, the sweet onion from Georgia and the first of the sweet varieties to appear in the market each year (late spring through midsummer); and Texas Sweets, New Mexico Sweet Onions, Hawaiian Maui Onions, and Walla Wallas from Washington, all of which are harvested in the summer and early fall. In the winter, we get good sweet onions from South America. All of these onions are meant to be eaten raw and should always be only lightly cooked for best flavor.

- Add the sliced onion and sauté 5 minutes or until softened.
- Add the mushrooms. Sauté about 3 minutes more or just until the mushrooms are cooked but still firm. Sprinkle in the parsley and salt.
- Stir in the sausage.
- Whisk together the eggs, hot-pepper sauce, and 1 cup cheese. Pour over the vegetables.
- Sprinkle over the remaining cheese.
- Place the skillet in a preheated 375-degree oven and bake for 15 to 20 minutes, or until a knife inserted near the middle comes out clean and the mixture is puffed.
- Cut into wedges and serve immediately.
- Serves 6-8.

Bacon and Onion Quiche

Quiche is not as popular a brunch or luncheon dish as it was, but this classic savory French pie is always well received when properly executed and filled with an interesting combination of flavors. This particular recipe is ideal for brunch. If you don't have a food processor and don't want to go to the trouble of making the French butter pastry, simply make a basic American-style crust using vegetable shortening. One final word about this recipe: buy a flavorful, good-quality bacon. My favorites are the ones smoked with apple wood.

    1 recipe Pâte Brisée (see below)
    6 strips thick-cut peppered bacon, diced
    4 large eggs
    ½ cup light cream
    Pinch freshly grated nutmeg
    ½ tsp. salt
    Dash freshly ground black pepper
    3 tomatoes, peeled and seeded
    3 tbsp. butter
    2 medium onions, halved and thinly sliced
    ½ tsp. dried oregano
    Pinch sugar

1 tsp. salt
¼ tsp. freshly ground black pepper
2 tbsp. chopped flat-leaf parsley
¾ cup grated Emmenthaler (or other natural
   Swiss) cheese

- Make the pastry according to the following recipe and prebake it as directed. Set aside to cool.
- Brown the bacon, stirring, in a heavy skillet. Remove with a slotted spoon to a paper-towel-lined dish.
- Whisk together the eggs, cream, nutmeg, ½ tsp. salt, and dash pepper. Set aside.
- Coarsely chop the tomatoes; set aside.
- Melt the butter in a heavy skillet and sauté the onions until just tender.
- Add the tomatoes and stir until the excess liquid is evaporated. Season with oregano, sugar, 1 tsp. salt, and ¼ tsp. pepper. Stir in the parsley.
- Spoon the tomato mixture, cheese, and bacon into the bottom of the prebaked pastry.
- Pour over the egg mixture.
- Bake in a preheated 375-degree oven for 30 to 35 minutes or until puffed and golden.

Pâte Brisée

1½ cups unbleached flour
½ tsp. salt
1 egg yolk
1 stick cold unsalted butter, cut into 8 pieces
4 to 5 tbsp. ice water

- Blend together the flour, salt, egg yolk, and butter, either with two table knives or the steel cutting blade of the food processor, until the mixture resembles coarse meal.
- Add the ice water and process or stir until pastry is moist. Pat into a disc and wrap in plastic wrap. Chill for at least 2 hours.
- Let the pastry warm up enough to be pliable, and roll out on a lightly floured surface to a large, thin (about ⅛ in. thickness) circle. Roll this around the pastry rolling pin and gently place into an 11-in. removable-bottom tart pan. Gently fit loosely into

pan, letting dough fall into place. Roll off the excess and press remaining pastry firmly onto sides of pan. Cover with parchment paper and pour in pie weights.

• Bake in bottom third of a preheated 400-degree oven for 10 minutes. Remove the paper and weights and bake about 2 minutes longer, just until the dough is set and baked. Let cool before filling.

Note: Removable-bottom tart pans are originally from France and can be found in specialty kitchen stores. They are designed with a bottom and sides that separate. After the quiche is baked and properly cooled, set it on something smaller in diameter and allow the sides to fall away. The bottom will still hold the quiche. It looks prettier and is easier to serve when the sides of the pastry are no longer covered by the pan. If you don't have an 11-in. removable-bottom tart pan, bake this quiche in a 10-in. pie pan.

Ham and Leek Tart

The time and energy required to make this tart are sure to be rewarded when you hear the compliments from your guests. In fact, if you have a food processor for making the pastry dough, it isn't a complicated dish at all. It is a good brunch main dish because it can be made entirely ahead. It is, however, preferable to make and prebake the pastry and have the ingredients for the filling ready to assemble so that all that remains in the morning is to mix the filling, pour it into the pastry shell, and bake. There is a flavor and texture advantage to serving such a tart fresh from the oven. After telling you that, I will say that I have made it the night before, served it warmed in a preheated 300-degree oven for 15 to 20 minutes, and heard no complaints. A dish of seasonal fresh fruit and some well-chilled champagne are all that are needed to complete the brunch menu. It's perfect for a small group.

    1 recipe Pâte Brisée (see above)
    2 medium leeks
    2 tbsp. olive oil
    1 tbsp. unsalted butter
    1½ tsp. chopped fresh thyme leaves (or ½ tsp.
       dried)
    Pinch salt

Washing leeks properly and thoroughly is important because they grow in sandy soil and often contain a lot of grit. Cut away the tough part of the green top. (Wash and save for flavoring stocks.) Trim the root end. Slice and wash thoroughly by soaking in lukewarm water. To leave it whole, place the trimmed leek on a cutting board and cut, lengthwise, three-fourths of the way through. Soak in lukewarm water for a few minutes. Then, hold under a steady stream of lukewarm water, pulling away the layers with your thumbs. Rinse away all of the grit.

Lukewarm water does the best job of washing away grit from herbs and vegetables. It is also more comfortable on the hands.

4 oz. thinly sliced prosciutto or Westphalian ham, cut into julienne strips
1 tbsp. flour
4 large eggs
1 cup heavy cream
⅛ tsp. cayenne pepper
½ tsp. salt

- Prepare the pastry according to the recipe above.
- Trim the leeks and slice crosswise into ¼-in. rounds. Put them into a sink of lukewarm water and wash thoroughly. Drain.
- Heat the oil and butter together in a heavy skillet. Sauté the leeks, stirring, until just tender. Season with thyme and a pinch of salt. Stir in the ham.
- Sprinkle over the flour and cook 2 minutes longer, stirring—without browning the flour. Place the leek mixture in the pre-baked pastry, distributing evenly.
- Whisk together the eggs, cream, pepper, and salt. Pour over the leek mixture just before ready to bake.
- Bake in the bottom third of a preheated 375-degree oven for about 30 minutes or until puffed and golden.
- Let cool 10 minutes before serving. Serve warm.
- Serves 8.

Crustless Quiche

This recipe goes back a number of years to when quiche was on every restaurant's menu. I taught classes at Cincinnati's first real gourmet kitchen shop and cooking school, a charming place called Hurrah! One of my most popular classes was "Quiches, Soufflés, and Omelets." This quick and easy recipe is not a real "quiche" but was a favorite of my students. It is still as a standby for a quick Sunday brunch entree.

2 tbsp. butter
1 medium onion, halved and thinly sliced
1½ cups cubed ham
½ cup chopped parsley
1 cup shredded Swiss cheese
6 eggs
1½ cups half and half
½ cup biscuit mix
1 tsp. salt
¼ tsp. hot pepper sauce
Dash nutmeg

- Melt the butter in a skillet. Add the onion and sauté for 2 to 3 minutes, stirring.
- Stir in the ham and parsley.
- Spoon into a buttered 9- or 10-in. pie pan. Sprinkle over the cheese.
- In a blender, blend the eggs, cream, biscuit mix, salt, and seasonings. Pour into the pie pan.
- Bake in the center of a preheated 375-degree oven for 35 to 45 minutes or until puffed and golden brown.
- Let cool about 10 minutes before cutting into wedges.
- Serves 8.

Flat-leaf or Italian parsley is always preferable as a flavoring ingredient because it has considerably more flavor than the curly variety.

Ham and Asparagus Gougere

Even a novice cook need not be intimidated by the French name or the number of ingredients and steps in this most delicious dish. A gougere is based on that delightfully light and elegant pastry, pâte à chou, which is the same pastry used for cream puffs. A food processor makes the pastry foolproof. The filling is not at all difficult and can, in fact, be made the night before, covered, and stored in the refrigerator. This pretty dish is an excellent main-course choice for brunch for a small group and makes a lovely presentation when it comes out of the oven to go directly onto your table. It's a dish I have often served for a spring brunch, just when the first asparagus comes into season. It is perfect for an Easter brunch as well as an elegant way to use up leftover ham. Just add some fresh fruit for a lovely, complete meal.

Pâte à Chou

1 cup water
1 stick butter or margarine, cut into 8 pieces
¼ tsp. salt
1 cup all-purpose flour
4 large eggs
½ cup shredded Swiss cheese

- Place the water, butter, and salt in a small saucepan. Bring to a rolling boil. (The butter should be melted.) Stir in the flour all at once and stir vigorously until mixture forms a ball of dough that leaves the sides of the pan. Remove from heat and set aside to cool for 5 minutes. Put into the food processor with steel blade in place. Add the eggs. Process until mixture is shiny and very sticky. Add the cheese and process just to mix.

- Grease a 10- or 11-in. round baking dish and spoon the pastry in a ring around the edge. Make the filling and spoon the filling in the center. Top with the 1 cup cheese.

- Place in the center of a preheated 400-degree oven for 40 to 45 minutes or until the pastry is puffed and golden brown. Sprinkle with the parsley and serve at once.

Filling

4 tbsp. butter or margarine
1 large onion, thinly sliced
8 oz. fresh mushrooms, cleaned and sliced

2 tbsp. flour
½ cup chicken broth, heated
½ cup light cream or whole milk
1 tbsp. dry sherry
Salt, to taste
Generous dash hot pepper sauce
2 cups cubed cooked ham
**1 lb. asparagus, cut into 1-in. pieces and cooked
   until crisp-tender**
1 cup (4 oz.) shredded Swiss cheese
2 tbsp. chopped parsley

- Melt the butter in a large heavy pan. Over high heat, sauté the onion for 2 minutes, stirring. Add the mushrooms and sauté for 2 to 3 minutes, stirring. Reduce the heat to medium and add the flour. Cook, stirring constantly, for 2 minutes without browning. Whisk in the chicken broth and cook until thickened. Whisk in the cream and sherry and whisk until smooth and bubbly. Season to taste with the salt and hot pepper sauce. Remove from the heat and stir in the ham and asparagus. Spoon into the baking dish and follow the above directions.

- Serves 6-8.

Crepe Batter

I am well aware of the fact that crepes are not as fashionable in culinary circles in this country as they once were. But a perfectly done French pancake—all golden, thin, and delicate—will never go out of style. Furthermore, it is such an ideal main course for brunch any season of the year. It is also a good choice for the busy host or hostess who wants to do the cooking and still enjoy the guests. All of the preparation can be done ahead. The actual crepes can be made days ahead. After they are cooled, freeze them in thin stacks in heavy-duty foil. They are then ready to be thawed overnight on the counter and popped into a hot oven in their foil package just long enough to be reheated. The warm crepes are easily separated, ready to be filled with your favorite fillings. The filling can be made the night before, covered tightly, and chilled. All that's left is to fill the crepes and bake them until hot through. A side dish of fresh marinated veggies or a colorful bowl of assorted fruits can be made ahead and chilled. And you can, indeed, enjoy the party along with your guests.

An easy way to cook asparagus that keeps its good flavor and texture is to roast it in a hot oven. Simply break away the tough ends and wash the asparagus. Drain well. Place in a single layer in a shallow baking pan. Sprinkle with just enough extra-virgin olive oil to lightly coat each spear. Season lightly with some coarse sea salt. Place the open pan in a preheated 450-500-degree oven. Roast for 10 to 15 minutes, depending on the thickness of the asparagus spears. (The thick ones are preferable.) When the asparagus is done, it should be crisp-tender.

It is not necessary to have a special crepe pan to make crepes. Any small skillet with shallow sides will do. The pan should have a nonstick coating or be seasoned by thickly coating the inside with vegetable oil and heating until very hot. Allow to cool and pour off the oil. Wipe out the skillet with a paper towel. Do not wash with detergent and hot water; rather, rinse with hot water alone and dry over a burner. Such a seasoned pan should be reserved only for crepes and omelets.

The following crepe batter is used for savory crepes. The batter is more likely to be lump free when made in the blender. The resting period is important for the proper texture of the finished crepe since it allows the flour particles to dissolve thoroughly in the liquid.

1 cup water
1 cup milk
4 large eggs
½ tsp. salt
2 cups all-purpose flour
4 tbsp. melted unsalted butter or margarine

- Place all the ingredients in the order listed into a blender. Cover and blend at top speed for 1 minute. Place in a covered container and let rest at least 2 hours at room temperature (or overnight in the refrigerator). The batter should be the consistency of heavy cream. If it is too thick, whisk in a bit more water or milk.

- Ladle just enough batter to lightly cover the bottom of a greased preheated crepe pan (or small skillet). Cook on the first side until the batter is completely set. Turn and cook for about 15 seconds on the second side. Invert the pan to remove each crepe to a side dish.

- Makes about 18 to 20 8- or 9-in. crepes.

Shrimp and Mushroom Crepes

1 recipe Crepe Batter (see above)
3 tbsp. butter or margarine
½ cup chopped onion
1 clove garlic, finely chopped
1 lb. fresh mushrooms, washed, trimmed, and
  thinly sliced
¼ cup dry sherry
1 lb. cooked shrimp (cut into pieces if large)
¼ cup chopped parsley
1½ tsp. fresh thyme leaves
2 tbsp. butter or margarine
2 tbsp. flour

1 cup milk, heated
½ tsp. salt
Dash nutmeg
Dash hot pepper sauce
1 cup shredded Swiss cheese
1 recipe Mornay Sauce (see below)
1 or 2 cups extra shredded Swiss cheese for top

- Make the Crepe Batter and cook 18 crepes ahead of time.
- Melt the 3 tbsp. butter or margarine in a large, heavy skillet. Over high heat, sauté the onion and garlic, stirring, for 3 minutes. Stir in the mushrooms and sauté for 2 to 3 minutes. Add the sherry and cook until all the liquid is evaporated. Remove from the heat and stir in the shrimp, parsley, and thyme. Set aside.
- In a heavy saucepan, melt the 2 tbsp. butter. Stir in the flour and cook, stirring, over medium heat for 2 minutes. Do not brown. Whisk in the milk and cook, stirring, until thickened. Season. Remove from heat and stir in the cheese, stirring until melted. Stir the sauce into the mushroom mixture.
- Reheat the crepes and fill by spooning a couple of large spoonfuls of the filling into the center of each crepe. Roll up and place, seam side down, in a shallow greased baking dish. Cover well and chill until ready to heat and serve.

Mornay Sauce

4 tbsp. butter or margarine
4 tbsp. flour
3 cups milk, heated
1 tsp. salt, or to taste
¼ tsp. hot pepper sauce
1 cup shredded Swiss cheese

- Melt the butter in a heavy saucepan. Stir in the flour and cook, stirring, over medium heat for 2 to 3 minutes. Do not brown. Whisk in the hot milk. Season. Off the heat, stir in the cheese until melted.
- To finish the crepes, spoon over just enough of the Mornay Sauce to cover each crepe; sprinkle with shredded Swiss cheese and bake in a 350 degree oven until hot through—about 20 minutes. Serve hot.
- Makes 18 filled crepes.

Marilyn's Souffléed Spoon Bread

This is a much-requested recipe from my "Quiches, Soufflés, and Omelets" classes. Spoon bread is a traditional Southern treat and this version uses the techniques of a soufflé to make it lighter and more elegant. It is a rich but very tasty treat.

> 3 cups milk (whole or 2 percent)
> ⅔ cup yellow cornmeal (preferably stone ground)
> 1 tsp. salt
> 1 tbsp. sugar
> 5 tbsp. unsalted butter or margarine
> 3 large egg yolks
> 5 large egg whites, room temperature
> 1 tsp. white vinegar

- Bring the milk to a slow boil in a heavy, nonreactive saucepan. Slowly stir in the cornmeal, 1 tbsp. at a time. (If a lump should form, use a whisk and beat until smooth.) Add the salt and sugar. Cook, stirring, until mixture thickens—about 5 minutes.

- Stir in the butter. Remove from heat.

- Beat the egg yolks until fluffy and lemon colored. Stir into the cornmeal mixture.

- Beat the egg whites with the vinegar until stiff peaks form. (Mixture should be shiny. Do not beat until dry.)

- Stir approximately one-fourth of the whites into the cornmeal mixture. With a rubber spatula, lightly fold in the remaining whites.

- Turn into a well-greased 1½-qt. (6-cup) soufflé dish (or any straight-sided casserole).

- Preheat the oven to 400 degrees. Place the dish in the center, reduce the heat to 375, and bake for 40 to 45 minutes or until mixture is golden and puffed.

- Serve immediately.

- Serves 8-10.

Rules for beating egg whites: Egg whites must be free of any yolk and should be room temperature for beating. Beat in a clean, dry bowl. As soon as they are stiff, and still shiny, cease beating.

Southern Buttermilk Biscuits

Down South where I grew up, it simply wasn't breakfast without biscuits. Nobody thought much about biscuits. They just made them, usually without consulting a recipe. Everybody's grandmother had the recipe in her head. But biscuits are a good example of a simple formula that always manages to be more difficult than it seems. I have encountered a lot of questions over the years about biscuit successes and failures. There is obviously no one simple answer. Starting with the right flour is certainly one of the answers. Soft wheat flour is a necessary ingredient to make a biscuit with the proper texture. It is not necessary to use buttermilk, but I think true Southern biscuits are made with buttermilk. (And if you do choose to use what we Southerners call sweet milk, leave out the baking soda.) The biscuit dough should be sticky and wet, so a heavily floured board is needed for the rolling and cutting step. If enough flour is added to make a firm, nonsticky dough, you are sure to have heavy biscuits. Oh well. As I often say to my radio-show callers, you are not making the atom bomb, just dinner. In this case, it is just biscuits and there is no question that one of the secrets is practice. All our grandmothers could vouch for that.

> 2 cups all-purpose soft wheat flour
> 2 tsp. baking powder
> ½ tsp. baking soda
> ½ tsp. salt
> ½ cup solid vegetable shortening (such as Crisco)
> 1 cup buttermilk
> ½ to ¾ cup extra flour, for flouring board and biscuit
>   cutter

- Into a mixing bowl, sift together the flour, baking powder, soda, and salt.

- Add the shortening. Using a wire pastry blender or two forks, quickly cut in the shortening until the mixture resembles very coarse meal. Pour in the milk. Lightly mix just until the milk is mixed in and a soft dough forms.

- Generously flour a large board. Turn the dough out onto the board, coating the bottom side. Quickly turn to coat the other side. Pat out with floured hands or gently roll with a floured rolling pin to ¹/₂- to ³/₄-in. thickness. Cut out with a 2¹/₂- to 3-in. biscuit cutter. Cut close together, using as much dough as possible to avoid reshaping and rolling again.

- Place the biscuits with sides touching in a greased 9-in. cake pan.
- Bake in the center of a preheated 450-degree oven for about 10 minutes, or until golden brown.
- Serve hot.
- Makes about 15 medium biscuits.

Note: For a variation, add ½ tsp. coarsely ground black pepper to the dry ingredients and 1 tbsp. finely shredded fresh basil leaves along with the buttermilk.

Southern Sausage Balls in Cream Gravy

I know that most of us are trying hard to eat healthier, which almost caused me to leave this recipe out of the book. I have limited myself to making it only once a year for my annual Christmas Brunch. But I reconsidered when I remembered how my guests always look forward to this dish. My dear friend and fellow Southerner Russ Wiles always loved this concoction and my much-loved brother-in-law Rege Jensen jealously guarded a batch I made up one holiday season at his house. Even if you only make this recipe once a year, it is worth having. It is a wonderful breakfast or brunch treat on a cold winter day. Be sure to use a good grade of flavorful, spicy pork sausage.

1 lb. spicy pork sausage
5 tbsp. butter or margarine
5 tbsp. flour
3 cups whole milk, heated
1 tsp. salt
½ tsp. freshly ground black pepper

- Form the sausage into small balls. Fry in a large, heavy skillet until cooked through and golden brown. Remove from the pan with a slotted spoon. Pour the sausage drippings from the pan. (Do not wipe out or wash.)
- Return the skillet to the heat and melt the butter or margarine. Add the flour and cook over medium heat, stirring constantly for 3 minutes.

- Whisk in the hot milk, salt, and pepper. Cook, stirring, until mixture bubbles and thickens. Add the cooked sausage balls and cook in the gravy for a few minutes.
- Serve hot over split Southern Buttermilk Biscuits.
- Makes 4 cups.

Beignets

I started my cooking career in New Orleans, and that experience has had a great influence on my recipe repertoire as well as my style of cooking. If you have ever visited that fascinating city, you know how much everyone loves their little French raised doughnuts called "beignets." If you go to visit, be sure to stop in a cafe to indulge in some of those sugar-coated treats with a cup of the traditional cafe au lait. Though you may have tried making your own beignets with the popular mix sold in New Orleans, the good news is that they are quite easily made from scratch. They are ideal, too, for a weekend-company breakfast, since the dough is best made the night before. It rises slowly in the refrigerator and the chilled dough is easily rolled and cut into squares, ready to toss into some hot oil for a very short cooking time. Remove to a paper-towel-lined tray for a short draining time and then sprinkle liberally with powdered sugar. Serve hot to what are guaranteed to be very happy guests!

½ cup boiling water
2 tbsp. vegetable shortening
¼ cup sugar
½ tsp. salt
½ cup evaporated milk
1 pkg. dry yeast
¼ cup warm water (105 to 115 degrees)
1 large egg, lightly beaten
3¼-3¾ cups all-purpose flour
Vegetable oil, for frying
Powdered sugar, sifted

- Pour the boiling water over the shortening, sugar, and salt.
- Stir until the shortening is melted. Add the milk and let stand until the mixtures cools to 115 degrees.

- Dissolve the yeast in the ¼ cup warm water and stir into the cooled milk mixture. Add the egg.
- Stir in 2 cups of the flour and beat well with a wooden spoon. Stir in enough flour to make a soft dough.
- Place in a greased bowl and cover with plastic wrap. Place in the refrigerator overnight.
- Pat or roll dough on a lightly floured surface to ¼-in. thickness. Cut into small squares—approximately 2 in. square.
- Heat about 4 in. vegetable oil in a deep skillet or saucepan to 375 degrees. Drop the doughnuts into the hot oil with the top surface down.
- When doughnuts float to the top, turn once and brown on the second side. Remove with a slotted spoon to a paper-towel-covered tray. Sprinkle with the powdered sugar while still hot.
- Serve immediately.
- Makes about 2½ dozen.

Golden-Raisin Scones

I never think my scones taste quite as good as many of the delicious ones I've enjoyed at tea time in England and Scotland. I'm sure one of the reasons is because our flours are different. Then there is that wonderfully indulgent clotted cream they always serve to spread on the scones! One year during a stay in a fabulous old country house in Devon, home of the famous Devonshire cream and butter, I enjoyed every calorie from my daily scones and clotted cream. Nevertheless, I always come back home and do my best to duplicate the highlights of those culinary adventures so I can share them with my students. I adapted this recipe for the food processor. I think these scones almost make up in ease and convenience for what they may lack in authenticity and I never seem to have any left over.

      3 cups all-purpose flour
      ⅓ cup sugar
      1 tbsp. baking powder
      1 tsp. salt
      1½ sticks (12 tbsp.) cold unsalted butter
      1 cup milk

¾ **cup golden raisins**
1 tsp. freshly grated orange rind
1 tbsp. milk
2 tbsp. sugar (coarse crystal, if available)

- In the food processor bowl, combine the flour, ⅓ cup sugar, baking powder, and salt.
- Cut the cold butter into 12 pieces and sprinkle over the top of the dry ingredients.
- Process, pulsing on and off, until the mixture resembles coarse fresh breadcrumbs.
- Add 1 cup milk, the raisins, and orange rind. Process for a few seconds, just until the dry ingredients are moistened (important not to overmix).
- Remove from the processor bowl directly onto a floured board. Knead lightly just to gather together into a smooth mass.
- Gently pat into a circle ½ in. thick.
- Cut with a 2½-3-in. floured biscuit cutter.
- Place the scones on an ungreased baking sheet. Using a soft-bristle pastry brush, brush the tops lightly with 1 tbsp. milk. Sprinkle with 2 tbsp. sugar.
- Bake in the upper third of a preheated 425-degree oven for about 12 minutes or until golden brown.
- Serve hot with butter and jam.
- Makes about 18.

Easy Batter Yeast Rolls

We Southerners are accustomed to eating freshly baked yeast rolls at all hours of the day. This is an old-fashioned recipe that I adapted to modern methods and ingredients: quick-rise yeast for faster rising and the food processor or mixer with dough hook for effortless mixing. They are really fast and easy enough to make in the morning to serve for a mid-day brunch, but it is even easier if the dough is made the night before and allowed a "cool rise" in the refrigerator. It will take a bit longer for the chilled dough to double and be ready to go into the oven, but it's a

When cutting biscuits or scones, be sure to push the cutter straight into the dough and lift straight up. Do not twist the cutter before removing it. Twisting it will press the edges of the dough together and inhibit rising. Cut biscuits as close together as possible, as twice-rolled dough tends to toughen.

convenient way to serve delicious hot bread for a late weekend breakfast or brunch. Try these rolls spread with plenty of butter and your favorite strawberry preserves.

> 2 pkg. quick-rise dry yeast
> 1 cup warm water (105 to 115 degrees)
> 1½ cups milk, scalded
> ¼ cup sugar
> 1½ tsp. salt
> 3 large eggs
> 1 stick unsalted butter or margarine, softened
> 5½ cups all-purpose flour

- Dissolve the yeast in warm water in a large mixer or food-processor bowl.
- Add the milk, which has been cooled to at least 115 degrees. Add the sugar, salt, eggs, butter, and 2½ cups of the flour.
- Mix for 1 minute, scraping sides of bowl, then beat for 2 minutes more.
- Add the remaining flour and mix until smooth.
- Cover the bowl and let rise in a warm place until doubled—about 45 minutes. (Or place a sheet of greased plastic wrap directly on top of the dough. Cover the bowl with foil and place in the refrigerator overnight.)
- Stir down with a wooden spoon. Spoon into well-greased muffin tins.
- Let rise until doubled—30 to 45 minutes (depending on temperature of dough).
- Bake in the center of a preheated 350-degree oven for 25-30 minutes or until golden brown. Let cool for 5 minutes in the pan before removing.
- Serve warm.
- Makes 18 large rolls.

Always scald milk in a nonreactive pan to prevent it from discoloring. It is "scalded" when bubbles form around the edge.

Yeast dough is best risen at a temperature of 90 to 95 degrees. An easy method: Place a pot of boiling water in the oven. Place the covered dough on the rack above it and close the oven door to contain the heat from the water.

One-Bowl Coffee Cake

Another quick and easy favorite, this tasty breakfast cake falls into my group of pantry-shelf recipes. That means that all of the ingredients are usually on hand, so you can decide on a lazy weekend morning that you are in the mood for a treat, simply get out all of the stuff, and throw it together. It requires only one bowl and one pan too! While it bakes, the aromas will stir even the sleepiest members of the household, and its warm broiled topping is simply scrumptious.

> 1⅓ cups sifted flour
> 4 tsp. baking powder
> 1 tsp. salt
> 1 tsp. cinnamon
> 1⅓ cups quick-cooking oats
> Grated rind of 1 orange
> ⅔ cup brown sugar
> 1 cup milk (whole or 2 percent)
> ⅔ cup melted butter or margarine
> 2 eggs, lightly beaten

- Sift together the flour, baking powder, salt, and cinnamon.
- Mix in the oats, rind, and sugar.
- Add the milk and butter to the eggs, and pour into the center of the dry ingredients. Stir just enough to moisten.
- Spread the batter into a greased 9-in. cake pan.
- Bake in a 450-degree oven for 30 minutes.

Topping

> ½ cup light brown sugar
> 2 tbsp. melted butter or margarine
> ½ cup chopped nuts (pecans or walnuts)

- Combine the ingredients and spread over the baked cake.
- Broil 3 minutes, or until the topping is bubbly.

The secret to fluffy quick breads, meaning bread, coffee cake, or muffins that are leavened with baking powder and/or baking soda, is to use a very light hand when mixing. After the dry ingredients are combined with the liquids, simply stir just enough to moisten. It is better to see a few flour particles than to overmix, which can result in a heavy finished product.

Peanut-Butter Muffins

I've always liked peanut butter for breakfast. It's delicious on toast, with or without jam. These muffins baked with plenty of peanut butter are even better. Serve them warm with your favorite jam. They don't need butter.

> **1 cup light brown sugar**
> **1 cup granulated sugar**
> **2 cups peanut butter, smooth or crunchy**
> **1 tbsp. butter or margarine**
> **3 eggs, separated**
> **2 cups sifted flour**
> **1 tsp. baking soda**
> **½ tsp. salt**
> **1¾ cups buttermilk or plain yogurt**

- In an electric mixer, cream together both sugars, peanut butter, and butter or margarine.
- Beat in the egg yolks.
- Sift together the dry ingredients.
- Add the dry ingredients alternately with the buttermilk to the creamed mixture.
- Beat the egg whites until soft peaks form.
- Stir one-fourth of the beaten egg whites into the peanut-butter mixture. Fold in the remaining egg whites.
- Fill greased muffin pans two-thirds full.
- Bake in a preheated 350-degree oven for 20 to 25 minutes.
- Makes 24 muffins.

Strawberry Muffins

This muffin recipe has been in my files since my New Orleans days. These muffins cannot qualify as light, but are they ever a treat! If you've ever had a typical Southern breakfast in one of the many great small bed-and-breakfast inns down South, then you may have tasted this muffin or something akin to it. It is truly a recipe worth trying when you are in the mood for a sweet morning treat.

> 2 sticks butter or margarine, softened
> 1½ cups sugar
> 3 eggs
> 1 tsp. baking soda
> 1 cup buttermilk or plain yogurt
> ½ cup golden raisins
> ½ cup chopped pecans
> 3 cups sifted flour
> 1 cup strawberry preserves

- In an electric mixer, cream together the butter and sugar until light and fluffy.
- Add the eggs, one at a time, beating after each addition.
- Stir the baking soda into the buttermilk or yogurt and add it to the bowl.
- Stir the raisins and nuts into the sifted flour.
- Fold in the flour mixture and stir in the preserves.
- Fill greased muffin pans two-thirds full.
- Bake in a preheated 350-degree oven for 20 minutes.
- Makes 24 muffins.

Pecan Pancakes Deluxe

If anything can qualify as real comfort food, it has to be a stack of home-made pancakes on a chilly morning. My Southern heritage comes to the fore again with my choice for a pancake recipe. If you've never tried them with pecans, you are missing a real treat. I love to serve these with maple syrup, but they are also good with a fruit syrup such as strawberry or blueberry.

> 1 egg, lightly beaten
> ½ cup powdered sugar
> ½ stick butter or margarine, melted
> ⅔ cup milk
> 1 cup all-purpose flour
> 2 tsp. baking powder
> ¼ tsp. baking soda
> ¼ tsp. salt
> ¼ tsp. allspice
> ½ cup chopped pecans

- Stir together the egg, sugar, butter, and milk.
- Sift the dry ingredients together and stir in the pecans.
- Add the liquid mixture to the dry ingredients. Stir to just blend. (Batter should be slightly lumpy.)
- Ladle onto a lightly greased preheated griddle or skillet.
- Cook 1 to 2 minutes per side, turning only once.
- Serve hot with butter and hot syrup.
- Makes about 15 3-in. pancakes.

Entertaining with Ease

Whether you are catering your own fancy party or have just invited a few friends for a glass of wine, there is the inevitable question: "What to serve them?" In this chapter I have endeavored to give you several good answers to that often nagging question. My aim has been to offer some attractive and tasty treats that will fill your entertaining needs and please the taste buds of your guests. I have concentrated on some of my favorites that don't require a tremendous commitment of time and energy. After all, my goal has always been to enjoy my own parties as much as my guests.

If your celebration calls for an array of party treats, choose an assortment that includes an interesting mix of hot and cold foods. Think about your time plan and select recipes you can make at various times preceding the party so that most of the food is prepped. This will give you those last few hours to calmly perform the other nonculinary preparations, such as setting an attractive table and arranging the flowers. Garnish each party dish simply and beautifully so your food makes a pleasing first impression. Remember, too, that everything on the plate must be edible. Finally, relax and have fun!

Appetizers Oysters Rockefeller

When I want a special appetizer featuring seafood, I usually go to my New Orleans file. Rockefeller sauce is truly a special treat, but serving this sauce in the traditional manner over fresh oysters on their shells on a bed of hot rock salt can get rather involved. So, simply eliminate the shells and salt and greatly simplify the preparation, serving, and eating of this special treat. The toast can be made hours ahead and stored in a tin or plastic bag. Like most full-bodied, rich sauces, the Rockefeller sauce actually improves in flavor when made hours ahead and chilled. Serve this as a first course at the table for a fancy dinner party or pass trays hot from the oven at a stand-up cocktail party. Either way, your guests are sure to be impressed.

> **24 thin slices French bread (no more than 2 to 3 in. in diameter)**
> **2 doz. large fresh oysters, with liquor**
> **1 recipe Rockefeller Sauce (see below)**
> **Freshly grated Parmigiano-Reggiano**

- Toast the bread slices until golden brown. Set aside.
- In a large skillet over medium heat, poach the oysters in their own liquor just until the edges begin to curl (only a couple of minutes). Remove from the heat.
- Using a slotted spoon to drain off the liquid, place an oyster on a slice of toast.
- Spoon over a large dollop of the Rockefeller Sauce.
- Sprinkle lightly with cheese.
- Repeat with remaining ingredients.
- Broil under a preheated broiler until the sauce is hot through.
- Serve hot.
- Makes 24 appetizers.

Rockefeller Sauce

4 tbsp. butter
2 stalks celery, chopped
6 green onions, chopped
1 cup parsley leaves
1 10-oz. pkg. frozen spinach, cooked and drained
1 tsp. anchovy paste

1 tbsp. Worcestershire sauce
½ tsp. hot pepper sauce, or to taste
¼ cup Herbsaint (or Pernod)
1 stick butter, softened
Salt and freshly ground black pepper, to taste

- Melt the 4 tbsp. butter in a skillet. Sauté the celery and onions just until the onions are softened. Stir in the parsley leaves.

- Squeeze as much liquid from the spinach as possible and stir into the onion mixture.

- Purée the mixture in a food processor. Add the remaining ingredients, including the softened butter, cut into pieces. Process until well mixed.

- Chill until ready to use.

Louisiana Shrimp Pâté with Cocktail Sauce

One of my students once asked me for a good party shrimp recipe that didn't require her to take out a second mortgage on the house in order to pay for the shrimp. This is the recipe I chose to give her. It will serve many more people than the same amount of regular boiled shrimp with sauce, and it has a delicious shrimp flavor. By the way, this cocktail sauce goes great with those boiled shrimp too.

2 lb. boiled shrimp, peeled and deveined
¼ cup chopped sweet salad onion
4 tbsp. softened butter or margarine
½ cup mayonnaise
2 tbsp. fresh lemon juice
½ tsp. hot pepper sauce
Salt, to taste
Extra mayonnaise, for greasing mold
1 recipe Cocktail Sauce (see below)
Parley sprigs and thinly sliced lemon, for
   garnish

- Finely chop the shrimp in a food processor.

- Add the onion, butter, mayonnaise, lemon juice, hot pepper sauce, and salt. Process until puréed.

When boiling shrimp in the shell, the water should be the same saltiness as the ocean. Any less salt will make the shrimp taste flat. In addition to enough salt, the secret to tasty boiled shrimp is some packaged Louisiana "Shrimp Boil," or make your own with some mustard seed, bay leaves, allspice, and dried hot red pepper. Add a lemon or lime, halved, and a medium onion, peeled and quartered. Simmer the mixture for 15 to 20 minutes, then bring it back to a rolling boil before adding the shrimp. The best tip of all for perfect boiled shrimp: Don't overcook it. Stop as soon as it curls and turns pink. Drain and cool.

- Line a ring mold (8- or 9-in.) with plastic wrap. Spoon in the shrimp mixture.
- Chill for several hours or until firm.
- Unmold onto a large plate and pour the Cocktail Sauce in the center.
- Garnish with parsley and lemon.
- Serve with bite-sized crisp toast or crackers for spreading.
- Serves 10-12.

Cocktail Sauce

1 cup bottled chili sauce
2 tbsp. grated horseradish
1 tbsp. fresh lemon juice

- Stir together to blend. Chill until ready to serve.

Shrimp Stuffed with Maine Lobster with Cajun Remoulade Sauce

Sid Jones is a talented local chef who comes up with one different appetizer after another. I love to "graze" at the charming bistro Encore, where Chef Sid runs the kitchen. This seafood appetizer is so delicious that I asked for the recipe for this book. Though not the simplest recipe, you can assemble it ahead of time and bake just before serving. The delicious Remoulade sauce will be even better if made ahead and allowed to chill several hours. If you don't have lobster, substitute crabmeat in the filling.

1 recipe Cajun Remoulade Sauce (see below)
8 large (16 to 20 count) shrimp, peeled and
   deveined with tail on
1 tbsp. olive oil
1 tbsp. finely chopped red bell pepper
1 tbsp. finely chopped green bell pepper
1 tbsp. finely chopped red onion
1 tsp. finely chopped garlic
1 egg yolk
1 tsp. mayonnaise
½ tsp. cayenne pepper
1 tbsp. fresh breadcrumbs (see tip)

½ tsp. Dijon mustard
4 oz. cooked lobster meat, chopped into small
 pieces
Salt and freshly ground black pepper, to taste
Mixed baby salad greens

- Make the Remoulade sauce, cover, and chill.

- With a small sharp knife, cut a slit starting at the tail of each shrimp along the back to the end, cutting only two-thirds through. Set aside.

- Heat the olive oil in a small skillet and sauté the peppers, onion, and garlic until tender, about 3 minutes. Pour into a bowl to cool slightly.

- Beat the egg yolk and mayonnaise together. Toss into the sautéed vegetables. Stir in the cayenne, breadcrumbs, mustard, lobster, salt, and pepper. Mix well and roll into 8 small balls. Stuff the shrimp with the lobster stuffing.

- Place in a greased baking pan and bake in a preheated 350-degree oven for 15 to 20 minutes.

- Arrange some salad greens on a plate and arrange the hot shrimp around the greens. Drizzle both greens and shimp with the Remoulade sauce.

- Serve immediately.

- Serves 2-4 as an appetizer.

Cajun Remoulade Sauce

½ cup mayonnaise
2 tbsp. ketchup
1 tsp. finely chopped garlic
½ tsp. lemon juice
1 tbsp. capers
1 tsp. cayenne pepper
1 tsp. whole-grain mustard

- Gently whisk all of the ingredients together. Cover and chill.

- Makes about ⅔ cup.

Fresh bread-crumbs are easily made in a food processor from day-old, firm bread. Simply tear the slices into large pieces and process for a few seconds or until the crumbs are the size you desire.

Chicken-Parsley Pâté

Of all the traditional party foods, nothing sounds more impressive than a homemade pâté. It is truly a fun, creative experience for the cook and looks so lovely on the party table. And since it must be made ahead, a pâté fits nicely into a well-planned party menu for the busy host or hostess. I suspect that one of the reasons even dedicated party givers don't make pâté is that it is usually loaded with such things as pork fat. This pâté is hardly diet food, but since it is based on lean chicken breasts, it is lighter in texture and calories than a traditional pork pâté. It is a versatile recipe that can be a first course for a dinner party or a part of a party buffet. For a cocktail party, slice it and then cut each slice in half. Serve it with some thin, crisp toast so that it can be eaten as finger food.

> 2 cups heavy cream
> 3 sprigs fresh thyme (or 1 tsp. dried)
> 2 bay leaves
> ¼ tsp. freshly grated nutmeg
> 1 tsp. black peppercorns
> 1 medium onion, peeled and quartered
> 1½ lb. boneless and skinless chicken breasts
> 1 tsp. salt
> ¼ tsp. hot pepper sauce
> 2 large egg whites
> ¾ cup chopped parsley

- Pour the cream into a nonreactive saucepan. Add the thyme, bay leaves, nutmeg, peppercorns, and onion. Scald. Remove from the heat and allow to sit for 30 minutes to infuse. Strain and chill the cream until it is very cold.

- Trim the chicken breasts and cut into 1-in. pieces. Cover and chill until very cold. Place in a food processor. Add the salt and hot pepper sauce. Chop finely.

- With the motor running and continuing to process the chicken, pour the cold cream slowly through the feed tube. (It should be taken up by the chicken as it is added.) Add the egg whites and process until mixture is light and fluffy.

- Fold in the parsley. Cook just a spoonful in the microwave and taste for seasonings.

- Oil a 6-cup loaf pan or pâté mold. Spoon in the chicken mixture and tap on the countertop to remove the air bubbles. Top with a piece of oiled parchment that is cut to fit the top of the pan. Cover the pan tightly with a double layer of heavy-duty foil, sealing well.

- Set the pan in a larger pan of hot water, with the water coming halfway up the sides of the pâté pan. Bake in a 325-degree oven for about 1 hour or until firm. Remove from the oven and the water bath. Cool. Cover with a smaller second pan and place weights in the smaller pan. Chill overnight.
- Remove the pâté from the pan. Slice into thin slices.
- Serve with the following Tangy Mustard Sauce and/or Cranberry-Apple Chutney.
- Serves 12-15.

Tangy Mustard Sauce

Here's a recipe that can be whipped together in a flash and is very versatile. It tastes good with any poultry- or pork-based pâté or smoked fish. You may use reduced-fat mayonnaise and sour cream if you are making "light" food. Spice it up with an especially hot mustard, or make it sweeter by simply drizzling in more honey until it tastes right to you. It will keep for several days in the refrigerator. After the party, the leftovers can do wonders for an ordinary ham or turkey sandwich.

> **1 cup mayonnaise**
> **½ cup Dijon mustard**
> **1 tsp. honey**
> **1 tsp. fresh lemon juice**
> **¼ cup sour cream**
> **Dash hot pepper sauce, to taste**

- Gently stir together all ingredients with a whisk until smooth.
- Cover and chill until ready to serve.
- Makes about 1½ cups sauce.

Cranberry-Apple Chutney

In the last few years, chefs in this country have discovered what the English have known for ages: chutneys add an exotic touch to even the plainest meat or poultry dishes. According to Webster, a chutney is "a spicy relish composed of spices, herbs, and fruits." We are also reminded that it was originally popular in India, which is obviously where the English discovered it. A homemade chutney has much to recommend it, not the least of which is the fact that it is so easily prepared. Even those of you with no experience at all in jams, pickles, and the like can cook up a successful chutney. As you can see from the following recipe, it is only matter of mixing everything in one pot and cooking it until it is done.

> Use Cranberry-Apple Chutney to make a quick appetizer that is especially appropriate for the holiday season. Simply spoon enough over some softened cream cheese to cover well. Spread onto crisp crackers.

2 cups water
2 cups sugar
2 tbsp. molasses
2 large Granny Smith apples, peeled and cut
     into small, thin slices
12 oz. fresh cranberries
1 cup golden raisins
⅓ cup red-wine vinegar
2 tbsp. finely chopped fresh gingerroot
2 tsp. hot curry powder
1 tsp. salt
½ tsp. hot pepper sauce

- In a heavy saucepan, bring the water and sugar to a boil. Boil until the sugar is dissolved.

- Add the molasses and apple slices. Bring to a boil. Reduce to a simmer and cook, uncovered, for 20 minutes, or until the apples are fork tender.

- Wash and stem the cranberries, and add them along with the remaining ingredients.

- Stir and bring back to a boil. Cook for 20 minutes longer.

- Store in a covered jar in the refrigerator until ready to serve.

- It is best when made a day or two before using. It will keep for several weeks in the refrigerator.

- Makes about 4 cups.

Curried Chicken Spread
with Apples and Almonds

Here is another dish featuring boneless chicken breasts and an Indian influence. This popular cut of poultry is so quick and easy to prepare, low in fat, and, when cooked properly, delicious. You may also use this recipe's chicken-poaching method to make a tasty chicken salad. I particularly like using this delicious curry-flavored spread for an autumn buffet when the apples are at their peak. It is great for winter holiday parties too.

> 2 whole boneless and skinless chicken breasts
> 2 cups chicken broth
> ½ cup dry white wine
> 1 tsp. black peppercorns
> 2 sprigs parsley
> 1 bay leaf
> 1 slice onion
> 2 green onions, cut into pieces
> ½ yellow delicious apple, peeled and cubed
> 4 tbsp. unsalted butter, softened
> 3 oz. cream cheese
> 1 tbsp. lemon juice
> ½ tsp. salt, or to taste
> 1 tsp. curry powder
> ¼ tsp. hot pepper sauce, or to taste
> Chopped parsley
> Toasted slivered almonds

- Trim the chicken breasts of all fat and gristle.

- In a skillet, heat together the broth, wine, peppercorns, parsley, bay leaf, and onion slice for 5 minutes.

- Add the chicken, cover with parchment paper, and poach for about 10 minutes, or until just cooked through. (Do not overcook.)

- Allow to cool for 10 to 15 minutes in the poaching liquid. Remove and cut into pieces.

- Chop the green onions coarsely in a food processor.

- Add the chicken and apple. Pulse on and off until the mixture is chopped.

Crudités for dipping: The following fresh vegetables look and taste best when blanched in a pot of rapidly boiling, salted water and then refreshed in very cold water. Drain well, pat dry, and chill until ready to serve.

Broccoli, florets and peeled and sliced stems—Blanch 1 minute

Cauliflower, florets—Blanch 1 minute

Asparagus, tender ends—Blanch 2 minutes

Green beans, small to medium sized, ends trimmed—Blanch 2 to 4 minutes (depending on size)

Snow peas, whole, with strings removed—Blanch 30 seconds

Fennel, bulb, sliced—Blanch 1 minute

The following vegetables are best raw, washed, cut into small, easy-to-eat strips, and chilled.

Carrots
Turnips
Zucchini
Yellow summer squash
Celery
Jicama
Other interesting additions to the "crudités platter":
Belgian endive leaves
Radicchio leaves
Medium-sized white mushrooms, firm and crisp and acidulated with lemon juice

- Add the butter, cream cheese, lemon juice, salt, curry powder, and hot pepper sauce. Process until smooth.
- Place in a crock or serving bowl. Top with chopped parsley and toasted almonds.
- Serve with thinly sliced French bread rounds or Melba toast for spreading.
- Serves 16-20.

Grilled Tomato-Basil Dip

One of my California friends, Sharon Shipley, cooking teacher and proprietor of "Mon Cheri" cooking school and catering company, got me started grilling tomatoes for sauces and dips. During tomato season, the grill tends to be in use a lot anyway, so why not toss on the tomatoes? It is not only practical but intensifies the delicious tomato flavor, while adding a hint of that intriguing "grilled outside" taste. Since this is obviously meant to be primarily a summertime party dip, fresh basil is likely to be around too and is another important component of this tasty dip.

5 ripe Roma tomatoes (or other small, firm, fresh tomatoes)
2 tbsp. olive oil
Salt, to taste
1 medium sweet salad onion
1 cup sour cream (regular or reduced fat)
3 oz. cream cheese, softened
2 tbsp. mayonnaise
3 tbsp. fresh chopped basil
1 small clove garlic, finely chopped
Hot pepper sauce, to taste
Whole basil leaves

- Core the tomatoes and cut in half lengthwise. Brush with olive oil and sprinkle the cut sides lightly with salt.
- Peel the onion and cut into 3 or 4 thick, lengthwise slices. Brush with olive oil.
- Grill the vegetables on a medium-hot grill until the tomatoes are cooked and soft. The onions should be "crisp-tender."

- Remove and cool.
- Peel and seed the tomatoes.
- Chop the tomatoes and onions.
- Whisk together the sour cream, cream cheese, and mayonnaise.
- Fold in the tomatoes, onions, chopped basil, and garlic. Season to taste with salt and hot pepper sauce.
- Serve immediately, or cover and chill until ready to serve.
- Garnish with whole basil leaves.
- Serve with crisp fresh vegetables (crudités) or corn chips for dipping.
- Makes about 2 cups.

Hot Beef and Cheese Appetizer Toasts

When I was living in Berlin in a charming, but tiny apartment, I was always on the lookout for easy party goodies that I could make in my little kitchen. This is my version of one I discovered in a German food magazine. I actually had my neighborhood butcher grind "beefsteak tartare" from a piece of beef tenderloin. Since I have returned to my food processor, I buy the beef and chop it finely with the steel cutting blade. These tasty toasts are great to serve on a chilly day.

1 lb. very lean beef (top round or tenderloin),
    finely ground
½ cup finely chopped onion
2 tbsp. chopped parsley leaves
1 tbsp. capers
1 tbsp. tomato paste
1 tsp. Dijon mustard
1 tsp. salt, or to taste
¼ to ½ tsp. freshly ground black pepper
1 egg, lightly beaten
6 oz. Emmenthaler or Gruyere cheese, shredded
6 to 8 slices firm white bread, crusts removed
    and toasted
Extra parsley leaves and capers, for garnish (if
    desired)

Artichoke leaves, cooked until tender and chilled

Radishes, big ones sliced or medium ones whole

Cucumbers, preferably the European type, which don't require peeling and seeding, cut into strips

The following vegetables are poor choices for serving with dips:

Cherry tomatoes—Too difficult to eat

Eggplant—Not good raw and wrong texture cooked

Wild mushrooms—Should never be eaten raw

Onions—Tend to be too strong in flavor, even the sweet salad varieties and the green ones

When a recipe calls for a small amount of tomato paste, the remainder in the can may be frozen for future use. Simply measure out tablespoon portions onto a waxed-paper-lined tray. Place, uncovered, in the freezer for about an hour, or until the tomato paste is frozen firm. Quickly remove to small freezer bags. When you are ready to use some paste, the frozen tablespoon dollops may be placed directly in a sauce or thawed in the microwave.

- With a fork, gently toss together the meat with the onion, parsley, capers, tomato paste, mustard, salt, and pepper.
- Stir in the egg and cheese.
- Spread the mixture onto one side of the toast.
- Place, spread side up, under a preheated broiler and broil for 3-5 minutes or until the mixture is hot through and bubbly.
- Cut into small triangles, fingers, or squares, if desired. (Or simply cut in half or into fourths.)
- Garnish with parsley leaves and capers, if desired.
- Serve warm.
- Serves 8-10.

Parmesan Rounds

This is a simple but very tasty little treat that features the great flavor of Italy's best cheese. Be sure you use the real thing. These delicious little toasts are a perfect accompaniment to a glass of wine.

1 loaf thinly sliced white sandwich bread
1 stick unsalted butter, softened
8 oz. cream cheese
¼ cup mayonnaise
½ cup finely chopped green onions
1 cup freshly shredded Parmigiano-Reggiano

- Cut the bread into small rounds. Using half of the butter, butter one side. Toast the buttered side under the broiler. Turn and toast second side. Cool.
- Whip together the cream cheese, mayonnaise, and onions with the remaining butter. Spread about 1 tsp. of the mixture on the buttered side of the bread. Dip into the cheese to coat.
- At serving time, broil until bubbly. Serve hot.
- Makes 24 small appetizers.

Bacon-Wrapped Stuffed Dates

These cocktail nibbles often appear on my holiday party table. This is a most appealing combination of sweet and salty tastes. Use the best bacon you can find. Thick-sliced bacon works best for this yummy treat.

> 12 pitted dates
> 12 slivers Parmigiano-Reggiano (to fit inside the
>   dates)
> 4 strips apple-wood-cured bacon, cut into thirds

- Place a sliver of cheese inside each date. Wrap each with 1 piece bacon and secure with a wooden toothpick.
- Place on a rack in a shallow baking pan and bake in a 350-degree oven for 15 to 18 minutes or until bacon is browned and crisp. Drain on paper towels and serve warm.
- Makes 12 appetizers.

Zippy Mexican Appetizer Pizzas

As my recipe files have grown, the percentage of Southwest/Mexican-inspired dishes has tended to increase faster than almost any other type of cuisine. There are good reasons for this. The most obvious is that I adore the flavors in this colorful cuisine. I have also had the pleasure of spending time in the parts of the world where these great flavors are everyday fare. A trip to Santa Fe was the inspiration for these fun appetizers that use the versatile flour tortilla for their "crust."

> 2 tbsp. olive oil
> 2 large yellow onions, peeled and thinly sliced
> 2 cloves garlic, finely chopped
> 2 mild green chiles, cored, seeded, and thinly
>   sliced crosswise
> 2 large jalapeño peppers, cored, seeded, and
>   thinly sliced crosswise
> 1 red bell pepper, cored, seeded, and cut into
>   thin rings
> 1 recipe Zippy Pizza Sauce (see below)
> 2 large flour tortillas
> ¼ cup chopped cilantro leaves
> 4 cups shredded jack cheese (1 lb.)

- Heat the olive oil in a large heavy skillet.
- Add the onions and garlic and sauté, stirring, for 5 or 6 minutes.
- Stir in all three kinds of peppers. Cook over medium-high heat for 5 more minutes, stirring.
- Remove from the heat and set aside.
- Make the sauce according to the following recipe.
- Place a tortilla on a lightly oiled baking sheet. Spread with a thin layer of the sauce.
- Top with half of the onion-pepper mixture.
- Sprinkle with half of the cilantro.
- Cover with 2 cups cheese.
- Repeat with the remaining ingredients.
- Bake the pizzas in the bottom of a preheated 450-degree oven for 10 to 15 minutes or until the tortillas are browned on the edges and the cheese is bubbly.
- Cut into small wedges. Serve hot.
- Makes 24 appetizers.

Fresh flour tortillas should be moist and very pliable when taken from their package. If they are dry and break when rolled, they are stale.

Zippy Pizza Sauce

1 tbsp. extra-virgin olive oil
1 large clove garlic, finely chopped
1 or 2 medium fresh jalapeño peppers, seeded and finely chopped
1 28-oz. can diced plum tomatoes, drained
Salt, to taste
Pinch sugar

- Heat the olive oil in a small heavy skillet.
- Sauté the garlic and peppers over medium heat, stirring, for 3 minutes.
- Stir in the tomatoes, salt, and sugar. Cook, uncovered, for 5 minutes.
- Taste and correct seasonings.
- Makes about 2$\frac{1}{2}$ cups.
- Store any leftover sauce in a covered container in the refrigerator. It keeps for several days.

Note: This is also good on regular pizza crust. For a quick hot "mini pizza," spread some sauce onto a toasted English muffin and top with cheese and any other desired toppings.

Bean and Cheese Quesadillas

This Southwest appetizer is a favorite at my house and definitely fun and easy to make. It is merely a "sandwich" made from two of those versatile flour tortillas. As the name quesadilla indicates, the filling always contains cheese, which can be combined with almost anything from seafood to vegetables. This one with cheese and refried beans is at the top of my list. Serve it topped with your favorite salsa, homemade or commercial. The Salsa Verde recipe goes very well with it.

1 recipe Refried Beans (see below)
6 extralarge flour tortillas
1 lb. shredded jack cheese
Vegetable oil, for browning
1 recipe Salsa Verde (see below)

- Spread Refried Beans over half of each tortilla, leaving a $1/2$-in. border around the edge.
- Sprinkle some cheese over the beans.
- Moisten the exposed edges of the tortillas with water and fold the unfilled sides over the filling. Press to seal the edges.
- Cover with plastic wrap and a damp towel to prevent drying until ready to cook and serve.
- Brush a griddle or heavy skillet with vegetable oil. Heat until hot.
- Grill the quesadillas on both sides until browned and crisp.
- Cut into wedges to serve.
- Serve warm with Salsa Verde (or your favorite salsa) to spoon over the top.

Refried Beans

Since I started making refried beans with good fruity olive oil instead of the traditional lard, I enjoy them much more. Not only do they have a much healthier makeup, but I like the flavor better.

2 cups cooked and seasoned pinto beans*
3 tbsp. extra-virgin olive oil
1 cup chopped onion
1 cup shredded jack cheese
1 tsp. sugar
½ tsp. hot pepper sauce

- Drain the beans, reserving the broth.
- Purée the beans in a food processor, adding liquid as needed to make a creamy mixture.
- Heat the oil in a heavy saucepan. Add the onion and cook until tender, stirring occasionally.
- Stir the puréed beans into the onions. Cook, stirring often, over low heat for 10 minutes.
- Off of the heat, stir in the cheese, sugar, and hot pepper sauce. Stir until cheese melts.
- Taste and correct seasonings.
- Serve hot.
- Makes about 2 cups.

*Canned pinto beans or dried beans that have been cooked in a seasoned broth may be used.

Salsa Verde

We in this country have embraced salsa as our own all-time favorite condiment. While the preferred salsa is usually the red tomato type, this "green" salsa offers another intriguing combination of flavors and can be used along with or in place of tomato salsa.

>   2 lb. fresh tomatillos
>   2 tbsp. olive oil
>   1 large yellow onion, chopped
>   3 cloves garlic, finely chopped
>   3 large fresh jalapeño peppers, seeded and
>   finely chopped, or to taste
>   1 4-oz. can chopped mild green chiles
>   1 tbsp. cider vinegar
>   1 tsp. sugar
>   Salt, to taste
>   ½ cup chopped fresh cilantro

- Remove the husks from the tomatillos. Rinse them to remove their stickiness. Cut in half and chop finely (easiest in the food processor). Place in a heavy nonreactive saucepan. Simmer, stirring occasionally for 15 minutes.

- Meanwhile, heat the olive oil in a skillet and add the onion, garlic, and jalapeño peppers. Sauté, stirring, for about 3 minutes, or just until the onion is tender. Remove from the heat.

- Stir in the chiles, vinegar, sugar, and salt. Add the cooled tomatillos and the cilantro.

- Taste and correct seasonings.

- Chill until ready to serve.

- Makes about 3 cups.

Spicy Chicken and Spinach Quesadillas with Lime-Cilantro Corn Salsa

This quesadilla is a favorite Sunday-night supper at my house. It is hearty and satisfying as well as filled with healthy ingredients. The corn salsa goes great on many Southwestern foods.

> 3 large boneless chicken breasts
> 3 tbsp. extra-virgin olive oil
> 2 chipotle peppers in adobo, finely chopped
> 1 tsp. adobo sauce
> 2 cloves garlic, finely chopped
> 1 tsp. salt
> 1 tbsp. lemon juice
> 1 lb. fresh spinach leaves
> 1 clove garlic, finely chopped
> Extra-virgin olive oil
> 12 oz. shredded mild cheese such as Monterey
>   Jack
> 6 medium flour tortillas
> Oil, for frying

- Wash, trim, and flatten the chicken breasts.
- Blend together the 3 tbsp. oil, chipotle peppers, sauce, 2 cloves garlic, salt, and lemon juice. Rub into chicken. Place in plastic bag and chill for 1 to 3 hours.
- Grill. Cool and cut into small pieces.
- Sauté the spinach with the 1 clove garlic in just enough oil to cover the bottom of a skillet, just until wilted. Remove and squeeze out excess liquid.
- Place some chicken, spinach, and cheese on one side of each tortilla. Fold over second side.
- Heat a small amount of oil in a heavy skillet. Brown each quesadilla on one side, turn, and brown second side.
- Cut each tortilla into 6 wedges. Serve hot with Lime-Cilantro Corn Salsa.
- Makes 36.

Lime-Cilantro Corn Salsa

3 tbsp. extra-virgin olive oil
1 cup chopped red onion
1½ cups fresh corn kernels
2 large jalapeño peppers, seeded and finely
  chopped
½ cup chopped fresh cilantro
1 tsp. salt, or to taste
2 tbsp. fresh lime juice

- Heat the oil in a skillet.
- Add the onion and cook over medium-high heat, stirring, for 2 minutes.
- Stir in the corn and cook, stirring, for 3 more minutes.
- Remove from the heat and stir in the jalapeños. Allow to cool.
- Stir in the remaining ingredients and chill.

Santa Fe Hot Bean Dip

This dip features the hearty flavors of roasted garlic and onion. Roasted onion can be a unique flavor addition to many dishes because cooking onions in dry heat intensifies their great flavor and brings out their natural sweetness. Try using roasted instead of sautéed onion and you will see what I mean. This bean dip can be made ahead and reheated in the microwave with good success.

2 tbsp. extra-virgin olive oil
1 tbsp. good chili powder
1 tsp. cumin
2 1-lb. cans pinto beans, drained
1 large roasted onion, chopped
3 cloves roasted garlic, chopped
½ tsp. hot pepper sauce
1½ cups shredded jack cheese
Salt, to taste
Chopped cilantro, for garnish

- Heat the olive oil in a heavy saucepan over medium heat.
- Add the chili powder and cumin. Stir the spices for 1 to 2 minutes. (Do not burn.)

To roast an onion, rub a large, unpeeled yellow onion with oil. Wrap in heavy-duty foil, crimping the top to close tightly. Place in a preheated 400-degree oven for 1 to 1½ hours, depending on the size of the onion. The onion will be soft when done. Cool and peel.

To roast garlic, cut the top off of a large, firm head of garlic. The tops of the cloves should be exposed. Place on a square of heavy-duty foil. Drizzle some olive oil over the garlic head and sprinkle with a bit of salt. Tightly close the foil, crimping the top. Place in a preheated 400-degree oven for about 30 minutes or until soft. Cool. Gentle pressure on the bottom of a roasted clove of garlic should easily push it out of its skin.

For a truly easy appetizer, toast some good French or Italian bread with a bit of olive oil brushed on it. Spread with a thin layer of roasted garlic. Sprinkle with a little salt (if desired). Garnish with some chopped fresh herbs such as basil or cilantro and/or sprinkle on a spoonful of diced fresh tomato.

- Purée the beans in a food processor and add to the saucepan.
- Stir in the onion and garlic. Cook for 5 minutes, stirring occasionally, over low heat.
- Stir in the hot pepper sauce and ½ cup cheese.
- Season to taste with salt.
- Place in a small casserole dish and sprinkle the remaining cheese over the top.
- At serving time, place in the microwave or a hot oven until hot through and the cheese is melted.
- Serve hot, garnished with cilantro, with tortilla chips for dipping.
- Serves 10-12.

Tex-Mex Crabmeat Nachos

I happily admit that I still thoroughly enjoy a good nacho. These crabmeat ones are not only good but a bit out of the ordinary, and appropriate for everything from a Sunday-afternoon football-game snack to a passed hors d'oeuvre at a fancy cocktail party. Be sure to use real crabmeat in this recipe.

> **Vegetable oil, for frying tortilla chips**
> **10 corn tortillas, cut into fourths**
> **3 tbsp. olive oil**
> **1 large sweet salad onion, chopped**
> **1 ripe large tomato, seeded and diced**
> **2 to 3 large jalapeño peppers, seeded and finely chopped**
> **½ cup chopped fresh cilantro**
> **8 oz. crabmeat (fresh or frozen)**
> **1 ripe large avocado, peeled and diced**
> **1 tbsp. fresh lime juice**
> **12 oz. jack cheese**

- Heat 3 or 4 in. vegetable oil to 365-370 degrees in a heavy skillet or saucepan.
- Fry the tortilla wedges until they are very crisp. Drain on paper towels.

- Heat the olive oil in a heavy skillet.
- Add the onion and sauté over high heat, stirring, for 2 minutes.
- Add the tomato and peppers. Cook for 2 more minutes.
- Remove from the heat and stir in the cilantro and crabmeat.
- Toss the avocado with the lime juice and gently toss into the crabmeat mixture.
- Arrange the tortilla chips on foil-lined baking sheets.
- Place a spoonful of the crabmeat mixture on each tortilla chip. Sprinkle with cheese to cover.
- Just before serving time, place the nachos in a preheated 450-degree oven for 2-3 minutes or until the cheese is melted.
- Serve immediately.
- Makes 40.

   Note: These may also be heated in the microwave. Take care not to overcook.

Sun-Dried Tomato Tapenade

Sun-dried tomatoes add great flavor to so many dishes. I like to chop them finely into a "tapenade" flavored with capers and some tasty roasted garlic. This tastes great spread on thinly sliced and toasted French bread, or in a somewhat more involved appetizer like our Sun-Dried Tomato and Mozzarella Triangles.

1 cup oil-packed sun-dried tomatoes, drained
2 tbsp. capers
3 cloves roasted garlic
¼ tsp. crushed hot red pepper
2 tbsp. chopped fresh cilantro or basil

- Place the tomatoes in a food processor. Add the capers and garlic.
- Process by turning on and off until the mixture is finely chopped—but not puréed.
- Remove from the processor bowl and stir in the pepper and cilantro or basil. Taste and correct seasonings.
- Makes about 1 cup.

Dried tomatoes may be purchased packed in oil or dry in bulk packages. Place the dry kind in a vegetable steamer and steam until they are plump—10 to 20 minutes depending on the size and degree of dryness. Place them in a jar and cover with some good olive oil. Allow to steep for several hours. Store in the refrigerator.

Roasted Red Pepper and Artichoke Tapenade

I am blessed with a lot of wonderful foodie friends and I am so glad Brett Stover is one of them. There is no one more fun to cook with than Brett and we have some roaring good times in our kitchens. Brett also gives wonderful parties with plenty of good food. This is one of his own party recipes.

> **1 clove garlic, chopped**
> **1 7-oz. jar roasted red bell peppers, drained**
> **1 6-oz. jar marinated artichoke hearts, drained**
> **¼ cup capers, drained**
> **½ cup finely chopped fresh flat-leaf parsley**
> **½ cup freshly grated Parmigiano-Reggiano**
> **⅓ cup extra-virgin olive oil**
> **1 tbsp. fresh lemon juice**
> **Salt and freshly ground black pepper, to taste**

- Turn on the food processor and drop the garlic through the center of the feed tube. Stop when the garlic is finely chopped. Scrape down the sides of the bowl with a spatula.

- Add the peppers, artichokes, capers, parsley, cheese, oil, and lemon juice. Pulse on and off until mixture is finely chopped.

- Remove and season to taste with salt and pepper.

- Serve with pita-bread triangles or crackers or as a vegetable dip.

- Makes about 1¾ cups.

Sun-Dried Tomato and Mozzarella Triangles

Frozen phyllo dough can make anyone look like an accomplished baker. The long, rectangular box found in the frozen-food case in the grocery store usually contains 24 paper-thin dough sheets. There are a few basic rules to follow (see tips), but with a little practice you can turn out very professional-looking appetizers using this versatile frozen pastry.

12 sheets frozen phyllo dough
Extra-virgin olive oil, for brushing on dough
1 recipe Sun-Dried Tomato Tapenade (see above)
1 lb. shredded mozzarella cheese

- Place 1 sheet of phyllo dough on a large cutting board.
- Using a soft-bristle pastry brush, brush lightly with some of the olive oil, oiling the edge first, then the center.
- Place a second sheet of phyllo directly on top of the first one, pressing carefully to smooth and seal the edges. Lightly brush some oil on the second sheet.
- Cut the dough into 4 lengthwise strips.
- Leaving a 1-in. margin on the end, place a spoonful of the tapenade and cheese at the end of each dough strip.
- Fold up, "flag fashion," to form a triangle that encases the tomato-cheese mixture.
- Seal the end with some more oil and lightly brush the top with oil.
- Repeat with the remaining phyllo dough.
- Place phyllo triangles on a parchment-paper-lined baking sheet.
- Bake in the upper third of a preheated 375-degree oven for 8 to 10 minutes, or until golden brown.
- Serve hot.
- Makes 24 appetizers.

Phyllo tips: Even though phyllo dough is frozen, the low moisture content prevents it from freezing hard. It requires only a couple of hours on the counter before it is ready to use.

Use a light, careful touch when unwrapping, unrolling, and laying out the delicate, thin sheets of phyllo dough.

While working with the phyllo, keep it covered with some plastic wrap and a damp dishtowel to prevent drying out beyond the point of being usable.

Always use an unsalted fat such as butter, margarine, or olive oil for layering the frozen phyllo-dough sheets. A spray can of olive oil may also be used.

Bacon and Onion Phyllo Rolls

The caramelized onion with bacon flavor makes a very tasty filling for these phyllo hors d'oeuvres. They are a delicious treat to serve, from brunch to evening cocktails. Make these up far ahead up to the baking stage, package, and freeze. Thaw about an hour on the countertop and they are ready to bake and serve. Pass these hot from the oven.

½ lb. sliced bacon, diced
1 tbsp. olive oil
2 cups sliced red Spanish onion
2 tsp. brown sugar
½ cup fresh breadcrumbs
Freshly ground black pepper, to taste
10 sheets frozen phyllo dough
1 stick butter or margarine, melted

- Fry the bacon pieces in a heavy skillet until crisp. Remove with a slotted spoon onto a paper-towel-lined plate.
- Pour the bacon fat from the skillet. Add 1 tbsp. olive oil and return to the heat.
- Add the onions and sugar to the skillet. Cook, stirring, over medium heat until the onions are caramelized, about 20 minutes.
- Remove from the heat and stir in the crisp bacon pieces, bread-crumbs, and pepper.
- Place 1 sheet of phyllo dough on a large cutting board. Using a soft-bristle pastry brush, lightly brush with the melted butter. Fold in half lengthwise.
- Lightly grease the top of the dough and cut, lengthwise, in half.
- Place 1 tsp. bacon filling on the end of each dough strip, leaving a 1-in. margin on the end and ½-in. margins on the edges. Fold the side margins into the center.
- Fold the end margin of each strip over the filling and roll up into a roll, sealing the edges with more butter.
- Repeat with the remaining ingredients.
- Place the rolls on a parchment-lined baking sheet.
- Bake in the upper third of a preheated 375-degree oven for 8 to 10 minutes, or until golden brown.
- Serve hot.
- Makes 20 appetizers.

Sensational Salads

A "salad" can be a simple bowl of lettuce with some dressing tossed into it or a baroque arrangement of meat, fruits, and fresh herbs, flavored with an exotic dressing. Whether it's simple or fancy, I love a good salad. I decided on "Sensational Salads" as the right title for this chapter because it turned out to be a lovely, tasty collection of salad recipes. So many so-called salads out there are not only *not* sensational but awful. Those are the ones that have often given salads a bad reputation: nothing but a bowl of limp iceberg lettuce torn into chunks that are far too large to eat, then garnished with a whole cherry tomato (my salad pet peeve). And finally those poor excuses for a salad are drenched in far too much heavy dressing, which drowns the top and, alas, does not even flavor the stuff in the bottom. You know what I am talking about. We've all had them and they are never enjoyable.

In any case, I think what you'll find here is a collection of pretty, versatile, nutritious, easy-to-make, elegant, and absolutely delicious salads. Take note of my tips along the way and your salads will be fresh, attractive, and tasty. I hope you will agree that these salads are indeed "sensational."

Favorite French Green Bean Salad

A few summers ago we spent three weeks in a country cottage in the enchanting Loire Valley. We shared the house and good times with Klaus and Barbara Jeziorkowski, two dear friends from Germany who also appreciate good food and wine. Needless to say, we thoroughly enjoyed taking advantage of the many great restaurants in that area of France. We also spent some fun hours tasting and learning about the elegant Loire wines. But without a doubt the most enjoyable part for me was going to the local farmers' markets and coming back to our postage-stamp-sized kitchen to see what we could create for dinner. The problem was the amount of food we managed to purchase. We especially couldn't resist the abundance and variety of fruits and vegetables. Haricots verts, those tiny little French green beans, were our biggest weakness. One day we bought two kilos! But before we left, the four of us managed to eat every single one. I created this salad on one of the last days with a pot of cold beans we simply couldn't bear to leave behind. (There were also olives and tomatoes in the refrigerator, not to mention the fabulous cold-pressed walnut oil we bought from a nice farmer.) Anyway, do buy the smallest beans you can find. You will, I'm afraid, be hard pressed to find beans as tiny or delicate as those we ate in France, but it's still likely to be one of your best bean salads.

2 cups water, lightly salted
1½ lb. young tender green beans
3 ripe medium tomatoes, cut into wedges
1 small sweet salad onion, halved and sliced
½ cup niçoise or kalamata whole black olives
½ cup whole small green olives
2 tbsp. coarsely chopped fresh basil leaves
½ cup walnut oil
2 tbsp. balsamic vinegar
1 heaping tsp. good Dijon mustard
Salt and freshly ground black pepper, to taste
Crisp lettuce leaves
Basil leaves, for garnish

- Boil the water. Cook the beans in the water, uncovered, for 3 to 6 minutes or until crisp-tender.
- Drain and refresh with cold water. Drain thoroughly and place in a large mixing bowl. Chill until very cold.

Salads are often served with olives with pits. It is much more elegant to pit the olives. To pit olives, place one or two on a well-anchored cutting board. Place the base of a chef's knife over the olive and rap the knife with the heel of your hand to pop the olive open. The pit can then be easily removed. If you choose to leave the olives whole with pits, you may want to alert your guests to that fact.

- Add the tomatoes and onion slices to the chilled beans along with the olives and chopped basil.
- Whisk together the oil, vinegar, mustard, salt, and pepper. (Or mix in the blender or food processor.) Toss the dressing into the salad.
- Taste and correct seasonings and serve, spooned onto crisp lettuce leaves. Garnish with a basil leaf or two.
- Serves 6-8.

Green Bean and Red Pepper Salad

A super summertime treat, this colorful vegetable combination will perk up even the dullest of plates. It is a must during Vidalia onion season but can be enjoyed year round with other sweet-onion varieties. The color combination can even lend a nice touch to a holiday buffet table.

2 lb. tender fresh green beans
2 cups water
1 large red bell pepper, cut into strips
1 large sweet salad onion, halved and thinly sliced
3 tbsp. chopped fresh dill (or 1 tbsp. dried)
⅓ cup extra-virgin olive oil
2 tsp. whole-grain Dijon mustard
½ tsp. salt, or to taste
¼ tsp. freshly ground black pepper
½ tsp. sugar
2 tbsp. red-wine vinegar
1 head red-tipped leaf lettuce, washed, dried,
    and chilled

- Wash and trim the ends from the beans.
- Bring the water to a rolling boil.
- Add the beans and stir. Cook, uncovered, for 3 to 6 minutes, depending on the size of the beans. They should be crisp-tender.
- Immediately pour into a colander to drain.
- Refresh with very cold water; drain very well.
- Toss the bell-pepper strips, onion slices, and dill with the beans.
- Whisk together the oil, mustard, salt, pepper, and sugar.
- Whisk in the vinegar.

Once green beans have been dressed with a dressing containing acidity (such as vinegar or lemon juice), they should be served immediately, because the acid will change the bright green color to a dull gray-green.

- Toss into the beans.
- Spoon the salad onto a bed of the leaf lettuce.
- Serve immediately.
- Serves 8-10.

Spicy Mixed Bean Salad

Some of us have always appreciated beans and have known them to be quite delicious and flavorful, not to mention versatile. Since it was recognized that "nutritious, high in fiber, and low in fat" could be added to their description, beans have enjoyed a steady increase in sales. This piquant salad is easy because it uses canned beans. My favorite brand is packed in glass jars. The salad is best when made several hours ahead to allow the flavors to blend and develop.

> 3 cups pinto beans, rinsed and drained
> 3 cups white beans, rinsed and drained
> 2 cups chopped celery
> 1 large cucumber
> 1 large sweet salad onion, chopped
> 12 cherry tomatoes, halved
> 1 or 2 medium to large fresh jalapeño peppers,
>   finely chopped
> ¼ cup chopped fresh cilantro leaves
> ½ cup extra-virgin olive oil
> 1 large clove garlic, finely chopped
> 1 tsp. chili powder
> 1 tsp. salt, or to taste
> 1 tsp. sugar
> 1 tsp. hot pepper sauce, or to taste
> ¼ cup red-wine or cider vinegar

Raw onions for salads can be soaked in ice water for 30 minutes to make them crisper and give them a milder flavor.

- Place the beans in a large bowl and gently toss in the celery.
- Peel, cut in half lengthwise, and seed the cucumber. Cut into thin slices.
- Toss the onion, tomatoes, cucumber, jalapeños, and cilantro in the bean mixture.
- In the olive oil, whisk the garlic, chili powder, salt, sugar, and hot pepper sauce.

- Whisk in the vinegar, whisking until the mixture is well blended.
- Pour the dressing over the bean mixture and gently toss.
- Serves 8-10.

Southern Black-Eyed Pea Salad

One of my Eastern friends once told me you have to be born with genuine Southern blood to appreciate black-eyed peas. Maybe so, but let's not be so sure before tasting this fun and delicious pea salad. We made it down home as a way to use up the ham and peas left over from Sunday dinner. Now I like to serve it as part of a picnic or summer supper buffet. It is good with or without the ham.

3 cups cooked black-eyed peas
1 cup chopped sweet salad onion
1 large red bell pepper, chopped
1-2 jalapeño peppers, finely chopped
8 oz. lean ham, cut into julienne strips
¼ cup chopped parsley
1 cup mayonnaise
1 tsp. hot pepper sauce
1 tbsp. Creole mustard (horseradish mustard)
2 tbsp. fresh lemon juice
1 tsp. salt
1 tsp. sugar
1 small head iceberg lettuce, washed and chilled
2 medium tomatoes, cut into small wedges and
    lightly salted
Parsley sprigs, for garnish

- Gently toss together the peas, onion, peppers, ham, and chopped parsley.
- Blend together the mayonnaise, hot pepper sauce, mustard, lemon juice, salt, and sugar in the blender or by stirring together with a whisk.
- Gently toss the dressing into the salad.
- Cut the lettuce into quarters. Slice into find shreds and spread onto a platter or in a shallow bowl.

Tips for better salads:

Wash and dry salad greens as soon as possible after they are purchased or picked from the garden.

To wash, submerge in lukewarm water and let sit until the grit sinks to the bottom. Lift out greens and spin dry in a salad spinner or dry well with white paper towels or soft dishtowels.

A salad spinner is a very handy gadget. It saves time and towels.

To store, place salad greens in a plastic bag with one or two soft white paper towels. Press out as much air as possible, seal, and place in the refrigerator crisper drawer. Properly washed and dried salad greens will keep for several days and will be crisp and ready to use when needed.

For an attractive tossed salad and one with interesting tastes and texture, use at least three different varieties of greens.

A tossed salad should always be tossed with its dressing before it is served. Use just enough dressing to lightly coat each leaf.

- Spoon the salad onto the lettuce.
- Place the tomato wedges around the edge of the salad and garnish with parsley sprigs.
- Serve at room temperature or chill until ready to serve.
- Serves 8.

Garbanzo and Green Olive Salad

By the time my good friend and cooking colleague Sharon Shipley gets around to writing her own cookbook, I will have used all of her favorite recipes in mine. Seriously, she is very generous to share some of her delicious creations and this one is a keeper. Filled with interesting flavors, this side salad featuring garbanzo beans can add interest to any picnic or party buffet. It also goes great with Mexican food.

> 1 cup large pimiento-stuffed green Spanish
>   olives, drained and sliced
> 2 1-lb. cans garbanzo beans, rinsed and drained
> ½ cup chopped onion
> ½ cup chopped celery
> 2 cloves garlic, finely chopped
> 2 tbsp. finely chopped fresh parsley
> 3 tbsp. fine lemon zest
> ¼ cup lemon juice
> ⅛ tsp. cayenne pepper, or to taste
> ⅓ cup extra-virgin olive oil
> Romaine lettuce leaves, washed, dried, and chilled
> 1 cup cherry tomatoes, halved and lightly salted

- Toss together the olives and garbanzos. Cover and chill for a couple of hours.
- Add the onion, celery, garlic, parsley, lemon zest, lemon juice, and cayenne.
- Slowly drizzle in the oil and mix lightly until all the ingredients are coated with oil.
- Line a salad bowl with the lettuce leaves.
- Spoon the salad onto the lettuce leaves and garnish with the halved tomatoes.
- Serves 8.

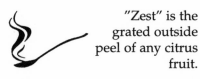

"Zest" is the grated outside peel of any citrus fruit.

Late Summer Squash Salad with Basil-Lemon Dressing

My weekly cooking column grew to a full-blown article on squash a couple of years ago. It was late summer when I was working on it, so this salad recipe went right from my kitchen to the article. It could also perhaps be titled "Trip to Farmers' Market." It is, nonetheless, easy, pretty, and very tasty. Fresh basil is an important flavor addition for the dressing.

3 small yellow summer squash, washed, trimmed, and cut into small strips
3 small zucchini, washed, trimmed, and cut into small strips
1 ripe large tomato, seeded and cut into small strips
1 cup cooked corn kernels*
½ cup chopped green onions
¼ cup chopped parsley
1 cup mayonnaise
½ cup plain yogurt or sour cream
1 tsp. Dijon mustard
¼ tsp. cayenne pepper, or to taste
1 tsp. salt, or to taste
2 tbsp. fresh lemon juice
2 tbsp. shredded fresh basil leaves
Small tomato wedges and whole basil leaves, for garnish

- Toss together the squash, zucchini, tomato, corn, green onions, and parsley.
- Whisk together the mayonnaise, yogurt, mustard, cayenne, salt, lemon juice, and basil. (For a reduced-fat dressing, use nonfat yogurt.)
- Toss the dressing into the vegetable mixture.
- Taste and correct seasonings.
- Chill until ready to serve. Garnish with the tomato wedges and basil leaves.
- Serves 8-10.

*Note: Fresh corn that is cooked and cut from the cob is best, but frozen whole kernels may be used.

Ham and Cheese Potato Salad
with Shallot-Herb Dressing

I couldn't offer a chapter on salads without including at least one potato salad. It surely must be America's number-one favorite as a side salad. No wonder, since it goes with almost everything. This one has even more to offer than the average potato salad. It's a casual main dish or a lovely addition to a buffet table. You can change it around to suit your needs. For a meatless but still hearty salad, just omit the ham. If you are looking for a good "just potato" salad, take out the cheese as well. It is the dressing that really makes this salad special.

2 lb. small red new potatoes, well scrubbed
1 recipe Shallot-Herb Dressing (see below)
3 cups cooked ham, cut into julienne strips
2 cups coarsely shredded Swiss cheese
½ cup oil-packed sun-dried tomatoes, drained
    and cut into small strips
½ cup thinly sliced green onions
3 tbsp. chopped flat-leaf parsley
1 tbsp. chopped fresh dill
Salt and freshly ground black pepper, to taste
1 small head romaine lettuce, washed and dried
Extra sprigs of parsley, for garnish

- Slice the unpeeled potatoes into thin slices, about ¼-in. thickness.
- Place in a steamer and steam for 8 minutes or just until fork tender.
- Make the dressing according to the following recipe.
- Remove the potatoes to a side dish and lightly toss with ½ cup dressing. Allow to sit for 30 minutes.
- In a large bowl, gently toss together the potatoes, ham, cheese, tomatoes, onions, chopped parsley, dill, salt, and pepper.
- Toss the remaining dressing into the salad.
- Taste and correct seasonings.
- At serving time, coarsely shred the romaine. Make a bed of the lettuce on a platter and spoon the salad over the top.
- Garnish with parsley sprigs.
- Serve at room temperature or chilled.
- Serves 8.

Shallot-Herb Dressing

2 shallots, peeled and finely chopped
½ cup dry white wine
¼ cup white-wine vinegar
1 cup mayonnaise
¼ cup chopped fresh parsley
3 tbsp. chopped fresh tarragon
¼ cup chopped fresh dill
½ tsp. hot pepper sauce
2 tsp. Dijon mustard
½ tsp. salt

- In a small nonreactive saucepan, boil together the shallots, wine, and vinegar until the liquid is reduced to ¼ cup. Cool.
- Whisk into the mayonnaise along with the herbs, hot pepper sauce, mustard, and salt.
- Chill until ready to serve.
- Makes about 1¼ cups.

Tropical Pork Tenderloin Salad with Ginger-Lime Dressing

As much as we all love a good chicken salad, it is nice to have a change now and then. A lean and tender pork tenderloin is a delicious alternative. This is a beautiful main dish for a casual summer dinner party, and all of the work may be done ahead.

2 pork tenderloins, 1½-2 lb. total
1 recipe Ginger-Lime Marinade (see below)
Crisp lettuce leaves
1 recipe Ginger-Lime Dressing (see below)
1 medium fresh pineapple, peeled and cut into
    pieces
2 cups seedless red grapes, halved
2 ripe avocados, peeled and sliced
½ cup pine nuts, toasted
½ cup toasted shredded coconut
Lime slices and mint leaves, for garnish

- Trim the tenderloins of all fat and silver skin.

- Place in a gallon-size, heavy-duty, zip-top plastic bag and pour over the marinade; seal tightly.
- Place in the refrigerator for several hours or overnight.
- Remove the tenderloins from the marinade and place on a hot grill, or roast on a rack in a shallow pan in a preheated 425-degree oven. Roast or grill for 20 to 25 minutes or until the pork reaches 150 degrees internal temperature.
- Remove and cool.
- Wrap and chill until ready to use.
- Line a large platter or large shallow bowl with the lettuce leaves.
- Slice the tenderloins into $1/4$-in. slices and toss in half of the dressing.
- Place in the center of the lettuce.
- Arrange the pineapple, grapes, and avocado in an attractive fashion around the pork. Drizzle with the remaining dressing.
- Sprinkle the pine nuts and coconut over the top and garnish with lime slices and mint leaves.
- Serve immediately.
- Serves 8-10.

Ginger-Lime Marinade

¼ cup peanut or vegetable oil
Juice and zest of 2 medium to large limes
1 large clove garlic, finely chopped
1 tbsp. finely chopped gingerroot
2 tbsp. chopped fresh cilantro leaves
2 tsp. salt
1 tsp. hot pepper sauce
1 tsp. sugar

- Whisk together until well blended or mix in the blender or food processor.

Ginger-Lime Dressing

¾ cup peanut oil
¼ cup fresh lime juice
1 tbsp. "hot and sweet" mustard
½ tsp. salt
1 tbsp. honey
1 tsp. grated gingerroot

- Whisk together until well blended or mix in the blender or food processor.
- Makes about 1 cup.

Fruited Chicken Salad with Lime-Macadamia Dressing

This is just the sort of attractive and delectable chicken salad you would expect to find at an elegant Southern "ladies luncheon." It would invariably be accompanied by a basket of piping-hot yeast rolls. Poaching the boneless breasts is quick and easy, and they are always juicy and tender. I really like this combination of fruit, but you can certainly create your own variation, since most any fruit goes nicely with this special macadamia dressing.

3 whole boneless and skinless chicken breasts
1 cup chicken broth
½ cup white wine
1 clove garlic, peeled and crushed
1 bay leaf
1 small pineapple, peeled and cut into pieces
2 cups seedless green grapes, halved
2 ripe mangos, peeled and cubed
½ cup dried apricots, cut into small strips
1 recipe Lime-Macadamia Dressing (see below)
Crisp lettuce leaves
Small bunches of grapes and lime slices, for
garnish

- Trim the chicken breasts of any fat. Place between two sheets of plastic wrap and flatten with a veal pounder.
- In a nonreactive skillet, combine the broth, wine, garlic, and bay leaf. Bring to a boil and boil for 5 minutes.
- Add the chicken. Cover with parchment paper and the skillet lid.
- Simmer for 8 to 10 minutes, or until the chicken is done. Do not overcook.

If you don't have a veal pounder, a bottle of wine may be used to flatten boneless chicken breasts.

- Let cool for 10 minutes in the liquid. Remove and slice, across the grain, into small strips.
- Toss together the pineapple, grapes, mangos, and apricots.
- Add the chicken.
- Make the dressing and toss into the salad mixture.
- Line a platter or shallow bowl with the lettuce leaves.
- Arrange the salad on the lettuce.
- Garnish with the grapes and lime slices.
- Serves 8-10.

Lime-Macadamia Dressing

½ cup walnut oil
¼ cup vegetable oil
¼ cup fresh lime juice
2 tbsp. apricot preserves
⅛ tsp. cayenne pepper
½ cup toasted and salted macadamia nuts

- In a food processor or blender, blend together all the ingredients except the nuts.
- Add the nuts and process just long enough to chop them finely.
- Makes about 1 cup.

Chicken Rice Salad
with Asian Dressing

I am happy to share the recipe for this tasty rice salad. The dish combines my two favorite types of rice: basmati (or our own domestic "Texmati") and wild rice, which is not rice at all but actually a seed. In any case, they are both flavorful whether served hot or cold. Having rice salad on the menu is a boon for the busy host or hostess, because it holds well in the refrigerator. This one is full of good flavors that only improve with the chilling. The lively flavor of the hot chili oil (available in Asian specialty stores or the special section of the grocery store) is an interesting touch.

> 1 cup raw long-grain wild rice
> Boiling water
> 2 whole boneless and skinless chicken breasts
> 2 tbsp. vegetable oil
> 1 tbsp. toasted-sesame oil
> 1 tsp. hot chili oil, or to taste
> Salt, to taste
> 1 cup raw basmati or Texmati rice
> ½ lb. fresh snow peas, washed and strung
> ½ cup chopped green onions
> 2 carrots, shredded
> 1 red bell pepper, cut into small strips
> 1 cup fresh bean sprouts, washed and dried
> ½ cup chopped fresh cilantro (or parsley)
> 1 recipe Asian Dressing (see below)
> Crisp lettuce leaves
> ½ cup sliced almonds, toasted

- One day ahead, put the wild rice in a glass measuring cup or bowl. Cover with 2 in. boiling water. Cover and allow to sit at room temperature for 12 to 24 hours. Drain and top with more boiling water. Cover loosely with waxed paper and place in microwave oven on high for 15 to 20 minutes or until the rice grains are tender but not mushy. Allow to sit for 10 minutes and drain off any excess water. Set aside.

- To finish, place the chicken breasts between two sheets of plastic wrap. Pound with a veal pounder (or some heavy flat object) to flatten chicken to an even thickness.

- Mix together the oils.

- Brush all surfaces of the chicken with the oil mixture and lightly salt.
- Grill or broil the chicken, turning once, just until done through—8 to 10 minutes, depending on size. Cool.
- Cut the chicken, across the grain, into bite-sized pieces.
- Cook the basmati rice according to package directions. Cool and fluff. Toss with the cooked wild rice.
- Blanch the snow peas for 30 seconds in lightly salted boiling water. Drain immediately and refresh with very cold water. Drain well and cut in half on the diagonal.
- Add the peas to the rice.
- Toss the green onions, carrots, red pepper, bean sprouts, and cilantro into the rice.
- Make the dressing.
- Add enough dressing to the rice mixture for good flavor.
- Toss the chicken with just enough dressing to coat.
- To serve, place the rice salad on a bed of lettuce leaves.
- Arrange the chicken on the rice.
- Sprinkle toasted almonds over the top.
- Serves 8 generously.

Asian Dressing

½ cup Chinese soy sauce
¼ cup peanut or vegetable oil
2 tbsp. toasted-sesame oil
1 tbsp. hot and sweet mustard
¼ cup rice-wine vinegar
Hot chili oil, to taste

- Whisk together or mix in the blender or food processor.

Smoked Turkey and Broccoli Salad

This is one of those dishes you can whip out of a grocery bag and into sup-per in no time (especially if you have a food processor to do the chopping). The turkey comes straight from the deli counter. The broccoli is quick and easy to prepare in the microwave or steamer, and the dressing is a snap. Toss it all up and serve! This is a good one to remember when it is your turn to contribute to "pot luck." It travels and keeps well, and you know everybody is interested in eating their share of broccoli these days.

> 1 large bunch fresh broccoli
> 1 lb. thickly sliced smoked turkey breast, cut
>   into small strips
> 1 cup coarsely chopped celery
> 1 large red bell pepper, cut into julienne strips
> 1 large red Spanish onion, halved and thinly
>   sliced
> ½ cup sliced black olives
> ¼ cup chopped parsley
> ¾ cup vegetable oil
> 1 tbsp. soy sauce
> ½ tsp. salt, or to taste
> ½ tsp. hot pepper sauce, or to taste
> 1 tsp. sugar
> ¼ cup cider vinegar
> Crisp leaf lettuce leaves
> Extra red pepper strips and parsley sprigs, for
>   garnish

- Wash and trim the broccoli. Cut into florets.
- Peel the tender part of the large stems. Cut into ¼-in. slices.
- Steam the florets for 2 minutes. Refresh in ice water and drain well.
- Steam the stems for 3 to 5 minutes or until crisp-tender. Refresh and drain.
- Toss the broccoli and turkey with the celery, bell pepper, onion, olives, and chopped parsley.
- Whisk together the oil, soy sauce, salt, hot pepper sauce, sugar, and vinegar until well blended. (Or process in a blender or food processor.)

- Toss enough dressing into the salad to coat all the ingredients.
- Pile onto a bed of crisp lettuce leaves.
- Garnish with strips of red pepper and parsley sprigs.
- Serve cold.
- Serves 6-8.

Avocado-Fruit Salad

Most salads rely on fresh seasonal ingredients. But the season for this one is not the usual summertime season. This is one of my favorite standbys for cold-weather meals. That is, of course, when citrus fruits are at their peak and the other ingredients are available as well. It looks so pretty, tastes great with roast chicken or turkey, and also complements a succulent slice of baked ham.

> **3 navel oranges**
> **3 large white or pink grapefruits**
> **3 ripe medium avocados**
> **Juice of ½ lemon**
> **½ cup peanut or vegetable oil**
> **¼ cup fresh lemon juice**
> **½ cup honey**
> **1 tsp. salt**
> **Dash hot pepper sauce**
> **1 tsp. celery seed**
> **Boston or Bibb lettuce leaves**
> **1 cup seedless red grapes, halved**
> **Watercress leaves, for garnish**

To peel an avocado, cut it in half lengthwise and remove the pit. Using a large spoon, scoop each avocado half, intact, from the peel. Place flat side down on a cutting board to slice or cube.

- With a sharp knife with a flexible blade, trim the ends of the oranges and grapefruits. Cut down, following the contour of each fruit, and remove a strip of peel with the white pith. Continue until the peels are all removed.
- Slice oranges and grapefruits crosswise into $^1/_8$-in. slices.
- Cut the avocados in half lengthwise. Scoop them out of the peels, intact, and slice into thin slices.
- Acidulate the avocados with juice from the ½ lemon.
- Make the dressing by placing the oil, lemon juice, honey, salt,

and hot pepper sauce in a food processor or blender and processing until very smooth.

- Add the celery seed and process a few seconds just to blend.
- To assemble, arrange the lettuce leaves on individual salad plates or one large plate.
- Arrange the oranges, grapefruits, avocados, and grapes on the lettuce in an attractive pattern.
- Drizzle over just enough dressing to lightly coat.
- Garnish with the watercress leaves.
- Serves 8.

Tuna Salad Deluxe

Yes, there had to be at least one tuna-salad recipe. I thought you'd want one with a little different twist. This one has its own personality, starting with the "chiffonade" of iceberg lettuce and spinach. It is a colorful base for the other flavorful ingredients that earn this salad the "deluxe" title. By the way, keep this Mustard Vinaigrette in mind for simple tossed green salads as well.

> 1 recipe Mustard Vinaigrette (see below)
> 1 lb. fresh tuna fillets, 1 in. thick
> 1 small head iceberg lettuce, washed, dried, chilled, and finely shredded
> 2 cups fresh spinach leaves, washed, dried, chilled, and finely shredded
> 2 ripe large tomatoes, cut into small wedges
> 1 medium cucumber, peeled, seeded, and thinly sliced
> 1 large red bell pepper, cored and thinly sliced
> ½ cup whole pitted kalamata olives
> 2 tbsp. capers
> 3 tbsp. chopped parsley

- Make the Mustard Vinaigrette.
- Place the tuna in a shallow dish (or plastic bag) and pour over half of the dressing.
- Cover and marinate in the refrigerator at least 1 hour.

- Remove the tuna from the marinade and broil under a hot preheated broiler for 10 minutes, turning once after 6 or 7 minutes. (Or grill for the same time on a hot grill.)
- Cover the fish and chill until ready to use.
- Toss together the shredded lettuce and spinach. Toss with half of the remaining dressing and place on a serving dish.
- Arrange the tomatoes, cucumbers, and peppers around the edge.
- Flake the tuna into large flakes and arrange in the middle of the plate.
- Sprinkle over the olives, capers, and parsley.
- Drizzle over the remaining dressing and serve.
- Serves 6.

Note: For a variation, substitute 2 7-oz. cans good-quality tuna for the fresh tuna. Drain the canned tuna, pour over $1/4$ cup dressing, and chill for 1 hour before adding to salad.

Mustard Vinaigrette
¾ cup extra-virgin olive oil
1 clove garlic, finely chopped
1 tbsp. Dijon mustard
1 tsp. salt, or to taste
½ tsp. coarsely ground black pepper
1 tsp. sugar
¼ cup red-wine vinegar

- Blend together the oil, garlic, mustard, salt, pepper, and sugar.
- Whisk in the vinegar. (Or blend all together in the blender or food processor.)
- Makes about 1 cup.

Calico Salad

The healthy ingredients in this salad are not the only reason to make it. It tastes good too and is a colorful, crunchy side salad for any meat, poultry, or fish from the grill.

1 bunch broccoli
Boiling salted water
3 cups (½ lb.) shredded cabbage
1 10-oz. pkg. frozen green peas, thawed
1 red bell pepper, cut into strips
½ cup vegetable oil
⅓ cup white vinegar
1 tsp. finely chopped onion
¾ tsp. paprika
1 tsp. celery seed
1 tsp. dry mustard
2 tbsp. honey
½ cup heavy cream
Salt, to taste
Hot pepper sauce, to taste
Boston or leaf lettuce

- Trim the broccoli; cut into florets, and set florets aside. Peel the stems and cut into thin slices.
- Blanch the broccoli stems in the water for 5 to 6 minutes or until crisp-tender. Add the florets and cook 1 minute. Drain and refresh with cold water. Dry on paper towels.
- Toss with the cabbage, peas, and red pepper.
- Mix together the oil, vinegar, onion, paprika, celery seed, mustard, honey, cream, salt, and hot pepper sauce and toss with the vegetables.
- Arrange on a bed of lettuce leaves.
- Serve immediately.
- Serves 8-10.

Crunchy Cole Slaw

There are times when nothing but cole slaw will do. It is a natural with fish. It is also the perfect side salad for a traditional American summer supper. This one goes a bit beyond "typical and traditional," with its extra-colorful ingredients, but it is definitely filled with good old-fashioned flavor.

> 1 small head green cabbage, finely shredded
> 4 medium carrots, peeled and shredded
> 1 cup thinly sliced celery
> 1 medium red bell pepper, chopped
> 1 small red Spanish onion, chopped
> ¼ cup chopped flat-leaf parsley
> 1 recipe Creamy Slaw Dressing (see below)

- Toss together all of the slaw ingredients.
- Chill until ready to serve.
- Make the Creamy Slaw Dressing and toss into the slaw before serving.
- Serves 8.

Creamy Slaw Dressing

1 cup mayonnaise
¼ cup yogurt (or reduced-fat sour cream)
1 tsp. sugar
1 tsp. dried dill
¼ tsp. hot pepper sauce
1 tsp. Dijon mustard
½ tsp. salt
1 tbsp. fresh lemon juice

- Mix together with a whisk until smooth.
- Cover and chill until ready to use.
- Makes about 1¼ cups.

Asparagus with Citrus Vinaigrette

I think fresh, tender asparagus may taste even better cold than hot. Buy nice plump spears for this recipe—they taste so much better than the skinny ones. This also makes an elegant side salad or light first course for a dinner party. Add some boiled shrimp and/or julienne strips of lean ham to turn this salad into a spring lunch. Also, please note that this is another good, basic vinaigrette that can be used for other vegetables or for tossed mixed greens.

> **1 lb. fresh asparagus**
> **Water to cover**
> **2 hard-cooked eggs, sieved**
> **½ cup chopped fresh parsley**
> **1 tsp. finely chopped lemon zest**
> **1 tsp. salt, or to taste**
> **¼ tsp. freshly ground black pepper**
> **1 recipe Citrus Vinaigrette (see below)**
> **Crisp Bibb lettuce leaves**

- Wash the asparagus and break off the tough ends.
- In a large nonreactive skillet, boil just enough water to cover the asparagus.
- Lightly salt the water and lay the asparagus in the boiling water. Cover with 2 layers of soft white paper towels.
- Simmer for 3 to 4 minutes (for thick spears).
- Remove immediately and refresh with ice water.
- Drain well.
- Toss the sieved eggs with the parsley and lemon zest.
- Season with salt and pepper.
- Make the Citrus Vinaigrette.
- Arrange the asparagus on a bed of lettuce leaves.
- Sprinkle over the egg mixture.
- Just before serving, drizzle lightly with the dressing.
- Serves 6.

Always add dressings with acid ingredients such as vinegar or lemon juice at the last minute to asparagus. The acidity will fade their bright green color.

To properly prepare hard-cooked eggs, cover with water in a saucepan with a tight-fitting lid. Bring to a boil with pan covered. Reduce to a simmer and cook for 10 minutes. Immediately drain and refresh with cold water to prevent overcooking. Overcooking causes an unattractive green ring to form around the yolk.

Citrus Vinaigrette

½ cup extra-virgin olive oil
1 tbsp. white-wine vinegar
1 tbsp. fresh lemon juice
1 tbsp. fresh orange juice
1 tsp. Dijon mustard
½ tsp. salt
Freshly ground black pepper, to taste

- Whisk together or blend in the blender or food processor.
- Makes about ⅔ cup.

Herbed Tabbouleh Salad

Here is my favorite version of a delicious and nutritious specialty from the Middle East.

2 cups ground bulgur wheat
4 cups boiling water
¼ cup extra-virgin olive oil
1 cup sliced kalamata olives
1 large red bell pepper, chopped
1 cup chopped flat-leaf parsley
½ cup fresh basil leaves, cut into strips
¼ cup thinly sliced green onions
1 cup coarsely chopped toasted pecans
Juice of 2 lemons
1½ tsp. salt
Freshly ground black pepper, to taste
1 small head romaine lettuce, coarsely shredded
    (optional)
Halved cherry tomatoes, lightly salted
Whole basil leaves

- Put the bulgur in a large bowl and pour over the boiling water.
- Let stand for at least 1 hour.
- Drain well and return to the bowl.
- Stir in the olive oil and olives.
- Toss in the red pepper, parsley, and basil strips.

- Stir in the green onions, pecans, and lemon juice.
- Season with the salt and pepper.
- Cover and chill until ready to serve, at least 4-5 hours.
- To serve, spoon onto a bed of romaine and garnish with the tomatoes and basil leaves.
- Serves 8-10.

Super Soups and Stews

What's my own most favorite food? It's probably not possible for me to come up with an honest, definitive answer. I am, however, confident in saying that I never tire of eating good soup. I enjoy all types of soup, from the spiciest chili to creamy, elegant soups. Now if you ask which soup I like best, I will have to tell you "all of the following." It wasn't easy tackling my overflowing soup file to choose recipes from a soup lover's collection. That's why this chapter is so long.

There is something special about a steaming bowl of aromatic soup. Isn't it always the first thing we think of when we're feeling under the weather and need to be nourished and nurtured? It's something everybody can make, too. A good soup brings together a combination of ingredients that taste even better together than they did alone. In soups, the whole is indeed greater than the sum of its parts. And finally, a soup recipe is a good choice for those of you caught up in today's typical busy lifestyles. It is one dish that usually actually improves when it is made ahead and reheated as needed. You Sunday-afternoon chefs should have a great time with this chapter. Pass the crackers!

Marilyn's Gazpacho

Dilled and Chilled
Summer Vegetable Soup

Guacamole Soup

Fish Soup
with Garlic Croutons

Oyster and Chicken Gumbo

Chicken Stock

Beef Stock

Easy Roasted Red Pepper Soup

Red bell peppers are so sweet and delicious as well as a beautiful addition to so many dishes. Roasting enhances their rich flavor, making them a great base for this pretty soup. This quick and easy soup is a perfect beginning to an elegant dinner menu.

**3 large red bell peppers, roasted, peeled, and
  seeded
28-oz. can chopped tomatoes
2 cloves garlic, finely chopped
3 tbsp. extra-virgin olive oil
3 cups chicken broth
1 cup heavy cream
1 tsp. salt
½ tsp. hot pepper sauce
Chopped parsley**

- Purée the peppers and tomatoes in a blender.
- Gently heat the garlic in the olive oil, taking care not to let it brown.
- Stir in the purée and broth and bring to a boil.
- Whip the cream with the salt and hot pepper sauce.
- Top each serving of hot soup with the whipped cream and a sprinkle of parsley.
- Serves 8.

Swiss Leek Soup

Leeks are a great flavor addition to so many soups. They star in this one, a rich and delicious cheese soup. I've often included this recipe in my annual January soup classes because it is so well suited to a frosty winter day.

3 tbsp. butter
4 large leeks, thinly sliced
4 stalks celery, thinly sliced
1 large onion, thinly sliced
¼ cup flour
7 cups chicken broth
2 cups shredded Swiss cheese (Emmenthaler)
1 cup shredded Gruyere cheese
Salt and freshly ground black pepper, to taste
Dash of freshly grated nutmeg
1 cup heavy cream
¼ cup dry sherry
Chopped parsley

- Heat the butter in a large heavy pot. Add the leeks, celery, and onion. Cook, stirring, for 6 to 8 minutes or until the leeks are tender.

- Stir in the flour and cook over medium heat for 2 minutes without browning.

- Whisk in the broth and cook for 20 minutes.

- Purée and return to the pot. Slowly stir in the cheeses until they are melted.

- Season with salt, pepper, and nutmeg. Whisk in the cream and reheat, but do not boil.

- Add the sherry. Sprinkle with parsley before serving.

- Serves 8-10.

Butternut Squash Soup with Ginger and Toasted Hazelnuts

Butternut squash is my favorite of the winter squashes. Many soup recipes I've tried call for peeling and dicing the raw squash, a laborious task. I think you'll like my method of roasting the squash first. This not only makes for an easier recipe but also improves the rich squash flavor in this luscious soup.

> 1 large butternut squash (2½-3 lb.)
> Olive oil
> 2 tbsp. butter
> 2 tbsp. olive oil
> 2 large onions, chopped
> 1 tbsp. finely chopped fresh gingerroot
> ½ tsp. cayenne pepper, or to taste
> 2 tsp. salt
> 1 tbsp. dark brown sugar
> 3 sprigs fresh thyme
> 1 bay leaf
> 6 cups chicken broth
> 2 cups light cream (half and half)
> 1 cup crème fraiche
> ½ cup chopped toasted hazelnuts

- Cut the squash in half lengthwise. Line a baking sheet with foil. Brush the cut sides with some olive oil and place, cut sides down, on the baking sheet. Place in a preheated 375-degree oven for 1 hour or until fork tender. Cool. Scoop out the seeds and discard. Remove the pulp and reserve.

- In a large heavy pot, melt the butter with the oil. Add the onions and sauté for 5 minutes or until tender. Stir in the ginger, cayenne, salt, and sugar.

- Make a bouquet garni from the thyme and bay leaf and add to the pot along with the broth. Bring to a boil. Add the squash and cook for 15 minutes.

- Remove the bouquet garni and purée the mixture. Return to the pot and whisk in the light cream. Reheat, but do not allow to boil.

- Serve hot in bowls, each topped with a dollop of crème fraiche and a small spoonful of the hazelnuts.

- Serves 8-10.

Yellow Squash Bisque

A "bisque" is simply "a thick cream soup," and this one fits that definition perfectly. It is, however, thickened with wonderfully healthful and flavorful vegetables. Aside from the squash itself, the carrots and potatoes serve as natural thickeners while adding plenty of nutritional value. I happen to find the contrast of the mild vegetables and the very spicy cayenne to be most appealing. (I confess that I often add even a bit more than called for here.) You can feel free to use less if you want a milder-flavored cream soup.

6 tbsp. butter
1 large yellow onion, chopped
1½ lb. yellow summer squash, washed, trimmed, and diced
2 medium (about 1 lb.) russet potatoes, peeled and diced
2 medium carrots, peeled and sliced
6 cups chicken broth
Salt, to taste
¼ tsp. cayenne pepper, or to taste
1 cup cream (heavy or light)
2 tbsp. chopped parsley, for garnish

- Melt the butter in a large, heavy pot.
- Sauté the onion in the butter, stirring, for 5 minutes.
- Stir in the squash and sauté, stirring, 5 minutes more.
- Add the potatoes, carrots, and broth.
- Bring to a boil and then simmer, uncovered, for 20 to 25 minutes, or until the carrots are tender.
- Season with the salt and cayenne.
- Purée the mixture in a blender or food processor.
- Return to the pot and stir in the cream.
- Reheat, but do not boil.
- To serve, sprinkle each bowl of soup with some chopped parsley.
- Serves 8.

Note: If the squash seeds are large, halve the squash, scrape out the seeds, and discard them before dicing the squash.

Cream of Parsley Soup

The first cooking school where I taught on a regular basis, Hurrah!, has long since closed its doors, but many happy memories remain behind. It was there where I first experienced teasing from the students about my obvious love for that delightful herb, parsley. One Christmas a student arrived with an enormous bouquet of lovely fresh parsley and ceremoniously presented it with a funny proclamation that said, among other good things, that she knew there was nothing I would like better. I honestly can't imagine cooking without it. This lovely soup does a delicious job of displaying parsley's inimitable fresh flavor.

> When making cream soups ahead of time, stop just before adding the cream. Cool and chill. When ready to serve, bring back to a boil, add the cream, and reheat just to serving temperature. This makes reheating much simpler and eliminates the chance of overheating and causing the cream to curdle.

2 tbsp. unsalted butter
2 tbsp. extra-virgin olive oil
2 medium yellow onions, chopped
1 tsp. curry powder
6 cups chicken broth
4 cups peeled and diced potatoes
2 cups flat-leaf parsley leaves
Salt and freshly ground white pepper, to taste
2 cups light cream
Extra chopped parsley, for garnish

- Melt the butter with the oil in a large, heavy, nonreactive soup pot.
- Add the onions and cook, stirring, over medium heat until translucent and tender.
- Add the curry powder and cook, stirring, for 2 to 3 minutes.
- Whisk in the broth.
- Add the potatoes and bring to a boil. Cook, partially covered, for 20 minutes.
- Add the parsley leaves and cook 10 minutes more.
- Purée in a blender or food processor and return to a clean pot.
- Season to taste with salt and pepper.
- Whisk in the cream and reheat to serving temperature. Do not boil.
- To serve, sprinkle with the extra chopped parsley.
- Serves 8.

Fresh Cream of Asparagus Soup

This classic and most elegant asparagus soup has been in my active file since my early days of studying French cooking. It is one of the first things I make when the tender spring asparagus appears in the market. If you wish to lighten it up a bit, you may substitute light cream for the richer heavy one, but I should warn you that you won't have the same velvety texture.

1 lb. fresh asparagus
3 tbsp. butter
1 cup chopped yellow onion
3 tbsp. flour
5 cups chicken broth
1 cup heavy cream
Salt and freshly ground black pepper, to taste
2 tbsp. chopped fresh parsley

- Break the tough ends from the asparagus and discard.
- Cut the tips from the tender ends and set aside.
- Cut the tender ends into small pieces.
- Melt the butter in a large heavy pot.
- Sauté the onion, stirring, for 3 to 4 minutes or until tender.
- Stir in the flour and cook, stirring, for 2 minutes. Do not allow to brown.
- Whisk in the broth.
- Add the asparagus pieces and cook, partially covered, for 20 minutes.
- Allow to cool slightly and purée in a blender.
- Return to the pot.
- Whisk in the cream. Reheat. Do not allow to boil.
- Season to taste with salt and pepper.
- Meanwhile, cook the tips in a small amount of water in the microwave or on the stove, for 2 minutes (should be crisp-tender).
- Add the cooked tips to the soup along with the parsley.
- Serve hot.
- Serves 8.

Easy Spinach Soup

You won't find an easier homemade soup. This is perfect for supper on a cold day and yet light enough for any season of the year. It's also a tasty way to serve one of our healthiest green vegetables.

2 10-oz. pkg. frozen chopped spinach, thawed
   and squeezed*
5 cups chicken broth
1 tsp. Worcestershire sauce
Dash hot pepper sauce
1 tsp. potato starch**
2 cups light cream (half and half)
Dash freshly grated nutmeg
Salt, to taste

• Stir together the spinach, broth, Worcestershire, and hot pepper sauce.

• Bring to a boil, stirring.

• Reduce the heat and simmer for 5 minutes.

• Whisk the potato starch in ¼ cup cream. Whisk into the soup and add the remaining cream.

• Bring back to a simmer, stirring until the soup thickens slightly.

• Add the nutmeg and salt.

• Serves 6-8.

*To thaw spinach, place packages in a dish overnight in the refrigerator or thaw in the microwave.

**For a thicker soup, add a second tsp. potato starch.

Creamy Green Pea Soup

I tend to prefer a fresh green pea soup over the perhaps more typical split-pea soup made from dried peas. This one is flavored with the elegant taste of fresh leeks and is especially delicate and flavorful. A small portion is an excellent beginning to an elegant dinner. Or add a salad or sandwich to make a complete delicious lunch or supper. This is a good choice for a soup to make on the weekend for planned leftovers later in the week since it reheats well. Its luscious flavors actually improve after a day or two in the refrigerator. Just take care to heat it over gentle heat and don't allow it to boil.

> **2 tbsp. butter**
> **3 medium leeks, washed, trimmed, and chopped**
> **2 10-oz. pkg. frozen tiny green peas**
> **5 cups chicken broth**
> **1 cup heavy cream**
> **Salt and freshly ground black pepper, to taste**
> **Herb-flavored croutons (see tip)**

• Melt the butter in a heavy pan that has a lid.

• Stir in the leeks.

• Cover the pan and reduce the heat to low to sweat the leeks until soft and tender, about 15 minutes.

• Raise the heat and stir in the peas and broth.

• Bring to a boil and cook, stirring occasionally, for 15 minutes.

• Purée the mixture in a blender.

• Return to the pan and whisk in the cream.

• Reheat, but do not boil.

• Season to taste with salt and pepper.

• Sprinkle in the croutons just before serving.

• Serves 6-8.

Instead of throwing away those last few slices of stale bread, make your own croutons for soups and salads. Simply cut the bread into cubes. Spread into a single layer on a shallow baking pan. Melt the appropriate amount of butter (or use some good fruity olive oil) and season with some finely chopped fresh garlic and an assortment of dried herbs. Some finely chopped fresh parsley is also good to include. Toss the bread cubes with the flavored butter or oil, just enough to lightly coat. Bake in a 325-degree oven, stirring a couple of times, until toasted. To dry completely, allow to sit in the turned-off oven until dry.

Red Cabbage Soup

This soup has the same full-bodied flavor one expects from a really good pot of red cabbage, or Rotkohl, from a good German kitchen. Leeks are always plentiful in Germany and are used in many soups there. Their flavor is an important part of this hearty but elegant soup.

Recipes that contain ingredients with high acid content (like vinegar, apples, and tomatoes) should be cooked in a nonreactive pot. These ingredients will react with uncoated or unlined aluminum or iron cookware. The result is a chemical reaction that can give the dish an unpleasant metallic taste. Foods high in acid can also pit and damage the pan.

2 tbsp. unsalted butter
2 tbsp. vegetable oil
3 leeks, trimmed, washed, and thinly sliced
1 clove garlic, finely chopped
¼ cup light brown sugar
½ cup red-wine vinegar
½ tsp. allspice
1 medium head red cabbage, quartered and shredded
1 small onion, peeled
3 whole cloves
1 bay leaf
7 cups chicken broth
1 cup diced lean ham (optional)
1 cup sour cream
1 tsp. salt, or to taste
½ tsp. freshly ground black pepper
3 tbsp. chopped fresh dill (or 1 tbsp. dried)

- In a large pot, heat the butter and oil together.
- Sauté the leeks and garlic, stirring, for 10 minutes.
- Stir in the sugar, vinegar, and allspice and stir until sugar is dissolved.
- Add the cabbage.
- Stud the onion with the cloves and add to the pot along with the bay leaf.
- Pour in the broth and bring to a boil.
- Simmer, uncovered, for 45 minutes.
- Remove the onion and bay leaf.
- Stir in the ham (if desired) and sour cream, and reheat until hot but not boiling.
- Add salt, pepper, and dill.
- Serves 8-10.

Cauliflower Soup

This is another soup that stems from my experience in Europe. It is my version of a soup I enjoyed in Copenhagen. It is an excellent way to enjoy this pretty and nutritious winter vegetable.

> 1 large head cauliflower
> 4 tbsp. butter
> 1 cup chopped onion
> ¼ cup flour
> 4 cups chicken broth
> 1 tsp. salt, or to taste
> Freshly grated nutmeg, to taste
> ¼ tsp. white pepper
> 2 oz. Roquefort cheese, crumbled
> 2 cups light cream (half and half)
> ¼ cup chopped parsley

- Remove the leaves and thick base of the cauliflower; wash and cut into florets; set aside.
- Melt the butter in a large, heavy pan and sauté the onions until tender, 4 to 5 minutes.
- Add the flour and cook for 2 minutes.
- Whisk in the broth.
- Add the cauliflower and seasonings and cook for about 20 minutes or until the cauliflower is tender.
- Purée in a blender or food processor and return to the pan.
- Whisk in the cheese and cream, stirring until the cheese is melted. Do not boil.
- Garnish with parsley.
- Serves 6-8.

Mushroom Velvet Soup

This has the flavor of a classic "cream of mushroom" with a slightly different touch. While most of the mushrooms are puréed, some nice firm sautéed slices are set aside to add some texture. Please note that a proper mushroom cream soup must not be too thick. Like this one, all good cream soups should be just thick enough to lightly coat a spoon. Once again, if you prefer to make a lighter version, substitute light cream.

> 6 tbsp. butter
> 1½ lb. mushrooms, thinly sliced
> Salt and white pepper, to taste
> 1 cup chopped green onions
> 2 cloves garlic, finely chopped
> 4 large shallots, finely chopped
> 6 cups chicken broth
> 1 tsp. lemon juice
> 1 cup heavy cream
> ¼ cup chopped parsley

- Heat 2 tbsp. of the butter in a skillet. Sauté over high heat 2 cups of the mushrooms until they are tender and lightly browned, stirring, for 6 to 8 minutes. Season to taste with salt and pepper; set aside.
- Heat the remaining butter in a large pot.
- Sauté the remaining mushrooms, onions, garlic, and shallots just until onions are tender, about 5 minutes.
- Add the broth, lemon juice, and more salt and pepper and simmer for 30 minutes.
- Purée the mixture in a blender or food processor.
- Return to a clean pot and add the cream.
- Reheat; do not boil.
- Taste and correct seasonings.
- To serve, spoon some of the mushrooms into a bowl and ladle over the soup.
- Garnish with parsley.
- Serves 8-10.

Easy Borscht

I love this hearty soup from the Baltic regions, but the original recipe is very time-consuming. So, I've developed my own, much simpler version, retaining the authentic flavors of the original but requiring about half the preparation time. This is a perfect cold-weather soup—make up a big pot of it on the weekend and have what I call at our house "the soup of the week." It's best with some hearty homemade beef stock but works fine with a quality canned one.

**6 tbsp. butter
2 cloves garlic, finely chopped
1½ cups thinly sliced onions
1 cup sliced celery
1 cup sliced carrots
1½ lb. fresh beets (3 cups grated)
8 cups beef stock
2 tbsp. red-wine vinegar
1 tbsp. fresh dill (or 1 tsp. dried)
Salt and freshly ground black pepper, to taste
3 cups shredded green cabbage
2 large red potatoes, peeled and cubed
Sour cream
Extra chopped fresh dill or parsley, for garnish**

- Melt the butter in a large pot.
- Cook the garlic, onions, celery, and carrots in the butter, stirring, for 10 minutes.
- Add the beets, 2 cups stock, vinegar, dill, salt, and pepper to the onion mixture.
- Simmer, partially covered, for 20 minutes.
- Add the remaining stock, cabbage, and potatoes.
- Simmer for 20 minutes more.
- Taste and correct seasonings.
- Serve topped with a generous dollop of sour cream sprinkled with dill or parsley.
- Serves 8.

Puréed Winter Vegetable Soup

I am so very fond of turnips, but my dear husband does not share that sentiment. However, after many years of marriage, I have made the interesting discovery that he will often eat what he cannot see. That is how this soup came to appear at our table. The smallest-diced turnips in a normal winter-vegetable soup would be discovered with disdain. When I offered this lovely, creamy version composed of unidentified vegetables, it was devoured with gusto. Maybe it will work for you too. Just in case it doesn't, you can substitute 3 parsnips for the turnips.

> 4 tbsp. butter
> 1½ cups chopped onion
> 6 cups chicken broth
> 2 large turnips, peeled and cubed
> 6 carrots, peeled and sliced
> 2 red potatoes, peeled and cubed
> 1 cup heavy cream
> Salt and freshly ground black pepper, to taste
> Dash freshly grated nutmeg
> Chopped parsley

- Heat the butter in a large, heavy pan.

- Sauté the onion, stirring, for 5 minutes.

- Add the broth and vegetables and cook until all the vegetables are fork tender—about 20 to 25 minutes.

- Purée in a blender or food processor.

- Return to the pan and whisk in the cream. Season with salt, pepper, and nutmeg.

- Reheat without boiling.

- Sprinkle with parsley to serve.

- Serves 8.

Creole Corn Soup

I never tire of eating corn. It appears in all forms in many of my favorite dishes, from Mexican corn flour to simple roasted ears. I am certainly an advocate of eating it on every possible occasion during its summer season, and that is the time when I like this soup best. But the good news is that you can use frozen corn in the heart of winter and produce an aromatic and tasty pot of corn soup. Simply substitute two 10-oz. packages of frozen whole-kernel corn for the fresh corn.

    10 ears fresh corn (white or yellow)
    3 tbsp. butter
    1 large onion, chopped
    2 stalks celery, chopped
    2 large tomatoes, peeled and chopped
    8 cups chicken broth
    1 tsp. salt, or to taste
    ¼ tsp. freshly ground black pepper
    3 tbsp. chopped parsley

- Cut the corn from the cob. Scrape the cob well. Set aside.
- Melt the butter in a large pot.
- Add the onion and celery and sauté, stirring, over high heat for 3 minutes.
- Stir in the tomatoes and cook 2 minutes more.
- Stir in the broth and simmer for 20 minutes.
- Add the corn and cook 5 minutes longer.
- Season to taste with salt and pepper.
- Add the parsley.
- Serves 8-10.

Hearty Vegetable Soup with Basil Meatballs

*I didn't want to offer you just any old standard sort of recipe for veg-
etable-beef soup, because not only are there already so many in print, but
don't you all have your favorite already? Those are the recipes that we
just "know" from eating at our mothers' and grandmothers' tables. This
one stands out not only because of its savory vegetable-beef soup flavor
but because the "beef" comes from succulent little meatballs. It is also
handy for you busy cooks because the cooking time is so much shorter
than a traditional vegetable-beef soup. The meatballs can also be made
the night before and chilled, ready to add. For that matter, the entire pot
of soup tastes best when made the day before.*

> 2 tbsp. butter
> 2 tbsp. olive oil
> 2 cups chopped onion
> 2 cloves garlic, finely chopped
> 1 cup chopped celery
> 1 cup chopped carrots
> 6 cups beef stock (homemade or canned)
> 1 cup tomato purée
> 2 large red potatoes, peeled and diced
> 1 recipe Basil Meatballs (see below)
> ½ cup chopped fresh parsley
> Salt and freshly ground black pepper, to taste

- Heat the butter and oil together in a large, heavy pot.
- Stir in the onion, garlic, and celery and cook, stirring, for 10 minutes.
- Stir in the carrots and cook for 2 to 3 minutes longer.
- Add the stock, tomato purée, and potatoes.
- Bring to a boil and then simmer, partially covered, for 20 minutes.
- Make the Basil Meatballs according to the following recipe. Add to the soup and cook 20 minutes longer.
- Add parsley, season to taste, and serve piping hot.

Basil Meatballs

1 lb. very lean ground beef
1 tsp. salt
½ tsp. freshly ground black pepper
2 tbsp. finely shredded fresh basil
¼ cup chopped fresh flat-leaf parsley
½ cup fresh breadcrumbs
1 egg, lightly beaten

- Using two forks, lightly toss together all ingredients.
- Form into tiny meatballs and add them to the soup.
- Serves 8-10.

Minestrone alla Genovese

I've never had a better assistant in the kitchen than Tori Houlihan. She is smart, organized, and great fun to be with. We've spent lots of hours together in several kitchens and she has helped me teach many a cooking class. Tori shares my love for a good bowl of soup and sent one of her hearty favorites for this book.

2 links Italian sausage, casing removed
3 tbsp. olive oil
1 clove garlic, crushed
½ cup diced onion
½ cup chopped carrot
¼ cup chopped green bell pepper
½ cup chopped celery (include some tops if possible)
1 cup diced potato
2 cups beef stock
2 cups water
28-oz. can diced Italian-style tomatoes
1 cup shredded cabbage
1 cup chopped fresh spinach or ½ pkg. frozen chopped spinach
1 cup shelled fresh peas or ½ pkg. frozen peas
14½-oz. can canellini beans, drained and rinsed

A melon baller is the perfect tool for making uniform little meatballs. For larger meatballs, use a small ice-cream scoop.

1 tbsp. finely chopped fresh sage (or 1 tsp. dried)
¼ cup chopped fresh flat-leaf parsley
1 tsp. salt
½ tsp. freshly ground black pepper
¼ cup long-grain white rice
¼ cup ditalini (Italian soup pasta)
2 tbsp. dry red wine
½ cup freshly shredded Pecorino Romano

- In a large Dutch oven, sauté the sausage in the olive oil for 5 minutes, breaking it into small pieces.

- Add the garlic, onion, carrots, green pepper, celery, and potatoes; sauté for 10 minutes.

- Stir in the stock, water, tomatoes, cabbage, spinach, peas, beans, sage, parsley, salt, and pepper.

- Bring to a boil, reduce heat, and simmer for 30 minutes.

- Add the rice; simmer for 10 minutes.

- Add ditalini and wine. Simmer for another 10 minutes, stirring occasionally.

- Serve hot with Pecorino Romano on the side.

- Serves 10.

Provençal Veal Stew with Rice

In my "soups and stews" classes, I've labeled this dish a "company stew" because it is a bit more elegant than a typical stew. The gremolata (the combination of garlic, lemon zest, and parsley) adds interesting flavor and the breadcrumbs finish it with an attractive topping. Prepare this "fancy" stew in a dish that can go from oven to table. A shallow dish is the best choice so there is more room for the topping to brown and add texture. You may substitute cubed pork loin for the veal.

2 lb. veal stew meat
Salt and freshly ground black pepper, to taste
Flour, for dredging
3 tbsp. olive oil
3 large shallots, thinly sliced
½ cup dry white wine
1 cup beef stock
16-oz. can chopped tomatoes, puréed
1 tsp. brown sugar
2 tbsp. shredded fresh basil leaves
½ cup fresh breadcrumbs
2 cloves garlic, finely chopped
Zest of 1 lemon
¼ cup chopped flat-leaf parsley
Cooked rice

- Season the cubed veal with salt and pepper. Dredge in flour, shaking off the excess.
- Heat the oil in a heavy pot and brown the veal over medium-high heat.
- Remove with a slotted spoon to a side dish when it is browned.
- Add the shallots to the pot and cook, stirring until they are golden brown.
- Pour in the wine and cook for 2 to 3 minutes, stirring.
- Pour in the stock.
- Add the tomatoes and sugar.
- Return the veal to the pot and simmer the mixture, uncovered, for 15 minutes.
- Sprinkle in the basil.

When browning any meat for stew, don't crowd the pan. If the cubes of meat are allowed to touch, they will not brown well.

- Transfer to a nice shallow dish, cover, and place in a 300-degree oven for 1 hour or until the veal is fork tender.
- Meanwhile, stir together the breadcrumbs, garlic, lemon zest, and parsley to make the gremolata mixture.
- When the veal is tender, sprinkle over the gremolata and leave uncovered in the oven for 15 minutes.
- Serve with rice.
- Serves 6-8.

Spicy Fresh Tomato Soup

If I had to pick a favorite flavor among vegetable soups, it would have to be tomato. That puts me in the majority in our country, because the last time I checked it was everybody's favorite. This one incorporates both my love for tomato soup and my undying devotion to the good flavors of the Southwestern kitchen. The cilantro and hot sauce enhance the tangy tomato flavor. The sour cream adds a creamy contrast and the corn chips are a most appetizing "crouton." For a heartier and more elegant rendition of this soup, add 6 to 8 ounces of crabmeat or cooked shrimp just before serving.

2 lb. fresh tomatoes, peeled and seeded
2 tbsp. extra-virgin olive oil
1 large onion, chopped
2 large stalks celery, chopped
2 large cloves garlic, finely chopped
2 tbsp. flour
3 cups chicken broth
1 bay leaf
½ tsp. hot pepper sauce, or to taste
1 tsp. salt, or to taste
1 tsp. fresh lime juice
¼ cup chopped fresh cilantro
1 cup sour cream
Small corn chips, crushed
Extra chopped cilantro, for garnish

- Finely chop the tomatoes in a blender or food processor and set aside.

- Heat the oil in a large nonreactive pot.
- Add the onion, celery, and garlic. Cook, stirring occasionally, over high heat for 5 minutes.
- Stir in the flour, reduce heat to medium, and cook, stirring constantly, for 2 minutes.
- Whisk in the broth.
- Add the tomatoes and bay leaf.
- Cook, uncovered, over medium heat for 15 minutes.
- Season to taste with the hot pepper sauce and salt.
- Stir in the lime juice and cilantro.
- Remove the bay leaf.
- Serve hot, topping each bowl with a dollop of sour cream, some crushed corn chips (for "croutons"), and a sprinkling of cilantro.
- Serves 8.

Carrot and Jalapeño Soup

Just plain cream of carrot soup can be a most satisfying eating experience, but jazz it up a bit with my favorite hot pepper for a real culinary treat!

4 tbsp. butter
1½ cups chopped onion
1 lb. carrots, peeled and sliced
2-3 jalapeño peppers, seeded and finely chopped
1 tsp. fresh thyme leaves (or ⅓ tsp. dried)
1 bay leaf
5 cups chicken broth
1 cup heavy cream
1 tsp. salt, or to taste
3 tbsp. chopped cilantro

- Melt the butter in a heavy pot over medium heat.
- Stir in the onion, carrots, and jalapeño peppers and sauté, stirring, for 10 minutes.
- Add the thyme, bay leaf, and broth and bring to a boil.

- Reduce the heat to low and cook, partially covered, until carrots are very tender—about 25 to 30 minutes.
- Purée in the pot with an immersion blender until smooth. Or purée in a blender or food processor and return to the pot.
- Whisk in the cream and salt.
- Reheat without boiling.
- Serve hot, topped with cilantro.
- Serves 6-8.

Tortilla Soup

After telling one of my foodie friends that I was working on a soup chapter for this book, she said, "I hope you have a good tortilla soup." It just so happens I do! I like this one with its succulent chunks of white meat of chicken because it is light and yet satisfying enough to make a meal. Pass a bowl of sour cream if you like it creamier and a bowl of hot tomato salsa if you like it hotter. Shredded cheese is another popular condiment for sprinkling over the top.

> 4 chicken breast halves (with skin and bones)
> 2 onions, quartered
> 1 clove garlic, crushed
> 2 stalks celery, cut up
> 1 tsp. whole peppercorns
> 2 sprigs parsley (or cilantro)
> 1 bay leaf
> 10 cups water
> 1 large onion, chopped
> 3 tbsp. olive oil
> 6 tomatoes, peeled, seeded, and chopped
> 2 tbsp. fresh lime juice
> 1 tsp. dried oregano leaves
> 1 tsp. hot pepper sauce, or to taste
> 1½ tsp. salt, or to taste
> 6 corn tortillas, cut into ½-in. strips, fried crisp, and drained

- In a stockpot, combine the chicken breasts with the onion quarters, garlic, celery, peppercorns, parsley, bay leaf, and water.

- Bring to a boil and cook, uncovered, for 30 minutes or until the chicken is tender.
- Remove the chicken, cool, and remove the skin and bones. Coarsely chop the meat and set aside.
- Strain the stock and put in a large nonreactive pot. Reduce over high heat to 6 cups (this takes 10-15 minutes).
- In a heavy skillet, sauté the chopped onion in olive oil until tender, about 5 minutes.
- Add the tomatoes and sauté 2 minutes.
- Add the tomato mixture to the reduced stock.
- Add the lime juice, oregano, hot pepper sauce, and salt. Simmer for 5 minutes.
- Return the chopped chicken to the pot and cook until heated through.
- Ladle into bowls and garnish with the tortilla strips.
- Serves 10-12.

Chili Beef Soup

Since I live in a city so steeped in chili culture and populated with chili lovers, any recipe with this flavor tends to be popular among my column readers and radio listeners. This is not actually "chili" but a wonderfully hearty soup with the appropriate flavors that has gotten a number of complimentary reviews from readers and listeners. Quick and easy, this is a recipe that uses ingredients mostly right out of your pantry.

    3 tbsp. olive oil
    3 tbsp. pure chili powder*
    2 tsp. cumin
    ¼ tsp. cayenne pepper, or to taste
    1 cup chopped onion
    2 cloves garlic, finely chopped
    1 lb. very lean beef, finely ground
    4-oz. can chopped mild green chiles
    1 can (15 oz.) Ro-tel** tomatoes, chopped (with juice)

28-oz. can plum tomatoes, chopped (with juice)
6 cups defatted beef stock
1 tsp. salt, or to taste
2 15-oz. cans pinto beans, drained and rinsed
1 pkg. corn tortillas, cut into strips
Oil, for frying
⅔ cup chopped fresh cilantro

- Heat the oil in a large, heavy pot over medium heat.
- Add the chili powder, cumin, and cayenne.
- Cook, stirring, for 2-3 minutes.
- Add the onion and garlic and sauté, stirring, until onion is tender, about 5 minutes.
- Add the beef and cook, stirring, until red is gone.
- Stir in the chiles.
- Add both types of tomatoes and the stock.
- Cook, partially covered, for 25 minutes.
- Add the salt.
- Stir in the beans and cook 20 minutes longer.
- Fry the tortilla strips in about 1 in. oil until very crisp but not brown. (Oil should be 365-75 degrees.)
- Drain thoroughly on soft white paper towels.
- Serve the soup with crispy tortilla strips and cilantro sprinkled over the top.
- Serves 8-10.

*For a milder flavor, use ancho chili powder. For a spicier flavor, use chipotle chili powder.

**These tomatoes include both mild and hot green chiles. They are usually found in the grocery store's Mexican section or with other canned tomatoes. Other brands of tomatoes with chiles are also available.

When using paper towels for draining surface fat from fried foods, or for any other cooking purpose where the food comes in contact with the paper towel, use only solid-white ones. They should also be absorbent and indicate that they can be used in cooking.

White Chicken Chili

Here is another super Sharon Shipley recipe. I am not sure of the origin of "white chili," but I first experienced it in California, that land of culinary innovations where Sharon plies her craft as cooking teacher and caterer extraordinaire.

1 lb. dried Great Northern white beans, rinsed
    and picked over
2 lb. boneless and skinless chicken breasts,
    diced
3 tbsp. olive oil
2 medium onions, chopped
4 large cloves garlic, finely chopped
1 tbsp. canned chopped jalapeño peppers (with
    juice)
1 tbsp. cumin
1 tsp. dried marjoram
1½ tsp. dried oregano leaves
½ tsp. cayenne pepper, or to taste
6 cups chicken broth
3 cups shredded white cheddar cheese (12 oz.)
Salt and freshly ground black pepper, to taste
Sour cream, tomato salsa, and chopped fresh
    cilantro, for garnish

- Place the beans in a large, heavy pot. Add enough cold water to cover by at least 3 in. and bring to a boil. Cover, remove from heat, and let sit for 1 hour. Drain.

- Place the chicken in a large saucepan with a lid. Add enough cold water to cover, put on the lid, and bring to a rolling boil. Remove from heat. (Do not remove lid.) Allow to sit for 15 minutes. Drain and chill.

- Heat the oil in a large pot over medium-high heat. Add the onions and sauté until tender, about 5 minutes.

- Stir in the garlic, jalapeño peppers, cumin, marjoram, oregano, and cayenne and sauté 2 minutes more.

- Add the beans and broth and bring to a boil.

- Reduce the heat and simmer for about 2 hours, or until beans are very tender. Check and stir occasionally.

- Add the chicken and 1 cup cheese and stir until cheese melts.
- Season with salt and pepper.
- Serve with remaining cheese, sour cream, salsa, and cilantro to sprinkle over the top.
- Serves 8-10.

Note: For a quick cooking method, substitute 2 16-oz. cans white beans, rinsed and drained. Add the beans to the broth and onion mixture. Cook, uncovered, for 20 minutes. Remove 1 cup of the mixture and purée in a blender or food processor. Return to the pot and finish the recipe as directed.

Green Chile Pork Stew

I call this a "stew" rather than "chili" because I based it on a classic Mexican dish that is usually referred to as a pork stew. My version is lighter in both fat content and spiciness than the original one. It has great flavors! And it's an ideal "make-ahead on the weekend" dish for ready-to-eat weekday suppers.

> 2 lb. pork loin, cut into 1-in. cubes
> ¼ cup extra-virgin olive oil
> 1 tbsp. cumin
> 2 cups chopped onion
> 3 cloves garlic, finely chopped
> 28-oz. can diced plum tomatoes (with juice)
> 1 cup chicken broth
> 1 tsp. salt, or to taste
> 3 poblano chiles, roasted, peeled, seeded, and chopped
> 3 anaheim chiles, roasted, peeled, seeded, and chopped
> 2-3 jalapeño peppers, seeded and finely chopped
> ½ tsp. oregano

- In a heavy pan over medium-high heat, brown the pork in the oil.
- Sprinkle over the cumin and cook, stirring, for 2 or 3 minutes longer.

- Add the onions and garlic and cook, stirring, until the onions are tender, about 5 minutes.
- Stir in the tomatoes, broth, and salt.
- Cover, reduce heat to low, and simmer for 30 minutes.
- Stir in the remaining ingredients and simmer 45 minutes longer, uncovered, stirring often. The pork should be tender enough to shred.
- Taste and correct seasonings.
- Serve spooned over crusty cornbread or a bed of fluffy rice.
- Serves 8.

Vegetarian Black Bean Chili

Beans are chock-full of good stuff like protein and fiber, making them the perfect basis for a soup without any added meat. Black beans have an especially elegant and pleasing flavor that doesn't need the support of the usual soup bone. The spices and vegetables in this recipe combined with these tasty little beans will make this rather large pot of soup disappear in a hurry. It keeps for a good week in the refrigerator. For a smoky, spicier flavor, use chipotle chili powder in this soup. Ancho chili powder lends a rich but milder flavor.

4 cups dried black beans, washed and drained
½ cup extra-virgin olive oil
2½ cups chopped onion
4 large cloves garlic, finely chopped
1 tbsp. cumin
1 tbsp. paprika
2 tbsp. pure chili powder
4-5 jalapeño peppers, seeded and finely
  chopped, to taste
3 large mild green chiles, seeded and finely
  chopped (anaheim or New Mexico)
2 28-oz. cans diced plum tomatoes (with juice)
2 tsp. oregano leaves
½-1 tsp. cayenne pepper, to taste

2 tsp. salt, or to taste
½ cup chopped fresh cilantro
2 cups shredded mild cheddar cheese
1 cup sour cream
½ cup chopped green onions

- Place the beans in a large pot and add enough water to cover by at least 3 in. Bring to a boil, cover, and simmer for about 2 hours or until just tender.
- Drain the beans and reserve 2 cups of the liquid.
- Heat the oil in the washed-out pot.
- Add the onions and garlic and sauté, stirring, for 5 minutes.
- Add the cumin, paprika, and chili powder. Continue to cook, stirring, for 5 more minutes.
- Add the peppers and cook a couple of minutes longer.
- Stir in the tomatoes, oregano, cayenne, and salt.
- Bring to a boil. Reduce heat to low and simmer, uncovered, for 20 minutes, stirring occasionally.
- Add the beans and the 2 cups bean liquid. Cook, partially covered, for 15 minutes.
- Stir in the cilantro.
- Taste and correct seasonings.
- Serve hot with the cheese, sour cream, and green onions to spoon over individual servings.
- Serves 12.

Tex-Mex Chili

This is the recipe I often use to illustrate a typical "Tex-Mex" dish for my cooking students. It differs from the types of chili we're used to eating in the Midwest in several ways. For instance, you will notice it has no beans or tomatoes, tomato paste, or tomato sauce, and it always uses chunks of meat instead of ground beef. It is an economical dish since it's best made with a less tender cut of beef. I usually use very lean chuck. For a change, you can substitute pork butt for all or half of the beef. Cook it until the meat literally falls apart when touched with a fork. This is the perfect dish for a cold day . . . or anytime you are hungry for some hearty victuals.

Typical chili spices like chili powder, cumin, and paprika lend a better flavor if they are first lightly "toasted" in the oil before any liquid is added.

3 tbsp. vegetable oil
2½ lb. cubed lean beef
2 cups chopped onions
3 cloves garlic, finely chopped
2 tbsp. sweet paprika (Hungarian is best)
1 tbsp. cumin
2 tsp. salt, or to taste
3¼ cups water
2 tsp. crushed hot red pepper, or to taste
1 tbsp. masa harina*

- Heat the oil in a heavy pan. Brown the beef thoroughly.
- Stir in the onions and garlic and cook, stirring, over medium heat for about 10 minutes.
- Add the paprika and cumin and cook, stirring constantly, for 2 more minutes.
- Add the salt, 3 cups of the water, and the pepper.
- Bring to a boil, cover, and cook over low heat for 3 hours or until the meat shreds easily with a fork. Or place in a 300-degree oven for 3 to 4 hours.
- Stir together the masa harina and remaining water.
- Stir into the chili and cook 10 minutes longer.
- Taste and correct seasonings.
- Serves 6-8.

*"Masa harina" is Mexican corn flour that is used to make corn tortillas. It is available in gourmet specialty stores and markets that sell Mexican and Spanish products.

Marilyn's Gazpacho

Chilled soups happen to be one of my culinary passions. I know they are not as popular in general as hot soup, but much of that may depend on the weather. On a hot summer day, a chilled soup is certain to be a welcome beginning for lunch, or serve it from a thermos as a fun and elegant first course for a picnic or backyard cookout. Since a cold soup must be made in advance, it is the perfect choice for an informal and relaxed meal.

Not meant to be the Spanish classic, this recipe is my own favorite rendition of this well-known cold tomato-vegetable soup. Not only are the flavors unique, but it is much lower in fat than the original and it's a great way to use some of the summertime produce.

> 3 large tomatoes, peeled, seeded, and chopped (reserve juice)
> 1 cucumber, peeled, seeded, and chopped
> 1 large sweet salad onion, finely chopped
> 3 mild green chiles, roasted, peeled, seeded, and chopped
> 2-3 pickled jalapeño peppers, chopped (to taste)
> 1 ripe medium to large avocado, peeled and coarsely chopped
> 4 cups tomato juice, chilled
> 2 tbsp. olive oil
> 2 tbsp. red-wine vinegar
> ½ cup chopped fresh cilantro
> Salt and hot pepper sauce, to taste
> Sour cream (optional)
> Extra chopped cilantro, for garnish

- Stir all the vegetables into the tomato juice.
- Add the oil, vinegar, and cilantro.
- Season to taste with salt and hot pepper sauce.
- Cover and chill for several hours.
- Taste and correct seasonings.
- If desired, serve topped with a dollop of sour cream and a sprinkle of cilantro.
- Serve 6-8.

Dilled and Chilled Summer Vegetable Soup

This cold soup came about when I went overboard at the farmers' market one day. I had these big, gorgeous cucumbers and some lovely potatoes, along with an avocado that had to be used that day. You may find it to be a rather motley assortment of ingredients, but try it before you pass judgment. This is a great light lunch on a hot day!

2 tbsp. butter
1 cup chopped yellow onion
2 large red potatoes, peeled and cubed
3 cups canned chicken broth
10 oz. fresh spinach, washed and stems removed
2 large cucumbers, peeled, seeded, and thickly
    sliced
¼ cup chopped fresh dill
1 tbsp. fresh lime juice
1 ripe large avocado, peeled and cubed
1 tsp. salt, or to taste
½ tsp. hot pepper sauce, or to taste
2 cups sour cream (or plain yogurt)
Sour cream, for garnish (or plain yogurt)
Extra chopped fresh dill, for garnish

- In a large, heavy, nonreactive pot, heat the butter over medium heat and add the onion.
- Cover and cook for 5 minutes.
- Stir in the potatoes and broth.
- Cook, partially covered, for about 20 minutes or until the potatoes are fork tender.
- Stir in the spinach and cucumbers. Cook for 5 minutes.
- Remove from the heat and cool.
- Stir in the dill, lime juice, avocado, salt, and hot pepper sauce.
- Purée in a blender or food processor.
- Remove to a large bowl and whisk in the sour cream.

- Taste and correct seasonings.
- Cover and chill for at least 2 hours.
- Serve in chilled bowls topped with a dollop of sour cream (or yogurt) and sprinkled with some dill.
- Serves 8-10.

Guacamole Soup

Here are the great flavors of that famous avocado mixture, but in a creamy soup. The acidity from the tomatoes and lime helps to maintain the pretty green color of the avocado. Serve this one ice cold. In fact, I like to serve it in glass bowls set into a larger bowl of crushed ice.

> 2 cups sour cream (regular or reduced fat)
> ½ cup light cream or whole milk
> 1 cup chicken broth, chilled
> 1 small sweet salad onion, coarsely chopped
> 2 large tomatoes, peeled, seeded, and coarsely chopped
> 3 ripe large avocados, peeled and coarsely chopped
> 2 tbsp. chopped fresh cilantro
> 1 tsp. salt
> 1 tsp. hot pepper sauce, or to taste
> 1 tbsp. fresh lime juice
> Extra chopped fresh cilantro, for garnish

- Place all the ingredients, except the garnish, in a blender in the order listed.
- Pulse on and off until the avocados are blended to a smooth consistency and the tomatoes are finely chopped.
- Cover and chill for at least 2 hours.
- Before serving, taste and correct seasonings.
- Serve sprinkled with cilantro.
- Serves 8.

Fish Soup with Garlic Croutons

This simple-to-make fish soup can be adapted to the "catch of the day" at your local fish market, just as long as the fish is very fresh and firm. It is wonderful with halibut, and I made a most delicate and elegant version of it with salmon. It is a light but filling soup and makes a great lunch or supper dish.

> 6 tbsp. extra-virgin olive oil
> 1 large yellow onion, chopped
> 3 large cloves garlic, finely chopped
> ½ cup chopped flat-leaf parsley
> 2 lb. firm fish fillets, cut into bite-sized chunks
> 2 tsp. salt, or to taste
> ¼ tsp. cayenne pepper
> 5 cups water
> ½ cup chopped celery
> ½ cup chopped carrots
> 28-oz. can plum tomatoes, coarsely chopped
>   (with juice)
> 1 tsp. lemon zest
> 8 1-in. slices Italian or French bread
> Extra-virgin olive oil
> 1 large clove garlic, peeled and halved
> 1 cup freshly grated Parmigiano-Reggiano
> Extra chopped parsley, for garnish

- In a large skillet, heat the 6 tbsp. oil until very hot.
- Add the onions and chopped garlic and cook over high heat, stirring, for about 5 minutes.
- Stir in the parsley and cook, stirring, a minute or two more.
- Add the fish and brown slightly on all sides.
- Remove the pan from the heat and season the fish with salt and cayenne.
- In a large pot, bring to a boil the water, celery, carrots, tomatoes, and lemon zest.
- Reduce the heat and simmer, uncovered, for 20 minutes.
- Pour the stock mixture into a blender or food processor and purée until smooth; return to the pot.
- Add the fish mixture to the stock. Simmer for 15 minutes. Taste and correct seasonings.

- Brush the bread on both sides with olive oil and rub with the cut side of the garlic. Toast on both sides under a broiler until golden brown and crisp.
- Place a piece of the toast in a soup bowl.
- Ladle over the hot soup and sprinkle with 2 tbsp. cheese.
- Garnish with a sprinkling of parsley.
- Serve immediately.
- Serves 8.

Oyster and Chicken Gumbo

The Louisiana Cajuns, who are some of the world's best cooks, call their rich soup "gumbo." I have noted that some people are under the impression that a proper gumbo must always contain okra. That is not the case, as is illustrated by this delicious recipe. For an elegant company soup, I suggest using only chicken breasts for this piquant gumbo. It is also very tasty with a combination of dark and white meat.

2 tsp. salt, or to taste
Freshly ground black pepper, to taste
3 lb. chicken pieces
¼ cup vegetable oil
3 tbsp. flour
1½ cups chopped onion
3 stalks celery, chopped
1 medium green bell pepper, chopped
3 cloves garlic, finely chopped
5 cups chicken broth, heated
1 tbsp. Worcestershire sauce
½-1 tsp. crushed hot red pepper, to taste
1 bay leaf
½ tsp. dried thyme leaves
¼ tsp. allspice
1 pt. fresh oysters, with liquor
¼ cup chopped flat-leaf parsley
½ cup chopped green onions
About 2 cups cooked long-grain white rice
Hot pepper sauce

- Salt and pepper the chicken pieces.
- Heat the oil in a heavy large pot and brown the chicken well. Remove to a side dish.
- Stir the flour into the pot and cook, on a very low setting, for 8 to 10 minutes or until the "roux" turns a light brown color.
- Add the onions, celery, green pepper, and garlic. Cook 5 minutes, stirring.
- Stir in the broth, Worcestershire sauce, spices, and reserved chicken.
- Cook, uncovered, 1½ hours.
- Discard the bay leaf.
- Remove the chicken, allow to cool, remove the skin and bones, and cut the meat into bite-sized pieces.
- Add the oysters, parsley, and green onions to the stock mixture with the cut-up chicken.
- Cook 5 minutes more.
- Spoon a large spoonful of rice into each soup bowl and ladle over the gumbo.
- Pass the hot pepper sauce.
- Serves 8-10.

To prevent lumps from forming when liquid is added to a roux (the cooked fat and flour combination), the liquid should be hot.

Bay leaves must always be removed before a dish is served. To prevent losing a bay leaf in a soup or stew, tie a long piece of kitchen twine around it. Place the bay leaf in the pot and tie the other end of the string around the pot handle.

Chicken Stock

A good pot of soup with chicken stock as its base doesn't necessarily mean that one has to start with homemade chicken stock. A homemade stock, however, does naturally add a better and fresher flavor. Chicken stock is actually quite simple, since it merely involves tossing everything into a pot and allowing it to cook. It's a good project to do in quantity on a lazy Sunday afternoon. Cool and store in freezer containers in the freezer. Thaw overnight in the refrigerator or in the microwave before making your soup.

    3- to 4-lb. chicken, cut up
    10 cups water
    2 carrots, sliced into 1-2-in. pieces
    3 stalks celery, sliced into 1-2-in. pieces
    2 large yellow onions, peeled and quartered

All stock is cooked in an open pot and should be kept at a very slow simmer during the entire cooking time. Skimming the surface on a regular basis removes the fat and film that naturally form.

For low-fat or fat-free stock, it is best made the day before. After it is chilled, the fat forms and hardens on the surface, making it easy to remove.

For "consommé" or a clear soup, stock can be clarified by combining 1 crushed eggshell and 1 egg white per 1 qt. stock. Heat the stock and swirl in the egg mixture. Allow to stand 20 minutes and strain through a double layer of cheesecloth or a strong white paper towel.

6 large sprigs parsley
3 sprigs thyme (or 1 tsp. dried thyme leaves)
1 tsp. whole black peppercorns
2 bay leaves

- Combine all of the ingredients in a large pot. Bring to a boil, uncovered.
- Reduce the heat and simmer for 45 minutes to 1 hour.
- Skim and strain.
- Return the stock to a clean pot. Cook over high heat to reduce by half.
- Season to taste with salt.
- Cool and pour into a covered container. Chill until ready to use.
- Makes 5-6 cups.

Beef Stock

A proper beef stock is somewhat more time-consuming and complicated than chicken stock, but the reward of outstanding flavor makes it worthwhile. Browning the bones to create the caramelized flavors and color is the most important technique to master. Professional chefs often do that in big baking pans in the oven, but for this amount I find it simpler to brown the bones and the vegetables on the stove in a stockpot. If you want to make your own beef stock and are in the market for a pot, buy a stainless steel one with a heavy bottom.

¼ cup vegetable oil
2 lb. beef shank, bone in
2 lb. veal knuckles or shanks
2-3 lb. beef bones, with marrow
3 carrots, washed, trimmed, and cut up
2 large onions, quartered
4 stalks celery, cut up
Bouquet garni of 3 sprigs parsley, 3 bay leaves, and 3 sprigs thyme (or substitute 1 tsp. thyme leaves)
1 tsp. whole black peppercorns
12 cups water
Salt, to taste

- In a large, heavy pot, heat the oil until very hot.
- Add all of the bones. Turn the heat to medium and brown the bones well, turning them often.
- Add all of the vegetables and continue to stir and cook until the vegetables are golden brown.
- Add the bouquet garni, peppercorns, and water.
- Bring to a boil, reduce heat to low, and simmer, uncovered, for 6 hours, skimming off the fat every 30 minutes or so.
- Season with salt.
- Cool and strain.
- Chill until ready to use. May be frozen for later use.
- Makes about 2 qt.

On the Lighter Side

My interest in writing about and talking about lighter, healthier cooking reflects the interests of my radio listeners, my column readers, and my cooking students. I hear so many of you express the wish to find ways to cut fat and calories in the food you cook and eat. It is unfortunate but true that fat delivers flavor, and when you cut back on fat you're bound to lose some of the tastes you love. So I look for ways to bring out the flavor in some simple dishes so that the fat can be reduced without being missed.

By including this special chapter, I am not proposing any sort of "diet" but simply modifying some basic favorites by reducing the amount of fat, as well as sometimes replacing a less healthy fat with one lower in saturated fat and cholesterol. Common sense is the best guide. Some of this eating healthier business is as simple as starting with healthy foods, cooking them properly, and seasoning them well. I chose the following "potpourri" of recipes from my files because they are all "on the light side." Some have been altered to make them "lighter" and others are favorites of mine that just happen to be good healthy food. Some last words of unsolicited advice: Don't worry about every bite of food you put in your mouth, but do try cooking and eating some lighter, healthier foods—you may like it. And don't forget to treat yourself to dessert every now and then! As I always say to my radio listeners: "moderation in all things, including moderation."

Chef Cornelius's Very Veggie Frittata

My foodie friend Neal O'Donnell traveled the globe for Corning products as "Chef Cornelius" and shared his special recipes with everyone from national television audiences to small groups gathered in department-store housewares sections. This is one of his favorites that fits very nicely into this chapter, because it is not only "on the lighter side" but is pretty and very tasty. It's a great weekend brunch entrée, and I love it for Sunday-night supper.

> When attempting to make some of your favorite recipes "lighter," look first at the fat content. Remember that just 1 little gram of fat has 9 calories, and many recipes can still taste great with their fat content considerably reduced.

> Instead of chopping fresh basil, roll the leaves together like a cigar, place on a cutting board, and slice crosswise into thin shreds. They look prettier and add great fresh flavor to a dish.

2 potatoes, peeled and cubed
1 tbsp. butter, or a mist of vegetable oil cooking spray
1 large onion, thinly sliced
1 large red bell pepper, thinly sliced
1 medium zucchini, coarsely shredded (about 2 cups)
2 tbsp. shredded fresh basil (or 1 tsp. dried)
Salt and freshly ground black pepper, to taste
6-8 oz. garlic and herb Neufchatel cheese, to taste
8 large eggs (or 4 whole eggs and 6 egg whites)
5-6 drops hot pepper sauce
2 tbsp. freshly grated Parmigiano-Reggiano

- Cook the potatoes in boiling water until just fork tender. Drain and set aside.
- Heat a 10-in. nonstick skillet that is greased with the butter or cooking spray.
- Add the onion and sauté 5 minutes or until soft.
- Add half the red pepper. Add the zucchini, basil, salt, and pepper. Sauté about 5 more minutes or until zucchini is just soft.
- Add the potatoes and then drop the cheese onto the vegetable mixture by the tbsp.
- Whisk together the eggs and hot pepper sauce. Pour over the vegetables and stir with a fork to cover the vegetables evenly. Make a decorative spokelike pattern on top with the reserved red pepper strips.
- Sprinkle with the grated cheese.

- Place the skillet in a preheated 350-degree oven and bake for 20 to 25 minutes or until a knife inserted near the middle comes out clean.
- Serve immediately.
- Serves 6-8.

Chicken Mexicana

Those of you who have experienced Mexican food only in restaurants—where they tend not to pay even the slightest attention to fat or calorie content—will be pleasantly surprised when you try this dish. Actually, dishes flavored with the interesting typical spices and herbs of the Mexican and Southwestern kitchen are delicious when prepared in a lighter fashion.

    3 mild green chiles*
    8 boneless and skinless chicken breast halves
    2 tbsp. extra-virgin olive oil
    1 cup chopped yellow onion
    1 tsp. cumin
    3 large tomatoes, peeled, seeded, and chopped (reserve juice)
    2 cloves garlic, finely chopped
    1 tsp. salt, or to taste
    2-3 large jalapeño peppers, stemmed, seeded, and finely chopped
    ¼ cup sliced pimiento-stuffed olives
    3 tbsp. chopped fresh cilantro
    Cilantro sprigs, for garnish

- Roast the chiles in a 450-degree oven for 20 to 25 minutes or until the skin is brown. Cool in a sealed plastic bag. Peel, seed, and chop. Set aside.
- Place the chicken breasts between two sheets of plastic wrap and flatten them.
- In a large, nonstick skillet that has a lid, heat 1 tbsp. oil until very hot but not smoking.
- Brown the chicken for 2 minutes on each side, turning once. Remove to a side dish.

- Add the remaining oil and the onion and cumin. Sauté, stirring, for 2 minutes.
- Stir in the tomatoes with their reserved juice and the garlic. Cook for 5 minutes.
- Add the salt, jalapeño peppers, and chiles.
- Cover and cook over low heat for 5 minutes.
- Return the chicken to the skillet, cover, and cook for about 8 minutes or until the chicken is cooked through.
- Add the olives and cilantro and cook for a couple of minutes longer.
- Garnish with cilantro sprigs.
- Serve with Mexican Rice Pilaf.
- Serves 8.

*You may substitute a 4-oz. can of mild green chiles for the 3 roasted chiles.

Note: If fresh tomatoes are out of season, substitute a 28-oz. can of chopped plum tomatoes.

Mexican Rice Pilaf

Rice is an important component of a light, healthy, and balanced diet. This rice dish, of course, goes perfectly with the Chicken Mexicana, but it is a good side dish to go with almost anything, especially a vegetable plate featuring beans and corn.

1 tbsp. extra-virgin olive oil
½ cup chopped yellow onion
1 large clove garlic, finely chopped
1 tsp. cumin
1 tbsp. good chili powder
2 cups long-grain white rice
2 cups defatted chicken broth
2 cups tomato juice
¼ tsp. hot pepper sauce, or to taste
Salt, to taste
½ cup chopped fresh cilantro (optional)

When using canned chicken broth, place the unopened can in the refrigerator for a few hours. Open and carefully spoon away the solidified fat from the top.

It takes less fat to "sweat" aromatic vegetables (like onion and garlic) than it does to "sauté" them. The sweating process takes place in a covered saucepan, and the steam created from the vegetables helps to cook them, requiring less fat than sautéing in an open pan.

- In a heavy saucepan (with a tight-fitting lid), heat the oil. Add the onion, garlic, cumin, and chili powder. Stir, cover the pan, and cook on low for 5 minutes.
- Stir in the rice, coating well.
- Add the broth, tomato juice, hot pepper sauce, and salt.
- Cover, bring to a boil, and reduce to simmer.
- Simmer for 25 minutes or until all the liquid is absorbed.
- Toss in the cilantro before serving.
- Serves 8.

Light and Lovely Summer Chicken Salad

Chicken salads run the gamut as far as their calorie content is concerned. We often order chicken salad because it is assumed to be one of the lighter offerings on the menu. We all know that chicken is, after all, low in fat and a salad is a healthy choice. But I hardly need to comment on how wrong that assumption can often be. A chicken salad that starts with grilled chicken slathered with oil, or with roasted chicken that includes the skin and is dressed with one of those creamy, indulgent dressings, may well compete with dessert for the high-calorie prize of the day. This recipe, on the other hand, lives up to its title, since it contains only well-trimmed and properly cooked boneless chicken breast paired with a low-fat dressing. It is a "summer" chicken salad because it not only features summer sweet salad onions and ripe tomatoes but there is no better choice for a hot summer's day lunch or supper.

4 boneless and skinless chicken breast halves
2 cups defatted chicken broth
¼ tsp. hot pepper sauce
1 small onion, quartered
3 sprigs parsley
2 sprigs thyme (or 1 tsp. dried)
1 bay leaf
½ cup dry white wine
¼ cup water
1 tbsp. sugar

⅓ cup cider vinegar
1 tbsp. mayonnaise
2 tbsp. chopped fresh basil
1 tbsp. chopped fresh flat-leaf parsley
½ tsp. salt
¼ tsp. hot pepper sauce
1 large Vidalia onion, thinly sliced
1 medium cucumber, peeled, seeded, and thinly
  sliced
1 small head romaine lettuce, washed, dried, and
  chilled
3 ripe large tomatoes, thinly sliced
Salt and freshly ground black pepper, to taste
Parsley sprigs or basil leaves, for garnish

- Rinse, dry, and trim the chicken. Flatten between two sheets of plastic wrap.
- In a nonreactive skillet, mix together the broth, ¼ tsp. hot pepper sauce, onion, parsley sprigs, thyme, bay leaf, and wine. Bring to a boil.
- Add the chicken and cover with parchment paper. Simmer for 8 to 10 minutes or just until chicken is done through. (Do not overcook.)
- Allow the chicken to cool in the poaching liquid, remove, and cut across the grain into ½-in. strips.
- Heat the water and sugar together until sugar dissolves. Set aside to cool completely.
- Stir the vinegar into the cooled sugar and water mixture.
- Whisk in the mayonnaise until smooth and add the basil, chopped parsley, salt, and ¼ tsp. hot pepper sauce.
- Toss together the chicken, sliced onion, and cucumber. Pour over two-thirds of the dressing and toss to coat.
- Shred the lettuce and pile onto a platter or in a shallow bowl.
- Arrange the sliced tomatoes around the edge and pile the chicken mixture in the center.
- Drizzle the remaining dressing over the tomatoes and season to taste with salt and pepper.
- Garnish with parsley sprigs or basil leaves.
- Serves 6-8.

Flemish Chicken with Asparagus

I also use fresh salmon fillets in this recipe. In that case, I substitute 2 cups good dry white wine and 1 cup water for the chicken broth in the poaching liquid. The other ingredients remain the same. The poaching time is approximately the same too, depending on the size of the fish fillets.

2 cups defatted chicken broth
1 cup dry white wine
1 tsp. whole black peppercorns
1 bay leaf
3 sprigs parsley
2 sprigs thyme (or 1 tsp. dried leaves)
1 medium yellow onion, peeled and quartered
1 stalk celery, cut up
1 medium carrot, peeled and cut up
1 clove garlic, crushed

- To make the poaching liquid, in a large nonreactive pan, bring to boil all of the ingredients.
- Simmer, uncovered, for 15 minutes.

Flemish Chicken

8 boneless and skinless chicken breast halves
4 medium carrots, peeled and cut into small julienne strips
2 lb. fresh asparagus, tough ends removed
2 tsp. cornstarch
1 cup reduced-fat sour cream (or plain yogurt)
Juice of ½ lemon
Salt and freshly ground black pepper, to taste
2 tbsp. chopped fresh parsley

- Rinse and pat dry the chicken. Flatten between two sheets of plastic wrap.
- Add the chicken to the poaching liquid, cover with parchment paper, and simmer gently for 8 to 10 minutes or until the chicken is just cooked through.
- Remove the chicken to a side dish, cover, and keep warm.
- Strain the poaching liquid and return to a clean pan.
- Reduce the poaching liquid to 2 cups over high heat.

Poaching is the perfect fat-free cooking method. A well-seasoned poaching liquid is important to infuse the food with extra flavor. It is preferable to start with a good homemade stock that has been reduced somewhat to further enhance the flavors. But if you can't make your own, use a good-quality canned broth or make some with a flavorful (and not too salty) stock base. A good dry white wine and fresh herbs are also good flavor contributions.

- Cook the carrots in the microwave 2 to 3 minutes or until crisp-tender. (Or blanch in a small amount of boiling, lightly salted water for 2 minutes.) Drain and refresh with ice water.
- Steam the asparagus for 3 to 5 minutes in the microwave or a vegetable steamer (just until crisp-tender). Refresh with ice water and drain well.
- Bring the reduced stock to a boil.
- Whisk the cornstarch into the sour cream. Gently whisk into the hot stock and cook just until thickened.
- Season with the lemon juice, salt, and pepper.
- Arrange the chicken on a serving plate and spoon over the sauce.
- Garnish with the carrots and asparagus.
- Sprinkle with the chopped parsley.
- Serve hot with some crusty French bread.
- Serves 8.

Summer Vegetable-Herb Pizza

"How," you ask yourself, "did pizza make it into this part of the book?" That's a worthy question, indeed, considering the high fat and calorie content of most of the pizza eaten in this country. I love sharing this recipe, because it is proof that almost any of our favorite foods can be altered to change their fat profile without sacrificing their appeal and good taste. This is a fun one to make for the family and you don't even need to tell them that it's good for them.

I prefer fresh tomatoes for this delicious fat-free pizza sauce. When they are not available, substitute canned Italian plum tomatoes.

2 tbsp. olive oil
1 clove garlic, finely chopped
1 yellow onion, thinly sliced
12 large mushrooms, washed, trimmed, and thinly sliced
1 red bell pepper, cored, seeded, and thinly sliced
1 medium zucchini, cut into julienne strips
1 carrot, peeled and shredded

1 tbsp. chopped fresh oregano
½ tsp. salt
1 recipe Fresh Tomato Pizza Sauce (see below)
1 recipe Pizza Crust (see below)
8 oz. part-skim mozzarella cheese, shredded
2 medium tomatoes, thinly sliced
4 oz. freshly grated Parmigiano-Reggiano

- In a large skillet, heat the oil and sauté the garlic and onion for 2 minutes.

- Add the mushrooms and cook, stirring, for 2 minutes.

- Add the red pepper, zucchini, and carrot and cook 1 minute longer, stirring.

- Stir in the oregano and salt and remove from heat.

- Spread the tomato sauce on the crust.

- Top with the mozzarella cheese.

- Arrange the vegetable mixture on top and put the sliced tomatoes on top of the vegetables.

- Sprinkle with the Parmigiano-Reggiano and bake in a preheated 425-degree oven on the bottom shelf for 20 to 25 minutes until bubbly and golden brown.

- Let stand for 10 minutes after removing from the oven before slicing.

- Makes 1 11-in. deep-dish pizza.

Fresh Tomato Pizza Sauce

4 large tomatoes, peeled, seeded, and coarsely
   chopped
½ cup canned tomato sauce
¼ cup tomato paste
2 tsp. chopped fresh oregano
1 tbsp. finely shredded fresh basil
¼ tsp. chopped fresh thyme
1 tsp. sugar (or sugar substitute*)
Salt, to taste
Generous dash hot pepper sauce

- Mix together all ingredients thoroughly.

Parmigiano-Reggiano is one of the best cheeses for flavoring dishes with a low fat and calorie content. It is not high in fat but high in great flavor, so a little of it goes a long way.

Pizza Crust

1 pkg. dry yeast
½ cup + 2 tbsp. warm water (110 degrees)
1½ cups + 2 tbsp. unbleached flour
¾ tsp. salt
2 tsp. olive oil
Extra oil, for oiling pan

- Stir the yeast into the warm water and let stand for 10 minutes.
- Put the flour and salt into a food processor (or mixer with dough hook) and mix for 1 or 2 minutes.
- Add the yeast mixture and mix until the mixture leaves the side of the bowl.
- Add the oil and process 1 minute longer in the processor or about 5 minutes in the mixer. (Dough should be smooth and elastic.)
- Place in a gallon-size plastic bag, seal, and chill for 1 hour.
- Roll out on a floured surface and place in an oiled 11-in. deep-dish pizza pan (or removable-bottom tart pan).
- Top as directed.

*I use Splenda®.

Spring Garden Spaghetti

Combining a seasonal favorite, fresh asparagus, with sweet onion and then adding extra color with carrots makes a colorful and healthy pasta dish. Serve it as a meatless main course with a tossed salad of mixed greens and some crusty Italian or French bread. For a heartier entrée, add some julienne strips of smoked chicken or turkey or some grilled shrimp or scallops. Substitute whole-wheat pasta for an even more nutritious dish.

1 lb. fresh asparagus, washed and tough ends
  removed
2 tbsp. extra-virgin olive oil
2 cloves garlic, finely chopped
2 medium Vidalia onions, coarsely chopped
3 medium carrots, peeled and coarsely shredded
2 tbsp. dry white wine

1 cup reduced-fat sour cream (or plain yogurt)
1 tbsp. chopped fresh dill (or 1 tsp. dried)
2 tbsp. chopped flat-leaf parsley
Salt and freshly ground black pepper, to taste
1 lb. spaghetti, cooked "al dente"
¼ cup freshly grated Parmigiano-Reggiano

- Cook the asparagus in a small amount of water, or in the microwave, for 3 to 4 minutes or until crisp-tender. Cut on the diagonal into 1-in. pieces. Set aside.

- Heat the oil in a large skillet.

- Add the garlic and onions and cook over high heat, stirring, for 5 minutes.

- Add the carrots and wine and cook on high until the wine is reduced by half.

- Stir in the sour cream and blend.

- Toss in the asparagus, dill, and parsley.

- Season with salt and pepper.

- Toss the vegetable mixture into the hot, freshly cooked, and drained spaghetti.

- Sprinkle over the cheese and serve immediately.

- Serves 6-8.

"Al dente" means literally "to the tooth." In other words, the pasta is still firm and chewy, rather than soft and mushy. Dried pasta is almost always cooked to this doneness.

Orange-Basil Pork Tenderloin

One of the good things that has happened to American pork is a fat reduction of about 30 percent. Take an already lean cut like the elegant tenderloin, and we now have pork that competes with white meat of chicken and fish for a low fat and calorie content. It is delicious, especially with a tangy sauce like this one. It is also a good choice for the busy cook with little time to spend in the kitchen.

I prefer this tenderloin cooked on the grill, but it can also be roasted in a hot (450-degree) oven. Roast on a rack that is placed in a shallow pan. Internal temperature should be between 145 and 150 degrees. After it is removed from the oven, it will continue to cook a bit, so cover it with a tent of foil and wait about 15 minutes before slicing.

2 pork tenderloins, well trimmed
1 tbsp. canola or olive oil
1 clove garlic, finely chopped
2 tbsp. fresh orange juice
1 tsp. freshly grated orange peel
1 tbsp. fresh lemon juice
2 tbsp. orange liqueur (optional)
¼ cup chopped fresh basil
½ tsp. hot pepper sauce, or to taste
2 tbsp. soy sauce
¼ cup chopped green onions
½ cup chicken broth
Basil leaves and thinly sliced oranges, for garnish

- Place the tenderloins in a heavy-duty gallon-size zip-top bag.
- Whisk together the oil, garlic, orange juice and peel, lemon juice, orange liqueur, basil, hot pepper sauce, and soy sauce.
- Pour the marinade into the bag and seal securely.
- Place in the refrigerator for several hours or overnight.
- Remove the pork and reserve the marinade.
- Grill the pork over a medium-hot grill for about 20 minutes or until it reaches 145 to 150 degrees internal temperature,
- Slice on the diagonal into ¼-in. slices.
- Simmer the marinade with the green onions and broth for 20 minutes.
- Nap the sliced meat with the sauce.
- Garnish with the basil leaves and orange slices.
- Serves 8.

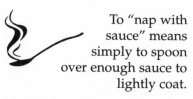

To "nap with sauce" means simply to spoon over enough sauce to lightly coat.

Lean Lemon Meatloaf

I receive varying degrees of response to my newspaper columns, from no apparent comment to loads of feedback. This favorite meatloaf recipe of mine may well hold the prize for causing the most fuss—all of it favorable—of any recipe I've ever featured in my column. We discussed it at length on the radio show and strangers stopped me on the street to say how much they appreciated having a new meatloaf recipe. Employees at the newspaper even told me about making it and enjoying it. I might add that it is one of my husband's very favorite dishes. I decided to include it in this chapter because most meatloaf is anything but light.

For this dish, I usually buy the leanest center-cut chuck or round steak and grind it in the food processor. If you don't have a food processor, ask your butcher to grind some very lean beef without the addition of any fat. Even though 3 tbsp. olive oil may look like a lot, some fat is needed for moisture and flavor, and you are replacing the beef fat with a healthier oil.

1½ cups chopped onion
1 large clove garlic, finely chopped
3 tbsp. extra-virgin olive oil
2 lb. very lean ground beef
1 egg + 1 egg white
2 tbsp. milk
1 cup breadcrumbs made from slightly stale bread
¼ cup chopped fresh flat-leaf parsley
1 tsp. salt, or to taste
¼ tsp. freshly ground black pepper
1 tsp. fine lemon zest
½ cup ketchup (or chili sauce)
2 tbsp. dark brown sugar
1 tbsp. Dijon mustard
1 tbsp. fresh lemon juice
½ tsp. hot pepper sauce
Thin lemon slices and parsley sprigs, for garnish

- Sauté the onion and garlic in the olive oil for about 3 minutes, stirring; remove from the heat and cool.

- With a fork, gently toss the onion mixture into the ground beef.

- Whisk the egg, egg white, and milk together.

- Stir in the breadcrumbs and toss into the meat mixture along with the parsley, salt, pepper, and lemon zest.

- Gently press the mixture into a nonstick (or lightly oiled) loaf pan to shape it. Invert into a lightly oiled, shallow baking pan.
- Mix together the remaining ingredients with a whisk or fork and spread evenly over the top of the loaf.
- Bake in a preheated 350-degree oven for 1 hour and 15 minutes or until done through.
- Let cool a few minutes before slicing.
- Garnish with lemon and parsley.
- Serves 6-8.

Southwestern Baked Tuna

Even diehard meat lovers like fresh tuna. It is firm textured and has a hearty yet mild flavor. This simple recipe is suitable for a fancy company meal and is convenient for the cook since it can be assembled ahead of time, chilled, and later popped into the oven.

> **4 fresh tuna fillets, cut 1-in. thick**
> **3 tbsp. extra-virgin olive oil**
> **1 large clove garlic, finely chopped**
> **1 tbsp. chili powder**
> **¼ tsp. cayenne pepper**
> **2 tsp. cumin**
> **1 cup fresh breadcrumbs**
> **1 tsp. dried oregano leaves**
> **2 tbsp. chopped fresh cilantro**
> **½ tsp. salt, or to taste**
> **Lime wedges**
> **Cilantro sprigs**

- Place the fish in a well-greased, shallow baking dish.
- Heat the olive oil in a heavy skillet over medium heat.
- Add the garlic and cook for 2 minutes. (Do not brown.)
- Add the chili powder, cayenne, and cumin and stir for 2 to 3 minutes.
- Remove from the heat.
- Toss in the breadcrumbs, oregano, chopped cilantro, and salt.

- Mix well and distribute the mixture evenly over the top of the fish.
- Bake in the top third of a preheated 450-degree oven for 10 to 12 minutes (or less time for rare tuna).
- Garnish with lime wedges and cilantro sprigs.
- Serves 4.

Zucchini-Mushroom Lasagna

Filled with energy-producing complex carbohydrates, pasta is satisfying for even the heartiest appetites. The problem with some of the traditional pasta dishes, such as lasagna, is that the sauces are often loaded with fat calories. This pretty vegetable lasagna is a great way to illustrate that even lasagna doesn't have to be a heavy, fat-laden dish.

The secret of this dish is its creamy, saucy texture, which comes from this lightened version of béchamel sauce. The good flavor comes from infusing the milk with aromatic onion, spices, and herbs before the sauce is made. Making it with low-fat milk cuts down considerably on the fat content.

2 tbsp. extra-virgin olive oil
2 medium yellow onions, thinly sliced
3 small to medium zucchini, thinly sliced
8 oz. fresh mushrooms, washed, dried, and
　　thinly sliced
2 cloves garlic, finely chopped
28-oz. can diced plum tomatoes, drained
4 tbsp. tomato paste
1 tsp. dried oregano
2 tbsp. chopped fresh parsley
Salt and freshly ground black pepper, to taste
9 lasagna noodles, cooked al dente and well
　　drained
1 recipe Light Béchamel Sauce (see below)
12 oz. part-skim mozzarella cheese, shredded (3
　　cups)
4 oz. freshly grated Parmigiano-Reggiano (1 cup)
Extra chopped parsley, for garnish

- Heat the oil in a large skillet.
- Sauté the onions, stirring, for 3 to 4 minutes or just until tender.
- Stir in the zucchini, mushrooms, and garlic and cook over high heat, stirring, for 3 to 4 minutes.
- Stir in the tomatoes, tomato paste, oregano, and parsley.
- Cook for 10 minutes. Add salt and pepper.
- Place 3 lasagna noodles in the bottom of an oiled 13-by-9-in. dish.
- Cover with one-third of the béchamel sauce.
- Spoon over half of the zucchini-mushroom mixture.
- Sprinkle in one-third of the mozzarella and half of the Parmigiano-Reggiano.
- Top with 3 more noodles and repeat the same layering procedure once more.
- Finish with the remaining noodles, sauce, and mozzarella.
- Bake in the center of a preheated 375-degree oven for 40 minutes.
- Sprinkle with the chopped parsley before serving.
- Serves 8-10.

  Note: Substitute spinach noodles for a colorful version.

Light Béchamel Sauce

2 cups 1 percent milk
½ peeled small onion
3 sprigs parsley
½ tsp. whole black peppercorns
1 bay leaf
3 tbsp. margarine or light butter
4 tbsp. flour
½ tsp. salt, or to taste
Dash freshly grated nutmeg
Generous dash hot pepper sauce

- In a small nonreactive saucepan, heat together the milk, onion, parsley, peppercorns, and bay leaf.
- As soon as bubbles appear around the edge of the milk, remove from heat and allow to "steep" for 30 minutes. Strain.
- Melt the margarine in a heavy nonreactive saucepan.
- Stir in the flour.

- Cook, stirring constantly, over medium heat for a full 2 minutes. Do not allow to brown.
- Whisk in the strained, warm milk, whisking until the mixture thickens.
- Season with salt, nutmeg, and hot pepper sauce.

Zucchini and Red Pepper Sauté

We've cooked so much zucchini over the years on the radio show. When August rolls around and first-time zucchini planters discover the extent of their harvest, they call with panic in their voices. This leads to other helpful callers reassuring them with their own favorite recipes for using up their squash crop. As a result, I have amassed quite a zucchini file. This is a favorite light one that is quick, pretty, and tasty. It is a perfect side dish to accompany any grilled meat, poultry, or fish.

> 2 tbsp. extra-virgin olive oil
> 2 cloves garlic, finely chopped
> 6 to 8 small zucchini (about 2 lb.), cut into small julienne strips
> 1 large red bell pepper, cored and cut into small julienne strips
> 3 tbsp. fresh lemon juice
> 1 tbsp. shredded fresh basil
> ¼ cup chopped fresh flat-leaf parsley
> Salt and freshly ground black pepper, to taste

- Heat the olive oil in a heavy skillet and sauté the garlic for 1 minute. Do not brown.
- Add the zucchini and red pepper and toss around in the pan over medium-high heat for 5 minutes or until cooked but still crisp.
- Remove from the heat and toss in the lemon juice, basil, parsley, salt, and pepper.
- Serve immediately.
- Serves 8.

Gazpacho Salad with Light Basil Vinaigrette

A salad with the great fresh flavors of the popular cold soup is particularly good when tomatoes are in season. Unlike most fresh salads, this one is designed to be assembled hours ahead, making it a convenient menu choice for a busy day.

This light vinaigrette has many other uses. It is good on just a plain tomato salad, thinly sliced cucumber, tossed greens, or anytime you want a light salad dressing.

1 large cucumber, peeled, seeded, and thinly
    sliced
8 oz. mushrooms, washed, trimmed, and thinly
    sliced
1 medium red onion, peeled, halved, and thinly
    sliced
1 medium red bell pepper, cored and thinly
    sliced
1 recipe Light Basil Vinaigrette (see below)
4 medium tomatoes, thinly sliced
Salt and freshly ground black pepper, to taste
¼ cup sliced black olives
¼ cup chopped flat-leaf parsley

- Layer the cucumber, mushrooms, onion, and red pepper in a medium bowl.
- Sprinkle with half the vinaigrette.
- Arrange the tomatoes on top of the vegetable mixture.
- Season with salt and pepper.
- Pour over the remaining dressing and sprinkle over the olives.
- Cover with plastic wrap and refrigerate several hours or overnight.
- Sprinkle with parsley to garnish before serving.
- Serves 8.

Light Basil Vinaigrette

½ cup red-wine vinegar
2 tbsp. water
1 tsp. sugar
1 clove garlic, finely chopped
2 tbsp. extra-virgin olive oil
¼ cup shredded fresh basil
¼ cup chopped flat-leaf parsley
¼ tsp. hot pepper sauce
½ tsp. salt, or to taste

- In a small nonreactive pan, or a glass measuring cup if microwave is used, heat together the vinegar, water, sugar, and garlic just to boiling.
- Stir to dissolve the sugar, set aside, and allow to cool completely.
- Whisk the vinegar mixture together with the oil, basil, parsley, and hot pepper sauce. Add salt.
- Makes about ³/₄ cup.

Easy Homemade Pita Bread

Pita bread happens to be my favorite example of fat-free bread. It is also fun to make. Store it in the freezer for later use. Because of its shape it is also so versatile. Halve it and fill with plenty of healthy veggies (splashed with one of our light salad dressings). Cut it up and serve it with spreads or dips instead of using high-fat chips and crackers. Toast it for snacks and hors d'oeuvres.

My directions are for the old-fashioned method, but those of you who have a food processor or mixer with a dough hook can whip out this bread in no time at all.

1 pkg. dry yeast
1¼ cups warm water (110 degrees)
3-4 cups unbleached flour
2 tsp. salt

- Dissolve the yeast in the water in a large bowl.
- Stir in 2 cups of the flour and the salt.
- Beat well and add more flour, $\frac{1}{2}$ cup at a time, until a rough, stiff dough forms.
- Knead on a lightly floured board for 8 minutes, or until the dough is smooth and elastic.
- Divide the dough into 6 pieces and form each into a round ball.
- Flatten each ball with a rolling pin on a lightly floured surface into a disc that measures $\frac{1}{4}$ in. thick and 5 in. in diameter.
- Cover each disc with plastic wrap and a dishtowel and allow to sit for 45 minutes.
- Place (top side down) on a greased baking sheet and bake in a preheated very hot oven—450-500 degrees—for 12 to 15 minutes or until puffed and light brown.
- Cool slightly and place in a plastic bag while still warm. Seal the bag and allow the bread to soften.
- Makes 6 small round "loaves."

Paul Sturkey's Cucumber Salad

Paul Sturkey is a great chef and I am proud to call him a good friend. I've certainly eaten my share of his innovative and wonderfully tasty dishes in his outstanding restaurants, and he often pinch hits for me on the radio show when I am out of town. Chef Paul is also interested in the challenge of making food that comes up to his high standards yet manages to be healthy and nutritious. This is a recipe that he shared with me so I could share it with you in turn. He suggests serving it alongside spicy dishes to act as a cooling element and to refresh the palate.

$\frac{1}{4}$ **cup white-wine vinegar**
Juice of 1 lime
4 tbsp. chopped flat-leaf parsley
1 tbsp. cumin
1 tbsp. chopped fresh cilantro
1 tbsp. chopped fresh chives
2 small cucumbers, peeled and thinly sliced
$\frac{1}{2}$ **medium red Spanish onion, thinly sliced**

- Whisk together the vinegar, lime juice, parsley, cumin, cilantro, and chives.
- Combine the cucumbers and onion in a bowl.
- Pour over the vinegar mixture.
- Cover and refrigerate for at least 2 hours, or up to 3 days.
- Let everyone salt and pepper to their own taste at the table.
- Serves 4-6.

Broccoli and Red Pepper Salad

A few years ago I was honored to be a spokesperson for the local American Cancer Society. The theme that year was "The Great American Food Fight," an all-out effort to spread the word about the importance of good nutrition for maintaining good health. The first point on the brochure that was handed out at my speaking engagements was, "Eat more cabbage-family vegetables." I probably don't need to tell you that broccoli was at the very top of the list. This is a recipe that I developed for that program. It is not only good for you but looks festive on the plate, is nice and crunchy, and simply tastes good. It's a good side salad in cold weather when some of the summer salad ingredients are not available.

1 bunch fresh broccoli, washed
1 large red bell pepper, washed
3 heads Bibb lettuce, washed, dried, and chilled
¼ cup chopped fresh parsley
1 recipe Light Vinaigrette Dressing (see below)

- Cut the broccoli into florets and remove the coarse stems.
- Steam for about 3 minutes or until crisp-tender (in steamer or microwave). Drain well, cool, and chill.
- Stem and core the pepper. Cut into fourths lengthwise and cut each strip crosswise into very thin julienne strips.
- Line a large plate (or 6 salad plates) with crisp lettuce leaves.
- Arrange the broccoli on top.
- Top with pepper strips and sprinkle with chopped parsley.
- Drizzle the dressing over the salad.
- Serves 6.

LIVE! FROM MARILYN'S KITCHEN

Light Vinaigrette Dressing

2 tbsp. extra-virgin olive oil
¼ cup balsamic vinegar
1 tbsp. water
2 tsp. Dijon mustard
Pinch sugar
Salt and freshly ground black pepper, to taste

• Whisk together all ingredients (or blend in a blender or food processor).

Grill It!

It wasn't all that long ago when grilling simply meant building a fire in the little outdoor grill and tossing on some burgers, or maybe a steak on Saturday night for company. Now we enjoy grilling everything from fresh seafood to fresh vegetables. The demand for bigger and better grills keeps growing, and the outdoor gas grill has become one of the most popular home appliances. Our quest for eating healthier is yet another influence on the amount of grilling we do, because this dry cooking method is a way to cook delicious food that isn't so fat and calorie laden.

I have done a number of creative dishes on the grill in the last few years. This chapter is proof of that. So grill it . . . and enjoy it!

Sizzling Shrimp

I remember making these delightfully aromatic shrimp in my New Orleans days and folks would tend to want to eat them directly from the grill. Actually that was not such a bad idea, since these tasty barbecued shrimp are at their best when served sizzling hot. Two or three large shrimp on a small bamboo skewer served with some crunchy French bread (which can also be buttered and browned the last minute on the grill) makes a fun first course from the grill. If you are looking for something different for a light and elegant main course, add sea scallops and some firm, fresh fish fillets for a seafood "mixed grill."

½ **cup vegetable oil**
½ **cup ketchup**
2 **tsp. salt**
½ **tsp. paprika**
¼-½ **tsp. cayenne pepper, to taste**
2 **cloves garlic, finely chopped**
1 **small onion, finely chopped**
1 **tbsp. fresh lemon juice**
2 **lb. large peeled and deveined shrimp**

- Combine all of the sauce ingredients in a bowl or heavy-duty plastic bag.
- Add the shrimp. Place in the refrigerator and marinate overnight or for at least 3 hours.
- Remove the shrimp from the sauce. Reserve the sauce for basting the shrimp while it is cooking.
- Arrange the shrimp on bamboo (see tip) or metal skewers.
- Grill over a hot fire about 4 to 5 in. from the heat for 3 to 6 minutes, depending on the size of the shrimp.
- Baste both sides of the shrimp while they are grilling and turn only once during the cooking time.
- Serve immediately.
- Serves 8 as a first course or appetizer.

Bamboo skewers work well for all kebabs. They are inexpensive and disposable, making them handy for parties. They come in different lengths. Use the small ones for appetizer kebabs or saté and the longer ones for dinner kebabs. Always thread the food on two bamboo skewers that are side by side, so you get a better grip on the food. Bamboo skewers must be soaked for at least 30 minutes in water before using. This prevents them from catching fire on the grill.

Shrimp has a short cooking time. As soon as it turns pink and just begins to curl, it is done and should be immediately removed from the heat.

Grilled Fish Kebabs

Kebabs are fun food! They look colorful and festive. They are easy to do because they can be all prepared well ahead and they are quickly grilled. Even the flavor is different, since the pieces are smaller, allowing them to be well infused with marinades and seasonings. Plus, compared to larger pieces of fish, poultry, or meat, there is also more surface to brown and take on that special "grilled" flavor. Since they are already cut up, kebabs are also easy to eat and are perfect fun food for a cookout picnic or casual supper. Just add some bread and salad to complete the menu. There are several kebab recipes for you in this chapter. This one features fish instead of the usual meat or chicken. However, chunks of chicken may be substituted.

½ cup olive oil
2 tbsp. fresh lemon or lime juice
1 tsp. lemon or lime zest
2 tbsp. chopped onion
2 cloves garlic, finely chopped
2 tsp. kosher salt
½ tsp. coarsely ground black pepper
2 tsp. fresh thyme leaves (or 1 tsp. dried)
1½ lb. fresh firm fish (halibut, tuna, salmon)
12 medium mushrooms, washed and trimmed
1 medium green bell pepper, seeded and cut into
   1-in. pieces
1 medium red bell pepper, seeded and cut into 1-
   in. pieces
1 sweet salad onion (such as red Spanish or
   Vidalia), quartered and layers separated
1 fresh fennel bulb, sliced ¼ in. thick and layers
   separated
Thyme sprigs
Lemon or lime slices

- To make the marinade, combine the oil, juice, zest, onion, garlic, salt, pepper, and thyme and mix until well blended.
- Cut the fish into 2-in. cubes.
- Thread the fish and vegetables onto stainless steel or bamboo skewers.
- Place in a shallow glass or ceramic baking dish. Pour over the marinade.

The accepted rule for cooking fish by any method is 10 minutes total cooking time for each 1 in. of thickness. When grilling or broiling, turn only once, two-thirds of the way through the cooking time.

- Cover tightly and place in the refrigerator for 2 hours. (If kebabs are not covered with marinade, remove from refrigerator after 1 hour and turn.)
- Grease the grill rack (or spray with a nonstick spray).
- Preheat the grill to hot.
- Remove the kebabs from the marinade and place on the hot grill.
- Grill the kebabs for about 10 minutes, turning once.
- Serve immediately garnished with thyme and slices of lemon or lime.
- Makes 6 large kebabs.

Lime-Cilantro-Marinated Salmon with Avocado Salsa

Salmon is surely everybody's favorite fish. It used to be a regional treat or something we ordered in a restaurant. Since the fresh seafood distribution system has become much more sophisticated, we can all easily enjoy delicious fresh salmon at home anytime we want it. Salmon's great flavor is enhanced by flavorful marinades such as this one and is delicious served either hot off the grill or chilled. This time-saving "two recipes in one" offers you both options.

1 recipe Lime-Cilantro Marinade (see below)
9 1-in.-thick salmon fillets (approximately 6 oz. each)
Potatoes, for roasting
1 recipe Avocado Salsa (see below)

- Make the marinade according to the following recipe.
- Add the fish fillets. Turn several times to evenly coat the fish with the marinade.
- Place in the refrigerator and allow to marinate for at least 1 hour or as long as 3 hours.
- Place the fish on a greased preheated hot grill, or place on a special fish rack or grid and place the rack on the hot grill.
- Grill for 6 minutes on the first side. If the fillets are thicker or

thinner than 1 in., adjust the cooking time. Salmon may be cooked rare, medium, or well done, but do not overcook or it will be dry.

- Turn and cook for 3 to 4 minutes on the second side, for the fish to be cooked through but still moist. (Use a shorter time for rare or medium rare.)
- Serve two-thirds of the fish hot. Cool the remainder, wrap, and store in the refrigerator for making the Grilled Salmon Salad with Cilantro-Lime Dressing later (see recipe below).
- To complete the grilled salmon meal, roast some potatoes on the grill and serve with the following Avocado Salsa.
- Serves 6.

Lime-Cilantro Marinade

Zest and juice of 2 large limes
¼ cup chopped fresh cilantro
½ cup finely chopped onion
½ cup extra-virgin olive oil
½ tsp. coarsely ground black pepper
1 tbsp. kosher salt
½ tsp. sugar

- Mix together the marinade in a heavy-duty zip-top plastic bag (or double 2 regular plastic bags).

Avocado Salsa

2 ripe large avocados, peeled and chopped
2 medium tomatoes, washed, cored, and
  chopped
1 cup chopped sweet salad onion
¼ cup chopped fresh cilantro
1 tbsp. fresh lime juice
1 tsp. salt
½ tsp. hot pepper sauce, or to taste

- Toss together the avocados and tomatoes.
- Add the remaining ingredients. Gently toss together.
- Cover and chill for at least 1 hour.
- Makes about 3 cups.

If you grill a lot of fish, it is worth the investment to purchase a special fish rack, which helps to prevent fish from sticking to a hot grill rack as well as allowing you to turn the fish without it falling apart. You will find these handy grill accessories at specialty kitchen stores and stores that sell grills.

Grilled Salmon Salad with Cilantro-Lime Dressing

Here is the second part of the grilled salmon recipe. For those of us who lead busy lives, it doesn't take any longer to marinate and grill some extra while you are at it. It will save time, and the salmon for this salad improves in flavor as it chills overnight.

> 3 grilled Lime-Cilantro-Marinated Salmon fillets (see above)
> 1 medium sweet salad onion, halved and thinly sliced
> 2 medium cucumbers, peeled, seeded, and thinly sliced
> 1 recipe Cilantro-Lime Dressing (see below)
> 1 large head Boston lettuce
> 2 ripe medium tomatoes, cut into wedges
> 2 hard-cooked eggs, cut into wedges
> 2 tbsp. chopped fresh cilantro

All cucumbers, with the exception of the "European" variety, should be peeled before adding to salad. To peel and seed a cucumber, cut a slice from each end. Peel with a swivel vegetable peeler. Cut in half, lengthwise. Over a bowl or the kitchen sink, pull a teaspoon through the length of the inside of the cucumber half, removing the pulp and seeds.

To add extra crispness to cucumbers, soak them for 30 minutes in ice water. Drain well.

- Cut the salmon into bite-sized pieces.
- Toss the salmon, onion, and cucumbers with enough dressing to coat. Arrange on a bed of crisp lettuce leaves.
- Garnish with the tomato and egg wedges. Sprinkle the cilantro over the eggs and tomatoes.
- Chill until ready to serve.
- Serves 6.

Cilantro-Lime Dressing

1 cup mayonnaise
½ cup plain low-fat or nonfat yogurt
2 tbsp. fresh lime juice
1 tsp. finely grated lime zest
1 tsp. salt
1 tsp. hot pepper sauce, or to taste
1 tsp. honey
3 tbsp. chopped fresh cilantro
2 tbsp. finely chopped red Spanish onion

- Whisk together all of the ingredients gently until smooth.

- Cover and chill until ready to serve. (Flavor is best if made at least a couple of hours ahead.)
- Makes about $1^1/_2$ cups.

Sharon's Wild Rice Salad with Grilled Shrimp

Even though Sharon Shipley and I live across the country from one another, we stay in contact and are always exchanging recipes along with culinary successes and problems. Sharon is an experienced cooking teacher who is always trying out new recipes. I was most pleased when she sent this recipe to be included in this book. You will be too when you taste it!

1 stick unsalted butter
Zest and juice of 1 lime
$^1/_4$ cup finely chopped cilantro
$^1/_2$ tbsp. roasted garlic purée
2 tsp. cumin
1 tsp. salt
24 large peeled and deveined shrimp, tails intact
1 recipe Wild Rice Salad (see below)

- Melt the butter. Add the lime zest and juice, cilantro, garlic, cumin, and salt.
- Thread the shrimp onto double skewers; place in a shallow glass or ceramic dish. Pour over the marinade.
- Allow to marinate for 1 to 2 hours in the refrigerator.
- Just before serving, place a double handful of soaked mesquite on a grill fire. Place the shrimp skewers on the preheated hot grill and grill the shrimp just until done through, about 6 to 8 minutes.
- Remove the shrimp from the skewers and arrange the warm shrimp on the cold salad.
- Serves 6.

Wild Rice Salad

1 cup long-grain wild rice
1 medium red bell pepper
1 medium yellow bell pepper

1 lb. fresh asparagus, tough ends removed
3 tbsp. extra-virgin olive oil
Coarse sea salt
3 cloves garlic, finely chopped
½ tsp. fresh thyme leaves
2 fresh jalapeño peppers, seeded and finely chopped
½ cup tomato, seeded and diced
½ cup finely chopped green onions
½ cup chopped fresh cilantro
½ cup olive oil
⅓ cup white-wine vinegar
Salt and freshly ground black pepper, to taste

- A day ahead, place the rice in a glass bowl. Pour enough boiling water over the rice to cover by 3 to 4 in. Cover lightly and allow to sit at room temperature for at least 12 hours. Drain and add more boiling water. Place uncovered in the microwave oven for 15 to 20 minutes on high or until tender. Do not overcook and allow to become mushy. Drain off any remaining water and set aside to cool. Cover and chill.

- Roast the peppers on a hot grill or in a 450-degree oven until the skins blister and darken. Place them in a closed paper or plastic bag until cool enough to handle.

- Peel, core, seed, and cut the peppers into ³/₄-in. dice. Cover and chill.

- Place the asparagus in a shallow dish. Drizzle with 1 tbsp. olive oil. Sprinkle lightly with coarse salt. Toss with fingertips to coat with the oil.

- Grill the asparagus on a hot grill just until crisp-tender. Cool and cut on the diagonal into 1-in. pieces. Cover and chill.

- To finish, heat 2 tbsp. oil in a skillet over medium heat. Cook garlic, thyme, and jalapeño peppers, stirring. Remove and cool. Add to the rice and stir well.

- Toss in the peppers, asparagus, tomatoes, green onions, and cilantro.

- Whisk together the ¹/₂ cup olive oil and the vinegar. Season with salt and pepper.

- Toss the dressing into the rice. Cover and chill until ready to serve.

To roast a pepper on a grill, place the whole pepper on a hot grill. Allow the skin to darken and blister. Turn for even roasting. After about 15 minutes or when the pepper softens and the skin is charred, remove to a plastic bag and seal the top of the bag. Cool to room temperature in the bag to "sweat" the pepper and make the skin easy to remove. Peel off the skin (it comes off easily with your fingers). Remove the core and seeds.

Grilled Swordfish Steaks with Spicy Eggplant Chutney

Swordfish, with its mild flavor and firm meaty texture, is a natural for the grill and a guaranteed crowd pleaser. This is a simple and straight-forward grilled-fish recipe, but there are two reasons why I definitely wanted to include it here. First, it uses mayonnaise instead of oil to lubricate and flavor the fish for grilling, a handy little trick that all fish grillers should note. It works well for other fish as well. The second reason was to share this delicious recipe for eggplant chutney, which is also wonderful with grilled lamb as well as other types of grilled fish.

6 swordfish steaks, about 1 in. thick
Mayonnaise
Salt and freshly ground black pepper, to taste
1 recipe Spicy Eggplant Chutney (see below)

- Brush each side of the fish steaks with a generous amount of mayonnaise.
- Season lightly with salt and pepper and grill on a hot grill about 10 minutes per inch of fish, or less to keep the inside rare. Turn just once.
- Serve immediately with Spicy Eggplant Chutney spooned on the side.
- Serves 6.

Spicy Eggplant Chutney

1 medium (about 1 lb.) eggplant, washed and trimmed
Kosher salt
⅓ cup extra-virgin olive oil
1 large yellow onion, chopped
3 cloves garlic, finely chopped
1 tbsp. finely chopped fresh gingerroot
2 or 3 jalapeño peppers, seeded and finely chopped, to taste
2 large tomatoes, peeled, seeded, and coarsely chopped
1 tbsp. dark brown sugar
2 tbsp. chopped fresh parsley
3 tbsp. drained capers

The long, slender eggplants are preferable to the round, fat ones. For the freshest ones, look for firm, shiny skin and a green stem. The heavier ones will be firmer inside than ones the same size that do not weigh as much.

- Cube the unpeeled eggplant. Place in a colander and toss with enough salt to coat well. Allow to sit in the sink for 30 minutes. Rinse well with cool water and pat dry with paper towels.
- Heat half of the oil in a large skillet and sauté the eggplant, stirring for about 10 minutes or until just tender.
- Remove to a side dish.
- Add the remaining oil to the skillet and add the onion, garlic, ginger, and jalapeño peppers. Cook, stirring, for 5 minutes.
- Add the tomatoes and cook for 3 more minutes over high heat, stirring.
- Return the eggplant to the skillet and add the sugar, parsley, capers, and salt to taste.
- Cook a couple of minutes longer. Taste and correct seasonings. Add more salt if needed.
- This is best made a few hours before serving to blend flavors. It may be served hot, chilled, or at room temperature.
- Makes about 3 cups.

Sassy Chicken Kebabs with Black Bean Relish

Everybody's favorite cut of chicken is the boneless and skinless breast. It is easy to understand why what the French call suprême is the preferred cut: Low in fat and quick cooking, it is just right for today's health-conscious and hectic lifestyle. It can, however, also be dry and bland and lately I have noticed signs of "chicken burnout" among my radio listeners. They call my show looking for new ways to add some excitement to their frequently consumed chicken breasts. Here's one for you. Nobody will ever call this chicken dish boring. It is good without the Black Bean Relish too, but not as much fun. And just think of all the extra nourishment you are getting from those tasty little black beans.

> **4 whole boneless and skinless chicken breasts**
> **1 recipe Sassy Marinade (see below)**
> **1 large red bell pepper, halved lengthwise an seeded**

1 poblano pepper, halved lengthwise and seeded
1 large sweet salad onion, peeled
8 oz. medium mushrooms, washed, dried, and
**   trimmed**
1 recipe Black Bean Relish (see below)

- Cut the chicken into 2-in. cubes.
- Place the marinade in a heavy-duty zip-top plastic bag. Add the chicken. Chill for 1 to 3 hours.
- Cut the peppers into 2-in. pieces. Blanch for 1 minute in lightly salted boiling water. Immediately refresh in ice water. Pat dry with paper towels.
- Cut the onion in half crosswise and separate the sections. Cut into 2-in. pieces.
- To assemble the kebabs, drain the chicken from the marinade. Thread the chicken and vegetables alternately onto 8 long skewers.
- Place on a hot grill.
- Grill, turning once or twice, for 8-10 minutes or until the chicken is done through.
- Serve immediately with Black Bean Relish.
- Serves 8.

Sassy Marinade

¼ cup dry sherry
1 tbsp. fresh lemon juice
¼ cup dark brown sugar
½ cup vegetable oil
½ cup soy sauce
2 tbsp. finely chopped fresh gingerroot
2 large cloves garlic, finely chopped
2 or 3 jalapeño peppers, seeded and finely
**   chopped**
1 tsp. lemon zest

- Stir together until well mixed.

Black Bean Relish

3 cups cooked dried black beans or 2 1-lb. cans
**   black beans, drained and rinsed**
3 tbsp. extra-virgin olive oil

Dry beans should be rinsed well and soaked before cooking. They may be soaked overnight. Or use the short method: Pour the clean, dry beans in a pot and cover with about 1 in. water. Cover and bring to a boil. Remove from heat and allow to sit at room temperature for 1 hour. They are then ready to cook. Season the cooking water with salt, 1 bay leaf, and 2 small dried red chiles.

If you are flavoring dried beans with an ingredient high in acid such as tomatoes or lemon juice, wait until the beans have cooked long enough to become tender before adding the acidic ingredient.

2 tbsp. red-wine or sherry vinegar
¼ cup thinly sliced green onions (including crisp green tops)
1 tsp. cumin
1 tsp. chipotle chili powder
1 tbsp. chopped fresh jalapeño pepper
1 tsp. salt, or to taste
½ tsp. sugar

- Toss together all the ingredients.
- Cover and chill for at least 3 hours or until ready to serve.
- Taste and correct seasonings.
- Makes about 3 cups.

Grilled Chicken Salad with Sun-Dried Tomato Vinaigrette

Grills have become more sophisticated, giving us more precise control over the temperature, and that opens up a much wider range of menu possibilities. It also makes grilling outdoors quicker and easier, keeping the house cooler and not messing up the kitchen. All that aside, the biggest benefit is in the extra flavor grilled foods have. For example, compare boiled to grilled chicken: both the flavor and texture are altogether different. That's why I think making chicken salad from grilled chicken breast is a great idea!

1 recipe Basil Marinade (see below)
8 boneless and skinless chicken breast halves
2 roasted red bell peppers, peeled and cut into strips
1 large sweet salad onion, thinly sliced
1 large cucumber, peeled, seeded, and thinly sliced
¼ cup chopped parsley
1 recipe Sun-Dried Tomato Vinaigrette (see below)
Romaine lettuce leaves
2 tbsp. shredded fresh basil leaves

- Make the marinade according to the following recipe.
- Rinse, trim, and pound the chicken between 2 sheets of plastic wrap to flatten.
- Place the chicken in the marinade in a heavy plastic bag. Marinate for 1 to 3 hours in the refrigerator. (Oil may thicken or coagulate. If so, allow to sit at room temperature for 30 minutes before removing chicken.)
- Place the marinated chicken on a very hot grill. Grill for 8 to 10 minutes or until cooked through, turning once.
- Cut the chicken, across the grain, into small strips.
- Toss together the chicken, red peppers, onion, cucumber, and parsley.
- Toss in the vinaigrette.
- Arrange the lettuce on a platter or in a shallow bowl.
- Spoon the salad over the lettuce.
- Sprinkle the basil over the top of the salad.
- Serve immediately.
- Serves 8-10.

Basil Marinade

¼ cup extra-virgin olive oil
3 tbsp. shredded fresh basil leaves
¼ tsp. cayenne pepper
1 tbsp. fresh lemon juice
1 tsp. grated lemon rind
1 clove garlic, finely chopped
1 tsp. salt

- Stir together the ingredients or mix in a food processor.

Sun-Dried Tomato Vinaigrette

½ cup extra-virgin olive oil
1 clove garlic, finely chopped
3 tbsp. red-wine vinegar
1 tsp. honey
¼ tsp. hot pepper sauce
½ tsp. salt, or to taste
½ cup oil-packed sun-dried tomatoes, drained
   and cut into tiny strips

- Whisk together, or mix in a food processor, all of the ingredients except the tomatoes, until well blended.
- Stir in the tomatoes.

Zucchini Kebabs with Basil-Spinach Cheese Sauce

I brought this delectable sauce recipe back from one of my sojourns in Germany. I know it may not seem like typical German food, but the German kitchen is changing along with a unified Europe. In any case, I have enjoyed this flavorful goat-cheese sauce with pasta as well as simple grilled fish, but my favorite use is with these pretty vegetable kebabs. It makes a wonderful hot summer day meatless meal.

> **4 tender medium zucchini**
> **2 large red Spanish onions**
> **¼ cup extra-virgin olive oil**
> **¼ cup coarsely shredded basil leaves**
> **1 large clove garlic, finely chopped**
> **1 tsp. salt**
> **½ tsp. freshly ground black pepper**
> **1 recipe Basil-Spinach Cheese Sauce (see below)**

- Wash and trim the ends from the zucchini. Cut into ½-in. rounds.
- Peel the onions and cut into quarters. Separate into 1- or 2-layer pieces.
- In a large, shallow dish, mix together the oil, basil, garlic, salt, and pepper.
- Toss in the zucchini and onions.
- Allow to sit for 1 hour at room temperature.
- Thread the vegetables onto 8 doubled bamboo skewers.
- Grill on a hot grill, turning often, until crisp-tender, 8 to 10 minutes.
- Serve on a bed of Basil-Spinach Cheese Sauce.
- Serves 8.

Basil-Spinach Cheese Sauce

2 tbsp. butter
¼ cup chopped onion
1 tbsp. flour
1 cup chicken broth, heated
1 lb. fresh spinach leaves, blanched, refreshed,
**   squeezed dry, and chopped***
¼ cup shredded fresh basil leaves
4 oz. fresh goat cheese, cut into small cubes
Salt and freshly ground black pepper, to taste

• Melt the butter in a heavy saucepan over medium heat.

• Add the onion and sauté, stirring, for 3 minutes or until just tender.

• Stir in the flour. Cook, stirring, for a full 2 minutes without browning.

• Whisk in the broth. Cook, whisking, until mixture bubbles and is slightly thickened.

• Stir in the spinach and basil. Cook, stirring, for 2 minutes.

• Add the cheese and continue cooking and stirring until melted.

• Season with salt and pepper.

• Serve hot.

• Makes about 1¹/₂ cups sauce.

*A 10-oz. pkg. frozen, chopped spinach may be substituted. Thaw in the microwave, cool, and squeeze out the excess liquid.

Wrapped-Up Potatoes and Carrots

No doubt one of the real benefits of cooking dinner on the grill is the fun we have doing it. Perfect for casual entertaining, it allows the hosts to stay out of the kitchen and mingle with the guests. So why not plan to cook all of the hot food for your entire meal on the grill? For a tasty and aromatic vegetable dish, make a packet of these rosemary-seasoned potatoes and carrots for each diner and serve them with any entree from fish to lamb. With your salad in the refrigerator ready to toss, you can easily serve up a delicious dinner.

> **1 medium white baking potato, scrubbed**
> **2 medium carrots, peeled**
> **4 thick slices onion**
> **1 tbsp. extra-virgin olive oil**
> **Salt and freshly ground black pepper, to taste**
> **1 sprig rosemary**

- Cut the potato into $1/4$-in. slices.
- Cut the carrots on the diagonal into thin slices.
- On a large sheet of heavy-duty foil, arrange the potatoes, carrots, and onions alternately.
- Sprinkle with the oil.
- Season with salt and pepper.
- Place the rosemary sprig on top and seal well using the "drugstore wrap."*
- Place on a hot grill for 30 minutes. Serve hot.
- Serves 1.

*Use the "drugstore wrap" for wrapping food to go onto the grill. Leave an excess of foil on both sides of the food. Pull up these long ends and fold down over the food into several tight folds. Slide your hands in opposite directions downward and outward from the top of the "package," pressing out the excess air. Then fold each short end toward the center in several folds. (A tight seal is important.)

Grilled Caponata

If I could only have one vegetable dish, it would surely be caponata. I simply find this combination of veggies and flavors to be irresistible. I have a couple of versions of this recipe. The one printed in my first book, Cooking with Marilyn, is made in a skillet. I have since developed this updated version and I must admit to liking it even better. It requires considerably less oil to grill than to sauté, making it lower in fat and calories. The overall flavor also improves on the grill.

    2 small to medium eggplants, about 1 lb. each
    Extra-virgin olive oil
    1 large red bell pepper, halved
    1 large yellow bell pepper, halved
    1 large red Spanish onion (or other sweet salad onion), thickly sliced lengthwise
    6 fresh plum tomatoes, halved
    ½ cup golden raisins
    1 tbsp. light brown sugar
    ¼ cup red-wine vinegar
    4 cloves roasted garlic, chopped
    3 tbsp. capers
    3 tbsp. chopped flat-leaf parsley
    1 tbsp. chopped fresh basil leaves
    Salt, to taste
    ½ tsp. hot pepper sauce, or to taste

- Wash and trim stems from the eggplants. Cut in half lengthwise. Score the cut surface, cutting about ¼ in. into the eggplants.

- Brush the cut surface with olive oil, using just enough oil to coat.

- Place the eggplants, cut side down, on a medium-hot grill. Cover and cook 20 to 30 minutes or until tender when pierced with the tip of a sharp knife.

- Remove and cool.

- After the eggplants are on the grill, lightly brush the peppers and onion slices on both sides with olive oil. Grill both until crisp-tender, 10 to 15 minutes. Remove and cool.

- Lightly rub the cut surface of the tomatoes with oil. Place on the grill and grill for 10-15 minutes or until soft. Remove with a large spoon to a side dish. Cool and remove the peels.

- Scoop out the cooled eggplant pulp and chop coarsely.
- Chop the peppers and onions. Add to the eggplant.
- Chop the tomatoes and add to the mixture.
- Place the raisins and brown sugar in a measuring cup and pour over the vinegar. Heat in the microwave until boiling. Remove and allow to sit for 20 minutes. Add to the eggplant mixture.
- Add the garlic, capers, parsley, basil, salt, and hot pepper sauce.
- Cover and chill for several hours.
- Taste and correct seasonings.
- Serve chilled as a side dish with grilled fish, chicken, or lamb, or serve as an appetizer with thinly sliced bread or toast.
- Keeps for 2 weeks or longer, covered in the refrigerator.
- Makes about 6 cups.

Burgundy Burgers

Of course, we couldn't talk about grilling without including a burger recipe. All weekend chefs have their own special version of America's favorite food from the grill. This is one of mine and it is truly juicy and delicious. If it is a family picnic and you don't want to add the wine, simply omit it. For best results with this recipe, it is important to start with the leanest and freshest ground beef. I often buy lean chuck or round steak and grind it in a food processor.

1 medium yellow onion, finely chopped
½ stick (4 tbsp.) butter or margarine
3 lb. freshly ground lean beef
1 tbsp. Dijon mustard
1 large clove garlic, finely chopped
1 tsp. Worcestershire sauce
Generous dash hot pepper sauce, to taste
¼ cup chopped fresh parsley
½ cup dry red wine
½ tsp. salt
½ tsp. freshly ground black pepper

- Sauté the onion in the butter in a small skillet for 5 minutes. Cool completely.
- Place the beef in a large bowl and gently toss in the onion-butter mixture, the mustard, garlic, Worcestershire sauce, hot pepper sauce, parsley, wine, salt, and pepper. Toss just until well mixed.
- Using a very gentle touch, form into 8 patties.
- Chill, covered, until ready to grill.
- Grill on a preheated hot grill to desired doneness. Turn only once.
- Serves 8.

These rules apply to all burgers, whether plain or fancy: Form the patties with the lightest and gentlest touch possible. Never squeeze or press the ground beef, since this results in a dry, tough burger. Always grill on a hot, preheated grill. Turn the burgers only once about two-thirds of the way through the cooking time. Never press with the spatula while cooking.

Beer-Marinated Flank Steak

If you have been cooking as long as I have, you too can remember when flank steak was an inexpensive cut. Those were the days when almost everyone preferred that well-marbled T-bone. Times change and this "less tender" cut from the lean flank has become much in demand. Not only one of the lowest in fat, and therefore calories, of all of the beef cuts, flank steak is also full of good beef flavor. An aromatic marinade infuses it with extra delicious flavors to make it even tastier. This one is simple to make with everyday ingredients.

> 1½-2-lb. flank steak
> ¼ cup soy sauce
> 3 tbsp. vegetable oil
> 2 tbsp. dark brown sugar
> 1 medium onion, coarsely chopped
> 1 large clove garlic, finely chopped
> 1 tbsp. finely chopped fresh gingerroot
> ¼ tsp. hot pepper sauce
> 12-oz. can beer

- Trim all the visible fat from the steak.
- Mix together the soy sauce, oil, brown sugar, onion, garlic, ginger, and hot pepper sauce, stirring until sugar is dissolved.
- Pour over the beer. (Don't use flat beer; it should be fresh and bubbly.)
- Place the steak in a gallon-size heavy-duty plastic bag with a

zip top. (Or double 2 regular plastic bags.) Pour over the marinade. Seal and turn the bag several times to evenly coat the meat with the marinade.

- Place in the refrigerator for 24 hours.
- Remove the steak from the marinade. (Discard marinade.)
- Place the steak on a hot grill. Grill for a total of about 15 minutes for medium doneness, turning after 9 or 10 minutes. Check for desired doneness with an instant-read thermometer.
- Place steak on a cutting board. Slice on the diagonal, across the grain, into very thin slices. Serve immediately.
- Serves 4-6.

Slicing across the grain is very important for flank and brisket cuts of beef. Slicing with the grain makes the meat texture tough and difficult to chew.

Midnight Marinade

Millstone Coffee has been a sponsor of my "Cooking with Marilyn!" radio show and I created this recipe for them. You can see that its color gave it its name. Use this marinade to enhance the flavor of any beefsteak.

½ **cup Worcestershire sauce**
½ **cup strong brewed Millstone dark roast coffee**
¼ **cup vegetable oil**
3 **tbsp. balsamic vinegar**
3 **tbsp. dark brown sugar**
2 **tsp. salt**
½ **tsp. freshly ground black pepper**
1 **tsp. finely chopped garlic**
1 **tbsp. finely chopped fresh gingerroot**

- Mix together all of the ingredients. Place the steak in a heavy-duty zip-top plastic bag. Pour in the marinade. Seal and chill for 12 to 24 hours.
- Broil or grill steak as desired.
- Makes enough to marinate 2 large flank steaks.

Honey-Lime Marinade

We talk a lot about grilling on the radio show. It used to be just during the summer months but it now extends to all year round. Many of my listeners have shared their favorite marinades, and this is one of the most frequently requested. It is an excellent choice for both chicken and pork.

1/4 cup fresh lime juice
1 tbsp. lime zest
2 tbsp. finely chopped fresh gingerroot
2 tbsp. chopped fresh cilantro
2 tbsp. honey
3 tbsp. extra-virgin olive or vegetable oil
1/4 tsp. cayenne pepper
2 tsp. salt
Lime slices
Cilantro sprigs

- Mix together all of the ingredients.
- Place the chicken or pork in a heavy-duty zip-top plastic bag and pour over the marinade. Seal and place in the refrigerator.
- Pork tenderloin and thick pork chops should be marinated 6 to 8 hours, a whole pork loin overnight, chicken with bones 6 to 8 hours, and boneless breasts at least 1 to 3 hours.
- Makes 2/3 cup.

Grilled Steak and Potato Salad with Green Peppercorn Dressing

I think everybody agrees there is no better steak than a properly grilled one. So why not transfer that incomparable flavor to a great main-dish salad to serve for an easy warm-weather supper? The obligatory potatoes to accompany the steak can be precooked hours ahead and finished on the grill, so that they, too, have a delicious grilled flavor. And speaking of flavor, my strong preference for potatoes in this salad are those tasty gold ones, called "Yukon Gold." White or red potatoes are good too.

2 lb. small yellow potatoes, scrubbed
Extra-virgin olive oil

Salt and freshly ground black pepper, to taste
2 lb. boneless top sirloin steak
8 oz. fresh mushrooms, washed, trimmed, and
   thinly sliced
2 tsp. lemon juice
2 large red bell peppers, cut into small strips
½ cup thinly sliced green onions
¼ cup chopped parsley
1 recipe Green Peppercorn Dressing (see below)
Romaine lettuce leaves, washed, chilled, and
   shredded
1 cup halved cherry tomatoes, lightly salted
Parsley sprigs

- Cook the potatoes in enough salted water to cover for 20 minutes, or until just tender enough to easily insert the tip of a small sharp knife. Drain and cool.

- Cut the potatoes in half. Brush the cut sides with olive oil and season with salt and pepper.

- Season the steak with salt and pepper.

- Grill the steak over a hot grill to a medium-rare doneness (or to your own desired doneness). A thick steak (2 in.) cooked to medium on a hot grill should take 18-20 minutes, turning once two-thirds of the way through the cooking time. However, the only accurate determination is to take the temperature with an instant-read thermometer.

- Toss the mushrooms with the lemon juice and set aside.

- Place the potatoes, cut side down, on the grill. Brush the peels with oil as they are grilling. Grill until golden brown. Turn and grill for a few minutes on the second side.

- Slice the steak, across the grain, into ¼-in.-thick strips, then cut the strips into bite-sized pieces.

- Cut the potatoes into 1-in. cubes.

- Toss the steak with the mushrooms, peppers, onions, and parsley.

- Gently toss in the potatoes and the dressing.

- Serve at room temperature or cover and chill until ready to serve.

- Spoon onto a bed of lettuce. Garnish with the tomatoes and parsley sprigs.

- Serves 8.

Green Peppercorn Dressing

2 cups mayonnaise (regular or reduced fat)
1 clove garlic, finely chopped
1 tbsp. water-packed green peppercorns, drained
2 tbsp. fresh lemon juice
1 tsp. Dijon mustard
1 tsp. sugar
½ tsp. salt

- Stir together all ingredients until mixed. Cover and chill until ready to use.
- Makes about 2¼ cups.

Beef Tenderloin with Red Wine-Shallot Sauce

For an occasion calling for something elegant from the grill, allow me to recommend a beautiful grilled tenderloin with a sauce straight from a French kitchen. Even though it certainly qualifies as fancy cuisine, this is not a difficult dish to prepare. The sauce can be made as long as a day or so ahead of time and will only improve in flavor. This tenderest of all cuts is always cooked at a high temperature and should go onto a pre-heated grill. It will probably cook quicker than you might expect, so check the internal temperature to make sure you're not overcooking it. If a whole tenderloin is too much for your occasion, serve beef fillets (cut at least 2 in. thick) and top them with this same luscious sauce.

¼ cup extra-virgin olive oil
3 cloves garlic, finely chopped
1 tsp. dried thyme leaves
1 tsp. coarse salt
1 tsp. coarsely ground black pepper
3-4 lb. well-trimmed beef tenderloin

- Mix together the oil, garlic, thyme, salt, and pepper.
- Place the beef in a shallow dish. Rub all the surfaces with the mixture. Cover and chill for at least 8 hours or as long as overnight.
- Place on the greased rack of a preheated hot grill.

- Grill for 20-25 minutes, turning only once, for medium-rare doneness—5-6 minutes less for rare and 8-10 minutes more for medium-well to well-done. (Test for desired doneness with an instant-read thermometer.)
- Remove to a cutting board. Allow to sit for 15 minutes before slicing into thick slices.
- Nap each slice with a spoonful of the sauce. Pass the remainder of the sauce.
- Serves 8-10 (depending on weight purchased).

Red Wine-Shallot Sauce

2 tbsp. butter
2 tbsp. finely chopped shallots
1 cup dry red wine
2 tbsp. chopped fresh parsley
2 tsp. fresh thyme leaves (or 1 tsp. dried)
1 small bay leaf
1 cup beef stock*
1 tbsp. tomato paste
1 tsp. fresh lemon juice
Salt and freshly ground black pepper, to taste

- Melt the butter in a small heavy pan.
- Add the shallots and sauté, stirring or shaking the pan, for 2-3 minutes.
- Stir in the wine, parsley, thyme, and bay leaf.
- Cook over high heat until reduced by half.
- Whisk in the stock and tomato paste and cook over high heat for about 15 minutes or until reduced and slightly thickened.
- Stir in the lemon juice and season with salt and pepper.
- Chill until ready to serve. Reheat just before serving.
- Makes about 1 cup.

*A good-quality canned beef stock may be used for this sauce.

Party Fajitas

Yes, I know that most real Mexicans have never heard of "fajitas." They are definitely American-style Mexican food and are often featured on Tex-Mex restaurant menus. Like many trendy foods, they are better in some restaurants than in others.

Fajitas are fun and easy to make at home on your grill, and with good fresh ingredients they are a tasty main dish. If you are having several people for an informal party, make all three: beef, pork, and chicken. By the time you add the garnishes, you have a complete dinner. (All you need is some Mexican beer or sangria.)

Fajitas are traditionally eaten as sandwiches, but usually sandwiches that have to be eaten with knife and fork. Here's how a fajita should be assembled. Place a few slices of meat in the center of a soft, warmed flour tortilla. Top with grilled onions. Spoon in some sour cream and salsa. Fold "burrito style": fold the sides of the tortilla in over the filling and, holding securely, roll up a third side to make a roll. Place, seam side down, on a plate. Spoon over more salsa, some guacamole, and more sour cream, if desired.

Both this piquant salsa and creamy guacamole can do double duty at a party. For appetizers, serve a bowl of each along with some crunchy tortilla chips for dipping. Save some back in the kitchen to go with the fajitas.

½ cup fresh lime juice
¼ cup fresh orange juice
½ cup olive or vegetable oil
¼ cup tequila (optional)
4 large cloves garlic, finely chopped
2 tsp. kosher salt
¼-½ tsp. cayenne pepper
2 lb. flank steak, pork tenderloin, or flattened
 boneless chicken breasts
3 medium yellow onions, peeled and halved
 lengthwise
Soft, warmed flour tortillas
Extra grilled onion slices
Sour cream
Salsa Verde (see index)
1 recipe Marilyn's Favorite Tomato Salsa (see below)
1 recipe Cilantro Guacamole (see below)

- Stir together the lime juice, orange juice, oil, tequila (if desired), garlic, salt, and pepper to make the marinade.
- Pour into a heavy-duty zip-top plastic bag or a shallow glass baking dish.
- Place the beef, pork, or chicken in the marinade. Add the onion halves.
- Seal the bag tightly or cover the dish with plastic wrap.
- Refrigerate at least 3 hours for the pork and chicken and at least 12 hours for the beef.
- Remove the onions from the marinade. Place, cut side down, on a preheated hot grill. Brush with some of marinade. Cook for 2-3 minutes. Turn and baste again with the marinade. Grill until browned and tender but not falling apart—about 8-10 minutes total.
- Place to the side of the grill, away from direct heat, to keep warm.
- Add the meat to hot grill. Grill the beef to the desired doneness. Grill the chicken and pork just until done through; do not overcook. For all three, cook on first side until about two-thirds done and turn.
- Keep warm until ready to slice. Slice across the grain into thin slices.
- Serve immediately with tortillas, grilled onion slices, and other toppings such as sour cream, Salsa Verde, Marilyn's Favorite Tomato Salsa, and Cilantro Guacamole.
- Serves 6.

Marilyn's Favorite Tomato Salsa

2 tbsp. extra-virgin olive oil
1 cup chopped yellow onion
2 large cloves garlic, finely chopped
4 large tomatoes, stems removed and coarsely chopped (or 7-8 fresh plum tomatoes)
3-4 large fresh jalapeño peppers, seeded and finely chopped, to taste
3 mild green chiles (such as anaheims), roasted, peeled, seeded, and chopped
3 tbsp. chopped fresh cilantro
1 tsp. salt, or to taste
1 tsp. sugar
2 tbsp. red-wine vinegar

- Heat the oil over medium heat in a heavy skillet. Cook the onions and garlic for 2 minutes. Remove from the heat and allow to cool.
- Stir together all the ingredients. Cover and chill for at least 2 hours before serving.
- Makes 3$^1/_2$-4 cups.

Cilantro Guacamole

3 ripe medium to large avocados
1 medium tomato, peeled, seeded, and coarsely
 chopped
$^1/_2$ cup finely chopped Vidalia or red Spanish onion
2 tbsp. fresh lime juice
$^1/_2$ tsp. salt, or to taste
$^1/_2$ tsp. hot pepper sauce, or to taste
3 tbsp. chopped fresh cilantro
Cilantro sprigs, for garnish

- Peel, seed, and mash the avocados.
- Stir in the tomato, onion, lime juice, salt, hot pepper sauce, and chopped cilantro.
- Cover and chill for at least 1 hour.
- Place in a serving dish. Garnish by making a "border" with the cilantro sprigs around the edge of the guacamole.
- Serve chilled.
- Makes 2$^1/_2$-3 cups.

To ripen avocados, place them in a brown paper bag and add an apple or ripe banana. Close the top securely and place in a warm, dark place. In 24 to 48 hours they are usually softened and ready to use.

Lemon-Mint Pork Loin with Peachy Pineapple Salsa

Leaner, quicker-cooking pork is great news for the health-conscious because it means that new and improved pork has less fat and fewer calories. It also means we can now cook it to no more than 160 degrees internal temperature, which is 25 to 30 degrees lower than the old method. I actually remove it from the grill at 145 to 150 degrees, place it on a heavy heat-proof platter, and allow it to sit on top of the grill for 15 minutes before slicing. The internal temperature will rise and the resting time also allows the juices to set, making for a very succulent and flavorful slice of today's elegant pork.

This fat-free fruit salsa is the perfect accompaniment for something as light as this pork tenderloin. Try it with grilled chicken breast, too.

3-4 lb. boneless pork tenderloin
½ cup extra-virgin olive oil
¼ cup fresh lemon juice
1 tbsp. lemon zest
2 large cloves garlic, finely chopped
1 tbsp. kosher salt
1 tsp. coarsely ground black pepper
½ cup chopped fresh mint leaves

- 24 hours ahead of time, trim away all of the fat from the pork.
- Mix together the remaining ingredients. Place the pork in a shallow dish or in a large plastic bag. Coat with the marinade, seal tightly, and chill.
- Place the pork on a preheated medium-hot grill.
- Grill, turning once or twice, until the internal temperature is 145 to 150 degrees.
- Let sit for a few minutes before slicing.
- Serve hot or cold with Peachy Pineapple Salsa.
- Serves 10-12.

Peachy Pineapple Salsa

2 cups diced fresh pineapple*
2 ripe large peaches, peeled and diced
2 tbsp. fresh lime juice
1 small to medium fresh jalapeño pepper, seeded and finely chopped
½ cup chopped Vidalia onion (or other sweet salad onion)
¼ tsp. salt
2 tbsp. chopped fresh cilantro

- Stir together all ingredients.
- Cover and chill for at least 2 hours.

*I do not recommend using canned pineapple. The flavor and acidity of fresh pineapple are essential for the success of this recipe. Nectarines or mangoes may be substituted for the peaches.

Red Wine-Marinated Butterflied Leg of Lamb

I have seldom encountered anyone who was indifferent to the flavor of lamb. When I ran a cooking school, it was always interesting to note audience reaction to the announcement that lamb was to be prepared. I got either cheers or boos, but never indifference. The exception was the class featuring this recipe, which converted many a cynic. When a boneless leg of lamb has all of the fat removed and is infused with a wonderfully aromatic marinade, the flavor changes drastically. The overall effect is simply delicious, and this very lean piece of meat has very little of what some may think of as that "strong lamb taste." So, even if you aren't a lamb-lover, you really should try this recipe. It may just change your mind.

1½ cups hearty, dry red wine such as a cabernet sauvignon
¼ cup olive oil
1 large yellow onion, sliced
3 large cloves garlic, crushed
½ cup chopped flat-leaf parsley
1 tbsp. chopped fresh rosemary leaves (or 1 tsp. dried)
1 tsp. good Dijon mustard
½ tsp. hot pepper sauce
½ tsp. freshly ground black pepper
2 tsp. salt
6-7-lb. leg of lamb, boned and trimmed of all visible fat

- 24 hours ahead of time, combine all of the ingredients except the lamb. Pour this marinade into a nonreactive dish or a large, heavy-duty plastic bag. Place the lamb in the marinade and put in the refrigerator.
- Remove the lamb from the marinade. Drain well.
- Spread out flat and grill over a medium-hot grill for about 25 minutes. Turn and cook until an instant-read thermometer inserted in the thickest part reads 140 degrees (for a medium doneness).
- Remove from the heat. Allow to sit on a cutting board for about 10 minutes. Slice, across the grain, into slices. Serve immediately.
- Serves 8-10.

When you want to add a smoked flavor to any meats, poultry, seafood, or vegetables on the grill, add soaked wood chips (or twigs) to the grill. The flavor varies with the type of wood. Some favorites are: hickory, mesquite, apple wood, grapevine, and dried basil stalks. Simply place a handful or two in a pot and cover with water. Soak for at least 30 minutes and as long as 1 hour for the larger hardwood chips. Drain. For best results, the wet chips can be placed on a screen wire grid above or to one side of the hot coals so that they get hot and smoke but don't burn up so quickly. This can be done on either a charcoal or gas grill that has a lid to close during the smoking process.

The only accurate method for determining degree of doneness in any grilled meat or poultry is to test the internal temperature. I highly recommend that anyone who enjoys grilling keep one of those small instant-read thermometers in a pocket. It can be used for everything from whole turkeys to small chops. Just be sure to insert it in the thickest part of the grilled meat or poultry, and avoid going through layers of fat or touching a bone. To avoid overcooking large cuts of beef, pork, and lamb, remove from the grill a few degrees short of the desired final temperature.

Center of the Meal

It has been my experience as a cooking teacher that there are now more people than ever who are interested in food and cooking. Sure, times have changed, and with more families all working away from home, daily dinners "from scratch" are not as common as they once were. But the genuine concern with nutrition and living a healthier lifestyle is sending many people to the food markets and into their kitchens.

There is no question that a great deal of satisfaction can and should be derived from the fun and enjoyment of creating something good to eat and feeding those special people in our lives. I hope you'll have fun serving the following dishes. Some are simple enough for a weekday family meal while others can be presented to guests at an elegant dinner party.

Curried Scallops

Scallops are a great choice for the busy cook who needs an elegant main dish in a hurry. I always prefer the large sea scallops (rather than the tiny "bay" scallops), which are in this easy recipe. I like this dish best served over a bed of fluffy, almond-scented rice, but it goes well with fresh pasta too. For a lighter version, simply serve it with some crunchy French bread and a tossed salad of crisp greens.

> 2 lb. sea scallops
> Salt and white pepper, to taste
> Flour, for dredging
> 6 tbsp. clarified butter
> 6 green onions, finely chopped
> 2 tbsp. Madras curry powder
> ½ cup dry white wine

- Wash the scallops and pat dry with paper towels.
- Season with salt and pepper and dredge in flour to lightly coat.
- Heat the butter in a heavy skillet.
- Add the scallops and cook quickly over high heat, turning once. Cook them a total of 3 to 5 minutes depending on their size. They should be seared and golden brown. Remove them to a side dish.
- Stir in the green onions and cook, stirring, for 3 minutes.
- Sprinkle in the curry and stir to blend in.
- Add the wine and cook on high until the wine is reduced by half.
- Return the scallops and cook, stirring, for 1 minute to reheat and to coat with the sauce.
- Serve with fluffy white rice that has toasted slivered almonds tossed into it.
- Serves 6-8.

Oyster and Artichoke Casserole

This is another favorite special supper dish from my New Orleans days. Either frozen artichoke hearts, which are cooked just until tender, or well-drained canned artichoke hearts may be used in this recipe. If you are feeling ambitious (or have a relative who owns an artichoke farm), you could, of course, use fresh artichoke hearts. Serve with crusty, fresh French bread so you can get up the last bit of irresistible sauce.

> 1 stick (4 oz.) unsalted butter or margarine
> ½ cup flour
> 3 cups milk, heated (you may use 2 percent)
> 2 tsp. salt, or to taste
> ½ tsp. hot pepper sauce, or to taste
> 2 tsp. Worcestershire sauce
> ½ cup dry sherry
> 1½ pt. fresh oysters, drained
> 16 artichoke hearts, quartered
> 1 cup fresh, lightly buttered breadcrumbs

- In a heavy saucepan over medium heat, melt the butter.
- Stir in the flour and cook, stirring constantly, for 3 minutes. Turn heat to medium low during this time if necessary to avoid browning.
- Whisk in the hot milk, raise the heat, and cook, stirring, until the mixture is very thick, about 1 or 2 minutes.
- Season the sauce with salt, hot pepper sauce, and Worcestershire.
- Stir in the sherry and cook 2 more minutes, stirring.
- Add the oysters and artichokes.
- Pour the mixture into a buttered 1½-qt. casserole.
- Top with breadcrumbs.
- Bake in a preheated 375-degree oven for 15 minutes or until bubbly and the top is golden brown.
- Serves 8.

Mediterranean Fish Fillets

Clara Jacobs and I have been good friends for years and we have eaten a lot of good food together, most of it at her house. Clara grew up in one of those Italian households where good food was an essential component of life, and she continued that tradition after she married Jake and had her own family. It is always a joy to receive an invitation to dine at their place. Clara loves to cook good food and she believes in having plenty of it. It is a standing joke between us that I never fail to say how relieved I am when I arrive at her house to discover that, in spite of my worries, there is going to be enough to eat. This is one of Clara's many great recipes.

> 6 fish fillets (catfish, flounder, etc.)
> ¼ cup extra-virgin olive oil
> Salt and freshly ground black pepper, to taste
> ¼ cup fresh lemon or lime juice
> 2 cloves garlic, finely chopped
> 2 tsp. finely chopped parsley
> 2 tsp. finely chopped basil
> Paprika

- Roll the fillets in the olive oil until covered on all sides.
- Season with salt and pepper.
- Place in a shallow baking dish, skin side down.
- Mix the lemon or lime juice, garlic, parsley, and basil and distribute evenly over the fish.
- Sprinkle the fish with paprika.
- Place in a preheated 400-degree oven and bake for 10 to 20 minutes, depending on the thickness of the fillets, until the fish is done through. Do not overcook.
- Serves 6.

Baked Fish Niçoise

Since fish has a relatively short cooking time and is not the best choice for cooking ahead and rewarming, a dish like this is always appreciated by the host or hostess who wants to be out of the kitchen when guests arrive. In other words, assemble it all well ahead of time with nothing more to do but step into the kitchen and pop it in the oven. For a casual meal, this is another main dish that needs only some good, crusty bread and a large tossed salad.

My first choice for this recipe is thick fillets of tuna, but any firm fish can be used.

¼ cup extra-virgin olive oil
2 large cloves garlic, finely chopped
2 large tomatoes, peeled, seeded, and coarsely
   chopped
2 tbsp. tomato paste
1 cup dry white wine
1 tsp. sweet paprika
1 tsp. chopped fresh thyme leaves (or ⅓ tsp. dried)
Salt and freshly ground black pepper, to taste
2 lb. tuna fillets, 1-2 in. thick
½ cup sliced black olives
1 lemon, very thinly sliced
Chopped parsley, for garnish

- Heat the oil in a medium skillet over medium heat.
- Add the garlic and cook for 1 minute without browning.
- Stir in the tomatoes, tomato paste, wine, paprika, and thyme.
- Cook, stirring, for 10 minutes.
- Season with salt and pepper.
- Grease a shallow baking dish and place the fish in it.
- Season the fish lightly with salt and pepper.
- Spoon over the sauce and sprinkle with the olives.
- Bake in a 400-degree oven for 10 to 12 minutes or until fish flakes easily with a fork. (Do not overcook.) For rare tuna, raise the oven temperature to 500 degrees and bake 5 or 6 minutes or to the desired doneness.
- Garnish with lemon slices and chopped parsley.
- Serves 6.

Fresh fish never has a "fishy" smell. Use fresh fish as soon as possible after it is purchased. To store it before use, keep it in the coldest part of the refrigerator or on a bed of ice in a pan.

Whole Fried Tilapia with Stir-Fried Gingered Vegetables

No doubt the most fun part of being a member of the food community is becoming friends with so many creative people. Paul Sturkey is a chef friend who always comes up with something delicious for me to try when I go to "Sturkey's" or "Encore," the two superb restaurants he runs with his talented pastry-chef wife, Pam. He never seems to lack for exciting new ideas, and each dish he sets before me always seem to be better than the last one I ate. He loves cooking fish and shares with us here one of his simple but delicious recipes. If tilapia isn't available, you may try this with other small whole fish such as trout or catfish.

> 4 whole tilapia, cleaned and fins removed
> 2 qt. vegetable oil, for frying
> 2 cups fine-ground yellow cornmeal or polenta
> ½ cup cornstarch
> Kosher salt and freshly ground black pepper, to taste
> 2 tbsp. toasted-sesame oil
> 3 cups very small julienne strips (2 in. long and ¼ in. thick) assorted vegetables (zucchini, yellow squash, carrots, peppers, leeks, etc.)
> 1 tbsp. finely chopped gingerroot
> ½ cup dry white wine
> 2 cups fish stock
> Pickled ginger, for garnish

- Wash the fish well in cold water.
- In a wok or large skillet (large enough to hold the oil and fish), heat the oil to 350 degrees.
- Combine the cornmeal and cornstarch and mix well.
- Season the fish with salt and pepper and dredge in the cornmeal mixture.
- Carefully place one fish in the hot oil and cook until it is golden brown, about 5 to 7 minutes.
- Place the fish on a cookie sheet and put into a warm oven (200 degrees).
- Cook the remaining fish and keep warm.

- In a separate wok or large, heavy skillet, heat the sesame oil to very hot but not smoking. Stir-fry the vegetables and ginger for 30 seconds.
- Add the wine and stock and bring to a boil over high heat. Reduce to simmer and cook for 2 minutes.
- Season to taste with salt and pepper.
- To serve, arrange a fish on each plate with some rice or mashed potatoes on the side. Nap with the vegetables and broth. Garnish with pickled ginger.
- Serves 4.

Lasagna with Sauce Bolognese

This is my favorite "traditional" lasagna recipe. The famous Italian meat sauce adds aromatic flavor, and the béchamel sauce (or white sauce) gives it a great creamy texture. It is important to use lean beef in the meat sauce so the lasagna won't be heavy and greasy. I often buy a very lean center-cut chuck and grind it myself. This lasagna is best made with fresh egg pasta but it is good, too, with dried pasta.

This is another good recipe for the busy host or hostess. Assemble it ahead and have it in the refrigerator ready to pop into the oven. (Remember that a chilled dish will take longer to cook, and take care not to put a chilled, breakable dish into a hot oven.)

2½ cups Bolognese Sauce (see below)
6 tbsp. butter
6 tbsp. flour
3 cups milk, heated
¼ tsp. salt
Freshly grated nutmeg
Dash hot pepper sauce
8 oz. freshly grated Parmigiano-Reggiano (2 cups)
12 oz. shredded mozzarella cheese (3 cups)
4 sheets blanched fresh egg pasta to fit pan
    (about 1 lb.) or 1 lb. dried lasagna noodles,
    cooked al dente and well drained

- Make the Bolognese Sauce according to the following recipe.
- Make the béchamel sauce by melting the butter in a heavy pan

over medium heat and stirring in the flour. Cook, stirring, for a full 2 minutes, without browning. Whisk in the milk, salt, nutmeg, and hot pepper sauce just until the sauce bubbles and thickens.

- Spread about 2 tbsp. Bolognese Sauce in the bottom of a 13-by-9-by-2-in. pan.
- Place a layer of pasta over the sauce.
- Top with more Bolognese Sauce to cover, spoon over one-third of the béchamel sauce, and sprinkle with $1/2$ cup Parmigiano-Reggiano and 1 cup mozzarella.
- Top with more pasta and layer with half of the remaining Bolognese Sauce, half of the remaining béchamel, $1/2$ cup Parmigiano-Reggiano, and half of the remaining mozzarella.
- Top with another layer of pasta and repeat a third layer just like the other two.
- Sprinkle the top layer with the remaining Parmigiano-Reggiano.
- Bake in a 375-degree oven for 25 to 30 minutes or until bubbly.
- Let sit 15 to 20 minutes before cutting.
- Serves 10-12.

Bolognese Sauce

3 tbsp. extra-virgin olive oil
1 tbsp. butter
1 cup chopped onion
2 cloves garlic, finely chopped
$1/2$ cup finely chopped carrot
$1/2$ cup finely chopped celery
2 lb. lean ground beef
2 tsp. kosher salt
$1/2$ tsp. freshly ground black pepper
1 cup dry white wine
28-oz. can crushed Italian plum tomatoes
$1/2$ cup chopped parsley

- Heat the oil and butter together in a heavy skillet.
- Sauté the vegetables in oil and butter until tender.
- Add the beef, salt, and pepper and cook until the red is gone.
- Add the wine and cook over high heat for 10 minutes, stirring often.
- Add the tomatoes and parsley and simmer, uncovered, for 30 minutes.
- Taste and correct seasonings.

Farfalle with Summer Sauce

I first got to know Toni Cashnelli when she was the food editor of the Cincinnati Enquirer, and it was under her tutelage that I began writing my first weekly food column, "Elegant but Easy," which I wrote for several years. Toni and I had some fun times setting up food pictures together as well as exchanging stories about our extremely intelligent cats. Toni always said she had no time to cook when she was food editor, but she did manage to submit this favorite recipe of hers, which she likes to toss together for a quick and light summer's day supper.

> 2½ lb. fresh plum tomatoes (or 2 28-oz. cans plum tomatoes, undrained and chopped)
> 3 tbsp. extra-virgin olive oil
> 2 medium carrots or 5 baby carrots, peeled and shredded
> 1½ cups chopped white onions
> 4 cloves garlic, finely chopped
> 1 generous bunch parsley, chopped
> ½ cup shredded fresh basil
> Salt and freshly ground black pepper, to taste
> 1 lb. farfalle (bow tie) pasta
> Freshly grated Parmigiano-Reggiano

- Peel, seed, and chop the tomatoes (if using fresh).
- Heat the olive oil in a large skillet and sauté the carrots, onions, and garlic about 10 minutes, until softened.
- Add the tomatoes, parsley, and basil and cook over medium heat, stirring occasionally, until tomatoes cook down—about 20 minutes.
- Add salt and pepper.
- Cook the pasta according to package directions and drain.
- Divide the pasta among 6 plates, top with the sauce, and pass the cheese.
- Serves 6.

Adding oil to the pasta water is not recommended for pasta that is to be served hot and tossed with a sauce. The oil may prevent the pot from boiling over, but it also coats the pasta and causes the sauce to slide off of it.

Cook 1 lb. pasta in 6-8 qt. rapidly boiling water. Add 3 tbsp. salt for this amount of water and pasta.

When adding salt to the pasta water, wait until the water boils before adding it. Otherwise, it takes that pot of water longer to come to a rolling boil—the stage it must be before adding the pasta.

Red Bell Peppers with Creole Eggplant Stuffing

Red bell peppers are not only pretty to look at, but their elegant, sweet flavor makes me prefer them over the green ones. Since they have become so readily available virtually year round, I have adapted many of my recipes to include them. If you enjoy both stuffed peppers and eggplant, you are certain to find this Creole-inspired dish a genuine treat. It can also be an excellent vegetarian dish. Simply omit the shrimp or ham.

    4 large red bell peppers
    1 1-lb. eggplant
    ½ cup extra-virgin olive oil
    1 cup chopped green onions
    2 ripe large tomatoes, peeled, seeded, and
        chopped
    2 large cloves garlic, finely chopped
    ¼ cup chopped fresh parsley
    2 tsp. chopped fresh thyme leaves (or ½ tsp.
        dried)
    ½ tsp. hot pepper sauce sauce, or to taste
    1 tsp. salt, or to taste
    8 oz. boiled shrimp, coarsely chopped (or 1 cup
        cubed lean cooked ham)
    1 cup fresh breadcrumbs
    ½ cup freshly grated Parmigiano-Reggiano

- Slice off the tops of the peppers, removing the stems and cores. Rinse out any extra seeds. Cut a very thin slice from each bottom (but not cutting into the pepper) so they sit up straight.

- Invert on a paper towel to drain.

- Cut the eggplant in half lengthwise and slash the cut surfaces several times. Brush generously with some of the olive oil.

- Place, cut side down, on a baking sheet.

- Bake in a 350-degree oven for 30 to 40 minutes or until fork tender.

- Remove and allow to cool. Scoop the cooled pulp from the shells.

- Discard the shells and chop the pulp. Set aside.

- Heat the remaining olive oil in a large skillet.

- Sauté the green onions for 5 minutes, stirring.

- Add the tomatoes and garlic and cook, stirring, about 5 minutes more or until most of the moisture has cooked from the tomatoes.
- Stir in the prepared eggplant along with the parsley, thyme, hot pepper sauce, and salt and cook 5 minutes more.
- Remove the skillet from the heat. Stir in the shrimp and half of the breadcrumbs.
- Taste and correct seasonings.
- Mix together the remaining breadcrumbs with the cheese. Top each pepper with some of the mixture.
- Lightly brush the outsides of the peppers with some olive oil.
- Place in a shallow baking dish. Bake in the middle of a pre-heated 350-degree oven for 30 minutes or until the stuffing is hot through and the tops are browned.
- Serves 4.

Miriam's Eggplant Casserole

Miriam is a beautiful, bright-eyed lady who came into our family a few years ago by marriage. My nephew Robert had the good fortune to meet her while living in Italy and returned to the States with her as his wife. Since then she has delighted us all with her homemade Italian food. This is a dish that she tossed together on a hot summer night when the family was together and several of us were in the kitchen. I remember thinking afterward that I wished I had paid more attention to what went into that wonderfully flavorful dish. It turns out that my sister Susan did ask and wrote it down, and she shared it for this book. When summer vegetables are in their prime, this makes an excellent meatless main dish. If you wish, add some cooked shrimp and/or cubed lean ham.

2 small eggplants, about 1 lb. each
2 tbsp. kosher salt
4 tbsp. extra-virgin olive oil
1 cup chopped onion
½ cup chopped celery
½ cup chopped green bell pepper
1 large clove garlic, finely chopped
1 tsp. dried oregano leaves

Yellow or brown-skinned onions are sweeter than the white-skinned onions and are preferable to use in any dish where onions are the dominant flavor, such as onion soup or onion sauce.

15-oz. can tomato sauce
1 tsp. salt, or to taste
½ tsp. coarsely ground black pepper
2 cups shredded part-skim mozzarella cheese

- Peel and cube the eggplants into 1-in. cubes. Place in a colander and toss with the salt to coat. Allow to sit for 30 minutes. Rinse well with cool water and pat dry with paper towels.
- Heat the oil in a large skillet (nonstick works best).
- Add the eggplant, onion, celery, green pepper, and garlic.
- Sauté, stirring constantly, over high heat until eggplant is tender.
- Remove from heat and stir in the oregano, tomato sauce, salt, and pepper.
- Pour into a 2-qt. shallow casserole.
- Bake in a 350-degree oven for 30 minutes.
- Remove from the oven and sprinkle the cheese over the top. Return to the oven and bake 10 minutes longer, or until the cheese is completely melted.
- Serve immediately.
- Serves 8.

Chicken Mole

Yes, I know at first glance this seems a rather odd assortment of ingredients. For that reason, I've always enjoyed preparing my version of this Mexican classic sauce for my students. For those who have never experienced a mole sauce, it is fun to see the look of delighted surprise on their faces when they taste this one. Don't expect this version to taste exactly like one you may have eaten in Mexico. It is milder and lighter and, in my opinion, more suited to North American tastes. It is something a bit out of the ordinary to do with boneless chicken breasts at your next dinner party.

4 whole boneless and skinless chicken breasts
Salt and freshly ground black pepper, to taste
Flour, for dredging
6 tbsp. extra-virgin olive oil

1 large yellow onion, chopped (about 1 cup)
2 cloves garlic, finely chopped
½ tsp. cumin
⅓ cup pure chili powder (ancho or chipotle)
¼ cup raisins
1 oz. unsweetened chocolate, cut into small pieces
¼ cup peanut butter
3 corn tortillas, toasted in oven, cooled, and broken up
1 tbsp. sesame seeds
¼ tsp. coriander
¼ tsp. ground cloves
2-3 cups chicken broth
½ cup tomato sauce
1 tbsp. sugar
Chopped cilantro, for garnish

- Rinse, trim, and flatten the chicken breasts between 2 sheets of plastic wrap.
- Season the chicken generously with salt and pepper and dredge in flour to coat lightly.
- Heat the oil in a large, heavy skillet and cook the chicken until browned and cooked through, about 10 to 12 minutes, turning once. Remove to a side dish and keep warm.
- Add the onions, garlic, cumin, and chili powder to the skillet and sauté until onions are tender, about 5 minutes.
- Stir in the raisins, chocolate, peanut butter, tortilla pieces, sesame seeds, coriander, cloves, 1 cup of the chicken broth, and the tomato sauce. Stir well.
- Purée the mixture in a blender or food processor.
- Return to the skillet and add enough of the remaining broth to make a medium-thick sauce.
- Stir in the sugar and cook, stirring occasionally, for 20 minutes. (Add more broth if necessary—sauce should be thick but not heavy.)
- Taste and correct seasonings.
- Spoon over the warm chicken breasts.
- Sprinkle with cilantro to garnish.
- Serve with rice cooked in chicken broth.
- Serves 8.

Store chocolate in a cool place. Chefs often store their good cooking chocolate in a wine cellar.

Chicken Tarragon

I find that more and more of my listeners and students are growing their own herbs. It is certainly not hard to do and it's so much fun to just pick a handful for jazzing up almost any dish you are cooking. I always look forward to the summer season, when I can pick plenty of one of my favorites, tarragon, for making this simple chicken dish. It is a super choice for a summer dinner party and tastes very good cold (if there is any left over) for lunch the next day.

Pick fresh herbs at least 1 hour before you wish to use them. Submerge them in lukewarm water to remove all soil. Place in a colander to drain. Gently wrap them in a soft, white paper towel, then place them in a resealable plastic bag. Chill until ready to use.

**4 whole chicken breasts, split into halves and
   skinned
1 tsp. salt, or to taste
½ tsp. freshly ground black pepper
½ cup flour
6 tbsp. vegetable oil
½ cup chopped fresh tarragon leaves
¾ cup dry white wine**

- Season the chicken with salt and pepper.
- Dredge in the flour, coating well.
- Heat the oil in a large, heavy skillet.
- Sauté the chicken in the hot oil, turning several times, until the chicken is golden brown on all sides. (This should take about 15 minutes.)
- Remove the chicken from the skillet and roll in the tarragon to coat well.
- Place in a shallow baking pan and pour over the wine.
- Place the pan in the center of a preheated 450-degree oven for 15 to 20 minutes or until the chicken is done through.
- Baste a couple of times by spooning the wine over the chicken.
- Serves 6-8.

French Chicken in Red Wine

Here's a recipe I brought back from a visit to France. A light red wine such as pinot noir is best for this elegantly flavored dish.

3 strips bacon, diced
3 tbsp. olive or vegetable oil
2 medium yellow onions, thinly sliced
1 2½-3-lb. chicken, cut into pieces
Flour seasoned with salt and freshly ground
    black pepper
2 large cloves garlic, finely chopped
1 bottle light red wine
2 cups chicken broth
Bouquet garni of 3 sprigs parsley, 1 bay leaf, and
    3 sprigs thyme
Salt and freshly ground black pepper, to taste
Chopped fresh parsley

- In a large, heavy pan, fry the bacon until crisp. Remove with a slotted spoon and set aside.

- Pour off the bacon fat. Add the vegetable oil to the pan and heat.

- Sauté the onions until just tender. Remove with a slotted spoon and set aside.

- Dredge the chicken pieces in the seasoned flour. Brown the chicken in the hot oil until golden brown on all sides.

- Return the onions to the pan. Stir in the garlic. Add the wine, chicken broth, and bouquet garni.

- Bring to a boil and cook, uncovered, for 1 hour. Stir occasionally.

- When chicken is fork tender, remove to a heated side dish. Strain the sauce and return to the pan. Cook over high heat for about 5 minutes to reduce slightly. Taste and correct seasonings.

- Pour the sauce over the chicken. Sprinkle with the bacon and some chopped parsley.

- Serve immediately with a salad and small boiled potatoes or some crusty French bread.

- Serves 4-6.

Never cook with a wine that you wouldn't enjoy drinking. After most of the alcohol cooks off, you have the flavor left, and that flavor should be rich and full bodied. Serve the same wine with the meal that you used to flavor the dish.

Musakhan (Chicken with Onions and Sumac on Flat Bread)

I met May Bsisu because she wanted to talk to me about a cookbook she is writing. I now count her among my close friends and have come to really appreciate her talents in the kitchen. An invitation to her house for some "May" food is very special. This is an example from her colorful collection of Mediterranean dishes. Even though this recipe may look complicated at first glance, it is great to make for a dinner party, and all of it can be cooked a day ahead and reheated. Sumac is a spice made from sumac berries that you will find at specialty Mediterranean food stores and in mail-order spice catalogues.

> **8-10 meaty chicken pieces* (3½-4 lb.)**
> **1 large onion, peeled and cut in wedges**
> **12 cardamom pods, cracked to expose seeds**
> **2 whole cinnamon sticks**
> **2 bay leaves**
> **Salt**
> **1½ tsp. freshly ground black pepper, or to taste**
> **5 lb. large onions**
> **1 cup extra-virgin olive oil**
> **½ cup sumac**
> **¾ cup pine nuts**
> **1½ tbsp. extra-virgin olive oil**
> **5 large rounds pita bread**
> **Chopped flat-leaf parsley, for garnish**

- Rinse the chicken pieces and trim away the excess fat and skin. Place in a large pot and add cold water to cover by 3 in. Add the onion, cardamom, cinnamon, bay leaves, 1 tsp. salt, and 1 tsp. pepper. Cover and bring to a boil. Reduce to simmer and cook for 1 hour. Skim the foam from the surface during the first 10 minutes of cooking.

- When the chicken is done, remove the pieces from the broth with a slotted spoon. Cool.

- Strain the broth and reserve.

- While the chicken is cooking, peel the onions and cut in half lengthwise (through the stem and root ends). Place, flat sides down, on a cutting board and slice into ⅛-in. slices.

- Pour 1 cup olive oil into a large, heavy saucepan and heat over high heat. Add the onion slices and stir well to coat them with the oil. When the onions are sizzling, reduce the heat to medium and stir in the sumac, dash salt, and $1/2$ tsp. pepper. Cook, uncovered, stirring occasionally, for 10 minutes.
- Add 1 cup reserved chicken broth and cover the pan. Reduce to simmer and cook for 45 minutes, stirring often. Remove from the heat and cool. Taste and salt to taste. Add more pepper, if desired.
- In a heavy skillet over medium heat, toast the pine nuts in $1^1/2$ tbsp. olive oil for just a couple of minutes or until pine nuts turn golden.
- Grease a large shallow baking pan and arrange the chicken pieces in the pan. Place in a 400-degree oven and bake for 30 minutes or until the chicken is lightly browned.
- While the chicken is baking, reheat the onions until hot.
- Split the pita bread in half and arrange on a large platter. Spread half the onions on the bread. Arrange half the chicken on top of the onions and sprinkle with half the pine nuts. Add a second layer of bread, onions, chicken, and pine nuts.
- Sprinkle with parsley before serving.
- Serves 8-10.

*Use a combination of white and dark meat chicken pieces.

Curried Turkey with Rice

Every November we do a lot of turkey preparation at the radio station. We start early in the month talking about fresh versus frozen birds and stuffed versus unstuffed and go into detail on all of the trimmings, working up to what we call "Marilyn's Turkey Repair Service" on Thanksgiving morning. It is perhaps our most popular show of the year. Then, as soon as the big day is over, we are flooded with calls about what to do with all that leftover turkey! I have collected quite an impressive batch of recipes featuring cooked turkey. This is, in my opinion, one of the better ones. It is also an excellent choice for a large buffet-style dinner party.

4 tbsp. butter or margarine
1 cup chopped onion
2 tsp. Madras curry powder
1 tsp. ancho chili powder
3 tbsp. flour
1 cup turkey or chicken broth, heated
1 clove garlic, finely chopped
1 tbsp. finely chopped gingerroot
½ cup chopped roasted cashews
½ cup flaked coconut
1 cup light cream (or plain yogurt)
3 cups diced or sliced cooked turkey
Salt and hot pepper sauce, to taste
3 cups cooked basmati or long-grain white rice
Chopped cilantro or parsley, for garnish

- Melt the butter or margarine in a heavy skillet or large saucepan.
- Stir in the onion, curry powder, and chili powder.
- Cook, stirring, over medium heat until the onion is tender, about 5 minutes.
- Stir in the flour and cook, stirring, for 2 to 3 minutes. Do not brown.
- Whisk in the broth and stir until the mixture thickens.
- Stir in the garlic and ginger and cook about 5 minutes more, stirring often.
- Stir in the cashews, coconut, and cream and cook just until the mixture is hot and bubbly.

- Fold in the turkey and continue to cook just until the turkey is heated through.
- Season to taste with salt and add a few drops hot pepper sauce.
- Remove from the heat and spoon over the rice.
- Sprinkle with cilantro or parsley.
- Serves 6-8.

Fillet of Pork with Caramelized Apples

A souvenir from one of my favorite summer vacations spent in the Loire valley, this combination of pork and apples sounds more as if it could have come from the Normandy region. Of course, it is possible that the chef who made it for me got it from there. But more importantly, it is a delicious way to prepare pork tenderloin. When the first crisp apples of autumn appear in the market, I get out this recipe.

> 2 small pork tenderloins (1½-2 lb.)
> 3 tbsp. extra-virgin olive oil
> 1 tsp. dried rosemary
> Salt and freshly ground black pepper, to taste
> 1 large yellow onion, halved and thinly sliced
> ½ cup apple cider*
> 2 tbsp. butter or margarine
> 2 large red-skinned cooking apples, cored and sliced
> 1 tbsp. sugar
> ¼ cup apple cider
> 1 red-skinned cooking apple, cored and sliced
> Juice of 1 lemon
> Parsley or watercress sprigs, for garnish

- Trim the tenderloins of all fat and skin. With a sharp knife, slice, across the grain, into ½-in. slices. Place the sliced pork between 2 pieces of waxed paper and flatten.
- Heat the oil in a large skillet. Brown the pork on both sides, turning once, and remove to a side dish. Season with rosemary, salt, and pepper.
- Pour off all but 1 tbsp. fat in the skillet. Add the onion to the skillet and sauté, stirring, until tender and golden.

- Pour in $1/2$ cup cider and reduce over high heat to 2-3 tbsp. liquid.
- Return the pork to the skillet and spoon over the sauce and onions, just long enough to heat through.
- Heat the butter for the apples in a separate skillet until it sizzles.
- Add the apple slices from the 2 apples, stirring to coat with butter. Sprinkle in the sugar and stir or toss in the skillet over heat until they are golden brown and coated with melted sugar.
- Arrange the pork on a plate and surround it with the cooked apples.
- Bring remaining cider to a boil in the skillet where the apples were cooked and stir to remove any particles from the bottom of the skillet.
- Spoon over the pork.
- Garnish with fresh apple slices coated with the lemon juice and sprigs of parsley or watercress.
- Serves 6-8.

*Hard cider was used in the original recipe, but fresh, nonalcoholic cider may also be used.

To serve fresh slices of apples or pears, "acidulate" them by coating lightly with fresh lemon juice. This prevents the fresh fruit from turning an unattractive dark color after being exposed to air.

Kentucky Bourbon-Marinated Pork Loin

This recipe came from a member of my radio audience. With a large number of Kentucky listeners, we get a lot of good regional recipes, which often call for flavoring with one of the delicious local bourbons. This recipe stood out from many others because of its robust flavor. By the way, leftover slices make a great cold pork sandwich.

5-6-lb. center-cut pork loin, boned
$1/2$ cup bourbon
$1/2$ cup light soy sauce
2 cloves garlic, finely chopped
3 tbsp. brown sugar
2 tbsp. dry mustard
2 tbsp. finely chopped gingerroot

- Trim the pork of all but $1/4$ in. fat.
- Mix together the remaining ingredients to make the marinade. Put the pork with the marinade into a heavy-duty reclosable plastic bag and seal. Refrigerate overnight.
- Place pork on a rack in a shallow pan and place in a preheated 425-degree oven for 30 minutes. Reduce the heat to 350 degrees and roast for about 1 hour longer or until the meat thermometer registers 150 degrees.
- Remove and let sit for 15 minutes before slicing.
- Serves 12.

Bohemian Goulash

Sometimes I feel as though I am writing my autobiography instead of a cookbook. So many recipes hold poignant memories of special people and places. This one holds cherished memories of my student days in Berlin, where I enjoyed so much wonderful ethnic food. This is my rendition of a dish my friends and I enjoyed eating on cold evenings in a charming and cozy neighborhood Hungarian restaurant. It secret is not unlike that of most successful recipes: use the finest ingredients. This dish needs some good, flavorful bacon, proper imported paprika, top-quality lean pork, and, of course, some tasty, fresh sauerkraut. If you enjoy this sort of food, I hope you won't hesitate to track down those good ingredients and make it. I promise you won't be sorry.

    8 strips thick-sliced apple-wood-smoked bacon,
       diced
    1 tbsp. butter
    3 cups chopped yellow onion
    3 tbsp. sweet Hungarian paprika
    3 lb. lean pork, cut into 1-in. cubes
    1 cup beef stock
    1 cup dry white wine
    2 lb. fresh sauerkraut, rinsed and drained
    2 tbsp. tomato paste
    1 tsp. caraway seeds
    Salt and freshly ground black pepper, to taste
    8 oz. noodles
    $1/2$ cup chopped parsley
    1 cup sour cream

- Blanch the bacon for 2 minutes in a small amount of boiling water; drain and place on paper towels to dry.
- In a large, heavy pot, melt the butter and stir in the bacon. Cook, stirring, until the bacon browns. Remove it with a slotted spoon.
- Add the onions and cook over medium heat, stirring until they are very tender and golden.
- Stir in the paprika and cook over low heat, stirring, for 2 to 3 minutes.
- Add the pork and stir well.
- Add the stock and wine and bring the mixture to a boil.
- Simmer, partially covered, for 1 hour or until the pork is fork tender.
- Stir in the sauerkraut, reserved bacon, tomato paste, and caraway seeds.
- Cook 30 minutes longer. (Pork should be very tender.)
- Taste and season with salt and pepper.
- Cook the noodles, drain, and toss with the parsley.
- Serve the goulash spooned over the noodles.
- Pass the sour cream to spoon over the top.
- Serves 8-10.

Easy Pork and Beef Enchiladas

My love for the foods of Mexico and the Southwest is quite obvious when I look at the number of such recipes that have accumulated in my files. I was cooking Mexican food for my students long before we had a good Mexican restaurant in Cincinnati (we have several now!) because that was the only way to get it. Some of my favorite recipes appear time and time again on my table and seem to just get better every time I make them. This one falls into that category. Once again I must comment on the importance of seeking out the proper ingredients. In this case that means good corn tortillas, good-quality, very lean pork and beef, and the best chili powder you can get your hands on. As a one-fork meal, this dish is a good choice for a large, casual dinner party. Just make a big bowl of fresh salsa and plenty of creamy guacamole and you've got a great dinner.

1 recipe Pork and Beef Enchilada Filling (see below)
1 recipe Easy Enchilada Sauce, warm (see below)
½ cup vegetable oil
16 corn tortillas
4 cups shredded jack cheese (1 lb.)
Tomato salsa
Guacamole

- Make the filling and sauce according to the following recipes.
- Heat the oil in a small skillet. Using tongs, place the tortillas into the hot oil, one at a time, for just a few seconds. (They should be very soft.)
- Immediately dip each hot, softened tortilla into the warm sauce, just coating the surface.
- Place flat on a tray for filling. Fill the center of each tortilla with about 3 tbsp. filling.
- Add 1 tbsp. cheese to each.
- Roll each enchilada and place, seam side down, in a shallow baking dish.
- Spoon over enough sauce to cover.
- Sprinkle with remaining cheese.
- Bake in a preheated 375-degree oven for about 15 minutes or until hot and bubbly.
- Serve hot and pass tomato salsa and guacamole to go with the enchiladas.
- Serves 8.

Pork and Beef Enchilada Filling

2 tbsp. vegetable oil
¾ lb. lean ground pork
¾ lb. lean ground beef
1 cup chopped onion
⅔ cup Easy Enchilada Sauce (see below)
Salt and hot pepper sauce, to taste

- Heat the oil in a medium, heavy skillet.
- Add the meats and onions and cook, stirring, until meats are cooked.
- Add the sauce and cook over low heat, stirring occasionally, for 10 minutes.
- Season to taste.

Easy Enchilada Sauce

3 tbsp. extra-virgin olive or vegetable oil
1½ cups chopped onion
¼ cup good mild chili powder
2 tsp. cumin
3 large cloves garlic, finely chopped
2 large fresh jalapeño peppers, seeded and
**   finely chopped**
28-oz. can crushed plum tomatoes
1 can (10 oz.) Ro-tel tomatoes, chopped
½ tsp. dried oregano leaves
1 tsp. sugar
1 tsp. salt, or to taste

- Heat the oil in a heavy skillet.
- Add the onion, chili powder, cumin, and garlic and cook, stirring, for 8 minutes.
- Add the jalapeño peppers and cook 2 minutes longer.
- Stir in both types of tomatoes and the oregano, sugar, and salt.
- Bring to a boil, reduce heat, and simmer for 20 minutes, stirring occasionally.
- For "chunky" sauce, serve as is. For smooth sauce, purée in a blender.
- Makes about 5 cups.

Ginger-Roasted Leg of Lamb

This recipe is very special to me. It came from my dear friend, the late Bert Greene. He interviewed Sukey and John Jamison of the Jamison Lamb Farm in Latrobe, Pennsylvania for his syndicated column in the New York Daily News. I tried their lamb, thought it was by far the best I had ever eaten, and invited them to be guests on my radio show. Since then we have become great friends and their lamb appears regularly on my table. Try this garlic- and ginger-studded leg of lamb recipe, one of Sukey's favorites. (The famous Jamison lamb is available by mail order, 800-237-5262, or through their Web site, www.jamisonfarm.com.)

> 5½-6-lb. leg of lamb
> 1-2 large cloves garlic, thinly sliced
> 1-in. piece gingerroot, peeled and cut into slivers
> 2 tbsp. Dijon mustard
> 1 tbsp. soy sauce
> ¼ cup olive oil
> 1 tbsp. lemon juice

- Trim most of the surface fat from the lamb.
- Using a small sharp knife or an ice pick, make small incisions in the surface of the lamb and fill each, alternating with a sliver of garlic or ginger. Continue until all the garlic and ginger are used.
- Mix together the mustard, soy sauce, oil, and lemon juice and spread over the top and sides of the lamb.
- Allow to sit at room temperature for 2 hours before roasting.
- Place on a rack in a shallow roasting pan and into a preheated 450-degree oven for 15 minutes.
- Reduce the heat to 325 degrees and roast about 1 hour for medium rare (longer if you prefer it medium to well).
- Allow to sit for 15 minutes before carving.
- Serves 8.

Cooking on the Radio

I've had numerous jobs in my career as a food professional. I've enjoyed them all, but none more than my job as host of the Cincinnati radio talk show, "Cooking with Marilyn!" It began in 1988 as a one-hour broadcast twice a week. As more and more people joined in by listening, calling, and sending in and asking for recipes, the show grew to a daily program. Times and management changed, and since 1995 I have been part of WKRC's "how-to Saturday" programming. It has become second nature to me now to sit down in front of that microphone on Saturday afternoon, answering questions from my listeners in Ohio, Kentucky, and Indiana and generally having fun, "cooking on the radio."

My good listeners have often heard me say that no one learns more on the show than I do. This is the way it works: Someone calls and asks a question. I do my best to answer it for them but every so often I get a question for which I honestly don't have a good answer. So, I ask for help from the listening audience. So far, I've always gotten a call from some good Samaritan with the answer, not only saving the day for me but helping their fellow listeners. In every sense, it is a community-recipe and food-fact exchange, and I love it. I know that a lot of other people do too, because they've told me so, and there is seldom a pause between callers in the three hours of air time.

This chapter is especially for my faithful listeners who have been a part of the radio show all these years. I have picked but a meager sampling of the recipes that have been, in some way or other, part of the show. Either I've received them in the mail or verbally on the radio or they are my own recipes I have shared over the air. Like the show itself, there is something for everyone: some recipes that are fun to make and whimsical, others that are outrageously indulgent treats, and ones that are more serious and even nutritious. If you want more, go to www.55krc.com, click on my name to get to my Web page, and you'll find all these and much, much more—all without even sending in a self-addressed stamped envelope. Enjoy!

Barb's Jezebel Sauce

Here is a good example of a recipe that initiated a lot of discussion several Saturday afternoons. Listener Barb shared it with us originally and told us that it was her favorite condiment with ham or pork roast. Another listener called to say she pours this sweet and spicy sauce over a block of cream cheese to serve as a spread for crackers. Then lots more listeners weighed in with other suggestions: use it as a glaze on ham or pork roast, or just eat on saltine crackers. Try it yourself and see if you can find other ways to use it.

12 oz. apricot preserves
12 oz. pineapple preserves
¼ cup prepared horseradish
1 tbsp. dry mustard
1 tsp. freshly ground black pepper

• Stir all the ingredients together. Chill until ready to use.
• Makes about 3 cups.

World's Best Bubbaque Sauce

Gene Archbold is a longtime friend who has been a spirited and interesting guest on the show. He is a wonderful cook who always comes up with recipes that are wild but generally work. This is a good example. Once you get past the wacky title of this one, you'll find it's actually a very good recipe. For best flavor, Gene recommends making it at least 24 hours ahead. He slow cooks pork and beef roasts for hours on the grill or in the smoker, shreds them, and adds the meat to this sauce to make a first-class barbecue sandwich. The recipe makes a lot, but it keeps well tightly covered in the refrigerator.

⅔ cup olive or vegetable oil
12 medium yellow or Vidalia onions, chopped
12 cloves garlic, finely chopped
1 cup flat-leaf parsley leaves
4 tbsp. shredded basil
3 tbsp. dried oregano leaves

5 tbsp. chili powder
1 tsp. ground cloves
2 tsp. onion powder
2 tsp. dry mustard
2 tsp. salt
1 tbsp. freshly ground black pepper
1 lemon, sliced
½ cup cider vinegar
1 cup brown sugar
12 fresh plum tomatoes, peeled and chopped (or
    2 28-oz. cans diced tomatoes with juice)
½ cup ketchup
1 cup Heinz 57 sauce
½ cup Worcestershire sauce
6 bottles dark beer or ale

- Heat the oil in a large, nonreactive pot. Add the onions, garlic, parsley, basil, oregano, chili powder, cloves, onion powder, dry mustard, salt, and pepper. Sauté for 10 minutes or until the onions are tender, stirring often.

- Add the remaining ingredients and simmer, uncovered, until mixture is thick enough to coat a spoon. Stir often.

- Makes about 12 cups.

Dilly Deviled Eggs

I have never met anyone who didn't like a good deviled egg. This recipe was given by a listener when I discussed the topic on the air. The fresh dill adds wonderful color as well as flavor to an old favorite.

1 dozen hard-cooked eggs, peeled
½ cup finely chopped sweet salad onion
⅓ cup chopped fresh dill
½ cup mayonnaise
¼ cup sour cream
¼ cup Dijon mustard
Salt and freshly ground black pepper, to taste

- Slice the eggs in half lengthwise. Remove yolks and mash.

- Stir the remaining ingredients into the yolks.
- Place in a pastry bag with large star tip. Pipe into the whites.
- Cover and chill.

Baked Jalapeño Poppers

The Saturday before "Super Bowl Sunday" is always a busy show, filled with callers seeking and sharing their favorite party recipes that have no redeeming qualities except they are fun to eat. Spicy foods have been very popular lately. This recipe got a lot of attention because it can be baked instead of fried like the original "poppers."

>1 lb. fresh jalapeño peppers
>8 oz. cream cheese, softened
>1 cup shredded sharp cheddar
>1 cup shredded jack cheese
>6 strips bacon, cooked crisp and crumbled
>¼ tsp. salt
>¼ tsp. garlic powder
>1 cup fresh breadcrumbs

- Cut the jalapeño peppers in half lengthwise and remove the stems, seeds, and white membranes.
- Blend together the cheeses until creamy.
- Stir in the bacon, salt, and garlic powder.
- Spoon about 2 tbsp. filling into each pepper half.
- Dip the filled tops in the breadcrumbs to coat.
- Place in a well-greased baking pan and bake in a preheated 300-degree oven for 20 to 40 minutes (longer baking time yields milder flavor).
- Serves 8-10 as an appetizer

Sauerkraut Balls

We were discussing party foods during the holiday season, when someone called for a good recipe for this Cincinnati specialty. Days later we were still receiving calls and recipes in the mail for this party treat from our German heritage. It seems as though everyone in the area thinks they make the best sauerkraut balls. So, I picked what seemed to be a representative recipe, tried it, and found it to be very good. Here it is.

1 lb. potatoes, peeled and cut into pieces
2 tbsp. butter or margarine
½ cup milk
1½ lb. fresh sauerkraut, squeezed dry
8 oz. lean cooked ham, chopped
¼ cup finely chopped parsley
2 green onions, finely chopped
1 tbsp. Dijon mustard
Salt and freshly ground black pepper, to taste
1 egg, well beaten
2 tbsp. cold water
Flour, for dredging
1 cup fine dry breadcrumbs
Vegetable oil, for frying

- Boil the potatoes in salted water until fork tender.
- Drain and return to the pan. Add the butter and allow it to melt.
- Pour in the milk and whip with a portable mixer, or use a potato masher, until the mixture is fluffy and smooth.
- Stir the sauerkraut, ham, parsley, onions, and mustard into the potatoes. Season with salt and pepper.
- Shape the mixture into 32 walnut-sized balls.
- Combine the egg with the water and blend thoroughly.
- Roll the sauerkraut balls in the flour to lightly coat, then dip in egg wash and coat with breadcrumbs.
- Place on a waxed-paper-lined tray and chill for at least 30 minutes.
- Deep-fry in 365-degree oil, or pan-fry until brown, and finish by baking in a 375-degree oven until done through.
- Serve hot.

Marilyn's Potato Pancakes

Another aspect of our area's German heritage is this staple: Kartoffelpuffer, or potato pancakes. We've "cooked" many versions of potato pancakes on the air. This is one of my own devising and it is a tried and true recipe. I developed it while living in Berlin and like to think it is quite authentic. Serve these delicate pancakes by themselves for brunch or supper with some good homemade applesauce or as a potato side dish. A food processor with a shredding disc makes this recipe very quick and easy. Don't forget the important step of squeezing the excess liquid from the raw shredded potatoes.

> 2½ lb. Idaho potatoes, peeled and shredded
> 2 large eggs
> ½ tsp. salt, or to taste
> 1 tsp. freshly ground black pepper
> 3 tbsp. flour
> ¼ cup milk
> ¼ cup finely chopped onion
> ½ cup shredded Swiss cheese
> 2 tbsp. chopped flat-leaf parsley
> Vegetable oil, for frying
> 1 recipe Homemade Applesauce (see below)

- Place the potatoes in a clean cloth and squeeze out their excess liquid. Set aside and prepare the batter.
- In a mixer or food processor, beat the eggs until frothy. Add the salt, pepper, and flour and beat well.
- Add the milk and mix well.
- Fold in the potatoes, onion, cheese, and parsley. Stir until well mixed.
- Heat about ¼ in. oil in a large, heavy skillet until very hot (but not smoking).
- Cook 1 pancake and taste and correct seasonings.
- Spoon the potato mixture into the hot oil to form pancakes about 3 in. in diameter. Cook on first side until golden brown. Turn once and brown the second side.
- Place on a baking sheet in a warm oven (175 degrees) until all of the pancakes are cooked.
- Serve hot with applesauce.
- Makes about 24 pancakes.

Homemade Applesauce

3 lb. tart cooking apples
½ tsp. lemon zest
1 cup dark brown sugar
Pinch cinnamon and nutmeg
1 tbsp. fresh lemon juice
2 tbsp. unsalted butter

- Core and peel the apples; cut into slices.
- Place with lemon zest in a large, heavy saucepan. Cook, covered, over low heat, stirring occasionally until very tender, about 30 minutes.
- Purée the apples and add the sugar, cinnamon, nutmeg, lemon juice, and butter. Cook, partially covered, over low heat for 10 minutes.
- Makes about 1 qt.

Southern Corn Pancakes

One miserable winter afternoon, we got onto a discussion of "cold-weather comfort food." A listener called in with this recipe and we were off and running. Try it and you'll see how appealing it can be when the weather is raw.

2 eggs, beaten
2 tbsp. sour cream
2 tbsp. butter, melted
1½ cups frozen corn, thawed
2 tsp. molasses
¼ cup flour
Salt and freshly ground black pepper, to taste
Clarified butter, for frying

- Combine the eggs, sour cream, melted butter, corn, molasses, flour, salt, and pepper, blending well.
- Heat the clarified butter in a heavy skillet. Ladle the batter in to make small pancakes.
- Keep warm in a 200-degree oven until all pancakes are made.
- Serve with Homemade Applesauce (see above) and sour cream.
- Serves 8.

Lemon-Basil Risotto Cakes

We've spent several shows talking about the wonderful Italian rice dish, risotto. One day I commented that I dearly loved rice cakes made with leftover risotto, and very shortly a good listener called in with this tasty recipe. The instructions here walk you through the full process of making a good risotto.

**2 cups chicken broth
3 tbsp. extra-virgin olive oil
¼ cup finely chopped shallots
1 tsp. lemon zest
1 cup uncooked arborio rice
1 cup dry white wine (Sauvignon Blanc)
¼ cup shredded Parmigiano-Reggiano
Salt and freshly ground black pepper, to taste
2 tbsp. shredded basil**

- Bring the broth to a simmer in a small saucepan.
- Heat 1 tbsp. oil in a heavy saucepan over medium heat. Sauté the shallots, stirring, until softened. Stir in the lemon zest and rice and stir for a minute to coat the rice with the oil.
- Add just enough hot broth to barely cover the rice. Cook over medium heat, stirring, until all of the broth is absorbed. Add the remaining broth, stirring until absorbed.
- Add the wine. Stir until it is absorbed.
- Total cooking time should be 18 to 20 minutes.
- Remove from the heat and stir in the cheese, salt, pepper, and basil.
- Chill until cold.
- Remove from the refrigerator and form into patties about 3 in. wide and ¼ in. thick.
- Heat the oven to 200 degrees.
- Heat the remaining oil over medium heat in a heavy skillet. Brown the cakes on both sides and place on a baking sheet. Place in the oven for a few minutes, or until warm through, before serving.
- Serves 6-8 as a side dish or first course.

Bruce's Popovers

Every week on the show there are new callers and new names. On the other hand, there are some names that appear on my monitor almost every Saturday. Bruce is one of them. He is a professional computer person and has established himself as the official "Cooking with Marilyn!" research department. He can always be counted on to supply our audience with high-tech information straight from the Internet. But Bruce is also a fine cook and he has shared many excellent recipes with us. This is a good example. It is an easy, foolproof popover recipe. Try it for Sunday brunch.

3 eggs
1 cup milk
3 tbsp. vegetable oil
1 cup sifted flour
½ tsp. salt

- Put all of the ingredients into a blender jar in the order listed.
- Blend on high speed for 1 minute. Stop and scrape the sides of the jar. Blend 1 minute more.
- Spray a muffin or popover pan with nonstick spray. Fill the cups ¹/₂ full.
- Place in a preheated 400-degree oven. Bake for 45 to 50 minutes.
- Makes 12 small popovers.

Chipotle Corn Bread

Here is another example of the spicy-food trend. We've baked a lot of corn bread on the radio, and the recipes that are the most fun are "jazzed up" with extra ingredients. A caller shared this one that has plenty of "jazz."

1 cup yellow cornmeal
1 cup all-purpose flour
¼ cup sugar
2 tsp. baking powder
1 tsp. baking soda
1 tsp. salt
1 cup grated Monterey jack cheese

1 cup buttermilk
3 large eggs
6 tbsp. (¾ stick) unsalted butter, melted and
   cooled
2 tbsp. finely chopped canned chipotle peppers
   in adobo*

- In a large mixing bowl, stir together the dry ingredient and cheese.
- In a separate bowl, whisk together the buttermilk, eggs, butter, and chipotles.
- Gently stir the buttermilk mixture into the dry mixture. Stir just until blended.
- Turn the batter into a well-greased 9-by-5-by-2¹/₂-in. loaf pan.
- Bake in a preheated 375-degree oven for 35 to 40 minutes or until a tester inserted into the center comes out clean.
- Cool in the pan on a rack for 15 minutes.
- Turn the bread out onto the rack and cool completely.
- Makes 1 loaf.

*Available in specialty food stores or in the Latin American/Mexican section of the grocery store.

German Pretzels

This is another good example of a recipe that reflects our local German heritage. We've gotten an amazing number of requests for pretzels over the years. It is interesting that they are still being made at home. Some require a lot of time and effort as well as hard-to-find ingredients. This recipe is relatively simple and got rave reviews for flavor.

1⅓ cups warm water (105-115 degrees)
2 tbsp. butter, softened
1½ tbsp. sugar
¾ tsp. salt
1 pkg. dry yeast
3½-4 cups flour
2 tbsp. baking soda
4 cups boiling water
Coarse salt

- In a mixer fitted with a dough hook, blend together the water, butter, sugar, salt, yeast, and enough flour to make a firm dough.
- Remove the dough to a greased bowl, turning to grease the top. Cover and allow to rise in a warm place until doubled.
- Punch down the dough. Pinch off pieces and roll with the palms of your hands into strips. Form the strips into pretzels. Place them on a greased baking sheet, cover, and allow to rise until doubled.
- Dissolve the baking soda in the pot of boiling water.
- Using a slotted spoon, dip each pretzel into the boiling water for a few seconds.
- Place the boiled pretzels on a greased baking sheet and sprinkle with the coarse salt.
- Bake in a preheated 475-degree oven for 12 to 15 minutes or until golden brown.
- Serve warm.
- Makes 12 large pretzels.

Reuben Pie

One day we got off on a "Reuben" discussion on the air. Someone called about a Reuben pie with the same flavors as the famous sandwich, a favorite in an area with such a strong German heritage. Then several people called in with their own recipes. This one was a particular favorite. It is fun and tasty, just the thing to have in the refrigerator to heat up and serve to the card players or after a football game, or just to eat while you're listening to the radio.

> **1 lb. fresh sauerkraut, rinsed and squeezed dry**
> **2 medium tomatoes, sliced ¼ in. thick**
> **3 tbsp. Thousand Island dressing**
> **1 lb. fully cooked smoked sausage, sliced**
> **8 oz. Swiss cheese, shredded**
> **2 tbsp. butter or margarine, melted**
> **10 crisp rye crackers, crushed**

- Spread the sauerkraut in a 9-in. round, glass pie plate.

- Top with the tomatoes and drizzle over the dressing.

- Cover with the sausage.

- Sprinkle with the cheese.

- Bake in a preheated 425-degree oven for 15 minutes.

- Drizzle the butter over the crackers and mix well.

- Remove the dish from the oven and sprinkle with the cracker mixture.

- Return to the oven for 10 to 15 minutes more.

- Cut into wedges to serve.

- Serves 4 as a main course or 8 as an appetizer.

Macaroni and Cheese

I reckon America's most beloved pasta dish has to be macaroni and cheese. We've talked about numerous versions of it over the years on my show. As I have often indicated on the air, this one is my favorite. I like the creamy cheese sauce based on a flavored béchamel (or white) sauce. Notice that this recipe calls for infusing the milk with extra flavor, making a wonderfully tasty béchamel sauce that you can use anytime a recipe calls for a béchamel or white sauce.

I have to dedicate this to my glamorous friend and fashion expert, Bette Sherman, who often listens to the show but seldom follows my cooking advice. She does, however, absolutely adore a good mac 'n' cheese.

3 cups milk, regular or 2 percent
1 small onion, quartered
1 bay leaf
2 sprigs parsley
½ tsp. dried oregano leaves
1 tsp. whole black peppercorns
6 tbsp. butter or margarine
6 tbsp. flour
1 lb. cheddar, shredded (4 cups)
Salt and hot pepper sauce, to taste
8 oz. elbow macaroni, cooked according to pkg.
   directions, drained

- Pour the milk into a nonreactive saucepan. Add the onion, bay leaf, parsley, oregano, and peppercorns. Heat until scalded. Remove from the heat and allow to sit for 30 minutes.

- Strain the milk, return to the pan, and reheat to scalding.

- In a medium, heavy saucepan, melt the butter or margarine.

- Stir in the flour. Cook over medium heat, stirring constantly, for 2 to 3 minutes without browning.

- Pour in the hot milk. Whisk until the mixture bubbles and thickens.

- Remove from the heat and stir in 3 cups cheese, stirring until melted.

- Season the cheese sauce with salt and hot pepper sauce.

- Fold in the cooked macaroni.

- Pour into a greased 1¹/₂-qt. casserole. Top with remaining cheese.

- Bake in the center of a preheated 350-degree oven for 25 to 30 minutes or until bubbly.

- Serve immediately.
- Serves 8.

Mustard and Herb Chicken

Marinades and flavor rubs are always a hot topic on my show and we spend a lot of time talking about them. Here's one especially for chicken that I got from a good listener. It is a chicken dish for all seasons. In the summertime, use the fresh herbs and grill it outdoors. In winter, convert it to the dried-herb version and broil it indoors. It's delicious both ways!

¾ cup Dijon mustard
3 cloves garlic, finely chopped
1 cup red-wine vinegar
2 tbsp. fresh lemon juice
½ tsp. salt, or to taste
1½ tsp. coarsely ground black pepper, or to taste
1½ cups extra-virgin olive oil
3 tbsp. chopped fresh tarragon (or 1 tbsp. dried)
2 tbsp. chopped fresh thyme (or 2 tsp. dried)
3 tbsp. chopped fresh parsley
4 small, broiler-sized chickens, halved (or 8
    chicken breasts)

- Place the mustard, garlic, vinegar, lemon juice, salt, and pepper in a blender or food processor. Process until well mixed.
- With the motor running, slowly pour in the olive oil, processing until all of the oil is incorporated.
- Add the herbs and pulse on and off to chop for just a few seconds.
- Place the chicken in a shallow glass or ceramic dish.
- Pour over the marinade.
- Cover and chill for at least 8 hours or as long as 24 hours.
- Remove the chicken from the marinade.
- Bake, broil, or grill the chicken until done.
- Serves 8.

Chicken Paprika with Fresh Broccoli and Parsley Noodles

This recipe came from a cooking class I taught in one of my favorite grocery stores, a loyal sponsor of my show. It is a very attractive "dinner in a dish" and can be quickly tossed together. It's elegant enough for company and a good way to get the family to eat their broccoli, too.

> **2 lb. boneless and skinless chicken breasts**
> **Salt and freshly ground black pepper, to taste**
> **½ cup flour**
> **2 tsp. paprika**
> **¼ cup vegetable oil**
> **1 medium yellow onion, thinly sliced**
> **1¼ cups chicken broth**
> **1 cup sour cream (regular or reduced fat)**
> **1 large bunch fresh broccoli**
> **1 recipe Parsley Noodles (see below)**
> **Parsley sprigs, for garnish**

- Wash, pat dry, and trim the chicken. Flatten to uniform thickness between 2 sheets of plastic wrap.

- Cut, crosswise, into ½-in. strips.

- Salt and pepper the chicken.

- Mix together the flour and paprika. Dredge the chicken in the flour mixture to coat lightly.

- Heat the oil in a large, heavy skillet until very hot.

- Quickly sauté the chicken, about 3 minutes, turning once.

- Using a slotted spoon, remove the chicken to a side dish.

- In the remaining oil (adding a bit more if necessary), sauté the onion, stirring, until tender.

- Pour in the chicken broth and cook over high heat for 5 minutes, stirring.

- Whisk in the sour cream.

- Return the chicken and cook just until the chicken is heated, 2 or 3 minutes.

- Taste and correct seasonings.

- Wash the broccoli and cut into florets, leaving a couple of inches of the tender stem attached.

- Steam in a steamer or in the microwave for 3 to 5 minutes, or until crisp-tender. Salt lightly to taste.
- Make the noodles according to the following recipe.
- Spoon the chicken over the noodles and arrange the broccoli around the noodles. Garnish with parsley sprigs.
- Serves 6-8.

Parsley Noodles

12-oz. pkg. egg noodles
2 tbsp. butter or margarine
Salt and freshly ground black pepper, to taste
½ cup chopped fresh parsley
2 tsp. chopped fresh dill (or ½ tsp. dried)

- Cook the noodles according to the package directions.
- Drain and return to the warm pot. Toss in the butter or margarine until melted.
- Season with salt and pepper. Toss in the parsley and dill.
- Serve immediately.
- Serves 6-8.

Marla's Chicken Salad

I've often said that chicken salad has to be the most popular main-dish salad. I don't have statistics to prove that, but my listeners certainly make a lot of chicken salads. This simple one appealed to many of them. It is so basic yet filled with good flavor, and the chicken breasts turn out to be very tender.

3 boneless and skinless chicken breast halves
1 tsp. salt
1 Granny Smith apple, peeled and finely chopped
1 tsp. fresh lemon juice
Hot pepper sauce, to taste
1 green onion, finely chopped
¾ cup mayonnaise

- Rinse, trim, and flatten the chicken. Place in a saucepan and cover by 2-3 in. water. Add the salt. Put a tight-fitting lid on the pan and bring to a rolling boil. Remove from the heat and allow to sit for 20 minutes.

- When the chicken is cool enough to handle, remove to a cutting board and chop finely. Put into a bowl and add the remaining ingredients.
- Taste and correct seasonings.
- Serves 4-6.

Bacon and Tomato Spaghetti

Like many of the recipes in my radio file, this one has no identifying name on it. So, I don't know who first contributed it, but what a great idea! It borrows one of our favorite flavor combinations from the popular sandwich for a good spaghetti dish. This recipe can also be put together very quickly for an easy, but filling, supper. Use some good, thick-sliced, flavorful bacon for the best results.

     8 strips bacon, diced
     ¼ cup vegetable oil
     1 large onion, chopped
     2 large stalks celery, chopped
     1 clove garlic, finely chopped
     ⅔ cup dry white wine
     **5 large tomatoes, peeled, seeded, and coarsely
       chopped**
     2 tbsp. tomato paste
     1 tsp. dried oregano leaves
     Salt and freshly ground black pepper, to taste
     1 lb. spaghetti
     6 oz. shredded Parmigiano-Reggiano
     2 tbsp. chopped flat-leaf parsley

- In a heavy skillet, brown the bacon. Remove with a slotted spoon. Pour off the fat.
- Add the oil to the skillet and heat until hot.
- Sauté the onion, celery, and garlic, stirring, for 5 minutes.
- Add the wine and cook over high until the liquid is reduced to about 1 tbsp.

- Stir in the tomatoes, tomato paste, and oregano. Reduce to low and simmer, uncovered, for 15 minutes, stirring occasionally.
- Season with salt and pepper and add the bacon to the sauce.
- Meanwhile, cook the spaghetti according to package directions, until tender but still firm. Drain.
- Toss the spaghetti into the sauce along with the cheese and parsley.
- Serve immediately.
- Serves 6-8.

Tuna Spaghetti

Pasta recipes are always much in demand, a trend that has steadily grown and certainly seems not to be slowing down with my listeners. We talked about this pasta recipe one day when someone called to request a spaghetti dish other than the usual one with tomato sauce and meatballs. It is one of my favorite "pantry shelf" recipes. Except for the fresh vegetables and herbs, you can keep these ingredients on hand in your pantry. In a pinch, you can substitute canned and/or dried ingredients for all of those items and get a quick meal together without going to the store.

¼ cup extra-virgin olive or vegetable oil
10 green onions, chopped
3 cloves garlic, finely chopped
4 medium tomatoes, peeled, seeded, and diced
¾ cup chopped parsley
2 tsp. shredded fresh basil (or 1 tsp. dried)
2 tsp. chopped fresh oregano (or 1 tsp. dried)
2 7-oz. cans tuna, drained
2 tbsp. fresh lemon juice
Salt and freshly ground black pepper, to taste
1 lb. spaghetti, cooked al dente
½ cup grated Parmigiano-Reggiano, or to taste

- Heat the oil in a large skillet.
- Add the onions and garlic and sauté over medium heat for 5 minutes.

- Add the tomatoes, parsley, basil, and oregano. Cook for 2 minutes, uncovered, over high heat, stirring occasionally.
- Add the tuna and lemon juice and stir just until hot.
- Season with salt and pepper.
- Place the spaghetti in a large heated bowl. Pour over the sauce and sprinkle in the cheese. Toss until mixed.
- Serve immediately.
- Serves 6-8.

Russ's Butter-Maple Leeks

This is a recipe that Russ Wiles created especially for his wife, Connie, on his charcoal grill. Don't even try to imagine what this rather unusual combination of flavors tastes like. Just try it. You'll be glad you did.

4 medium leeks
4 tbsp. butter
2 tbsp. real maple syrup
Salt and freshly ground black pepper, to taste

- Cut the roots off the leeks. Peel away the outside tough layers. Cut off the tough green ends, leaving the tender green parts.
- Slit the leeks, lengthwise, cutting $^{3}/_{4}$ of the way through.
- Wash thoroughly by submerging the leeks into a sink of lukewarm water and soaking. Then, hold under a steady stream of water and be sure that all of the grit is washed from between the layers.
- Cut the leeks in half, crosswise.
- Place each half in a sheet of heavy-duty aluminum foil with the cut side up.
- Cut the butter into thin slices and insert it into the leeks.
- Lightly drizzle the maple syrup over the butter.
- Season with a generous amount salt and pepper.
- Enclose each leek in its sheet of foil, sealing all of the edges well.
- Place on a hot grill. Cook for 10 minutes. Turn and cook about 10 minutes longer
- Serves 8.

Exceedingly Easy Fruit Dip

If I had an award for the shortest and simplest recipe called into the show, this one would surely be the winner. There were several variations when I got a request for a fruit dip, but this one was requested the most often. A number of folks said they use it for fresh strawberries. It makes an easy, but festive dessert, especially when the huge strawberries with stems are in the market.

8 oz. cream cheese, softened
7-oz. jar marshmallow cream

• Beat together with an electric mixer until fluffy.

No-Eggs Key Lime Pie

Other than recipes and general cooking information, one topic we often discuss on the show is food safety. In that category, the question most often asked is probably about eating raw eggs. Of course, it is not recommended practice, and when I tell callers that, they often express distress because they are about to make a delicious dessert that contains raw eggs. Often that dessert has been the perennially popular lemon or lime icebox pie. To solve the problem, a good Samaritan called in to share her recipe for a similar pie but without the eggs. It was a hit and we talked about it repeatedly in the weeks that followed. To make this creamy creation prettier, garnish it with thin slices of lime on the whipped-cream topping.

8 oz. cream cheese, softened
14-oz. can sweetened condensed milk
½ cup real key lime juice
½ tsp. vanilla
1 recipe Crumb Pie Crust (see below)
Sweetened whipped cream or topping

• Beat together the cheese and milk until smooth.
• Stir in the lime juice and vanilla, stirring until well mixed and smooth.
• Pour into the crust and chill until firm.
• Spread with whipped cream or topping before serving.
• Makes 1 9-in. pie.

Crumb Pie Crust

1½ cups graham-cracker crumbs
¼ cup sugar
6 tbsp. melted butter or margarine

- Stir together all of the ingredients until well blended.
- Press into a 9-in. pie pan, pressing firmly on the bottom and sides of the pan.
- Bake for 6 minutes in a preheated 375-degree oven.
- Cool and fill.
- Makes 1 9-in. pie crust.

Black Bottom Pecan Pie

There are times, such as the holiday baking season, when decadent desserts abound on the show. Just when I think they can't get any richer or sweeter, we get a recipe like this one. It got rave reviews from those who tried it. I, too, must admit that it is quite tasty. So if you're trying to gain weight, try it. The filling is quickly assembled and is best when made ahead of time. Seriously, this pie makes an ideal indulgent holiday dessert.

4 oz. sweet German chocolate
2 tbsp. butter
1 unbaked 9-in. pie shell
1 cup dark corn syrup
½ cup sugar
3 eggs, beaten
1 tsp. vanilla
1¼ cups pecan halves

- Break the chocolate into pieces.
- Put into a small, heavy saucepan and add the butter. Melt together over very gentle heat and whisk into a smooth, shiny mixture.
- Drizzle into the bottom of the pie shell. Spread evenly with a spatula.
- With an electric mixer, beat together the corn syrup, sugar, eggs, and vanilla. Beat until mixture is smooth.

- Stir in the pecans and pour into the pie shell.
- Bake in the lower third of a preheated 350-degree oven for 1 hour or until the filling is puffed and golden brown.
- Cool completely before slicing.
- Makes 1 9-in. pie.

Homemade Dog Biscuits

I've often said the radio show offers something for everyone. One cold winter day, I received a request for homemade dog biscuits. Someone wanted to bake these bone-shaped treats for a friend's dog as a Christmas present. (I thought it was an adorable gift idea.) I believe she had once seen such a recipe in print but couldn't locate it. Almost immediately, the phone lines filled to capacity with dog-biscuit bakers to the rescue. You will surely understand that I could not resist including this recipe as a finale to this chapter. Make up a batch for your favorite pooch.

2½ cups whole-wheat flour
½ cup powdered milk
4 tsp. beef bouillon
½ tsp. garlic salt
6 tbsp. shortening or meat drippings
1 egg, beaten
½ cup water

- In a food processor, mix together the flour, milk, bouillon, and salt.
- Add the shortening and cut in by pulsing the blade on and off.
- Add the egg and water and mix into a dough.
- Pat out dough on an oiled cookie sheet and cut with dog-bone-shaped cookie cutter. (Yes, they make them and you can find them in pet shops as well as gourmet gadget shops.)
- Bake 25 to 30 minutes at 350 degrees.
- Makes 24 small biscuits.

Sweet Treats

Life is uncertain. Eat dessert first! This is a slogan many people live by, but I've chosen to put this chapter in the traditional position as a fitting closing to my collection of recipes. Actually, I decided to call this section "Sweet Treats" because I view this batch of goodies as much more than just traditional desserts to be eaten after a meal. In England and Germany, I learned that some of the most enjoyable treats aren't even part of a meal but are best consumed in the afternoon with a cup of tea or coffee.

This collection of some good, sweet things to eat has come together from personal experiences both here and abroad. Some, as you will note, are gifts from generous recipe-sharing friends and radio listeners, and others are part of my Southern heritage. In the South, a special meal without a sweet delicacy at the end is unthinkable.

Sweets, like other foods, have their seasons. Often the ingredients dictate when to make them, such as in fresh summer-fruit desserts or those apple desserts that are at their best in the fall. You will notice, by the way, that I do have a passion for desserts with fruits and fruit flavors. In fact, as I was choosing the recipes to include here, it dawned on me that I seem to grow fonder of the simple, "real" desserts than the fancier ones that were part of my French training. I've included several of these "comfort food" favorites. Some are perfect for a snowy day and some are cooling treats for the dog days. I hope you enjoy them all.

Creamy Lemon Meringue Pie

In my opinion, it is hard to beat a good lemon dessert. I have lots of them in my cooking-class files, but this is a favorite that goes back to my Southern roots. I promise it will be a welcome treat any time of the year, but I usually think of it as perfect for a warm day. I guess it's because it reminds me of down-home church picnics and family reunions.

1 cup whole milk
1 cup sugar
¼ tsp. salt
5 tbsp. cornstarch
½ cup water
2 egg yolks
3 tbsp. butter, softened
½ cup fresh lemon juice
2 tsp. fine lemon zest
1 recipe Meringue (see below)
1 baked 9-in. pie shell (see Basic Pie Pastry
    recipe below)

- Heat together the milk, sugar, and salt in a double boiler until the milk is scalded.
- Whisk the cornstarch into the water and whisk into the milk mixture.
- Cook, stirring constantly, until the mixture thickens. Beat in the egg yolks, one at a time, and cook for 2 to 3 more minutes.
- Stir in the butter, lemon juice, and lemon zest and remove from the heat.
- Make the Meringue according to the following recipe.
- Pour the hot filling into the pie shell and top with the meringue, sealing well around the edges.
- Place in the upper third of a preheated 325-degree oven and bake for 15 minutes or until the meringue is golden brown.
- Cool and chill.
- Serves 8-10.

Meringue

3 egg whites, room temperature
½ tsp. cream of tartar
6 tbsp. sugar

- Beat the egg whites and cream of tartar in a clean, dry electric mixer bowl until frothy.
- Gradually add the sugar, beating constantly, until all sugar is incorporated and the meringue holds it shape in soft peaks. Do not overbeat.

Basic Pie Pastry

1 cup all-purpose flour
½ tsp. salt
⅓ cup vegetable shortening (Crisco), chilled
4-5 tbsp. ice water

- Pour the flour and salt into a small to medium mixing bowl.
- Add the shortening.
- With a pastry blender, or 2 table knives, cut the shortening into the flour mixture until the mixture resembles coarse meal.
- Add the ice water, 1 tbsp. at a time. Stir with a fork until all of the water is absorbed.
- Press the dough into a smooth disc. Wrap in plastic and chill for at least 1 hour in the refrigerator.
- Roll out on a lightly floured surface to a ⅛-in.-thick circle.
- Place the rolling pin at the top of the pastry circle. Roll toward you, rolling the pastry loosely around the rolling pin.
- Hold the rolling pin just above an 8- or 9-in. pie pan and quickly unroll the pastry into the pan.
- Gently press into the pan, taking care not to stretch the dough.
- Trim away the excess dough around rim, leaving about ½ to ¾ in. to roll under. Flute the dough at the rim with your fingers or press with tines of a fork.
- For an unbaked shell that is to be filled and baked, be sure there are no holes in the pastry.

Pie pastry tips:
—Measure properly. Use only dry measuring cups for the dry ingredients. Dip the cup into the flour (after you stir it, making sure it isn't packed down) and gently level the top of the cup with the back of a knife. Do not pack the flour into the cup.
—Too much flour makes pastry too dry to roll easily and creates a tough pie crust.
—Too much shortening makes it too crumbly and delicate so that it falls apart.
—Too much liquid affects the flaky texture, making it too heavy.
—Allowing the dough to rest for a couple of hours in the refrigerator makes it easier to roll. Wrap it tightly in plastic wrap before chilling.
—Always use a gentle touch when handling and rolling dough. Stretching the dough will cause it to shrink when it goes into the hot oven.

- For a shell that is baked and then filled (such as for my Creamy Lemon Meringue Pie recipe above), bake this pastry "blind" by covering it with parchment paper and filling it with metal pie weights or dry beans. (Metal pie weights are available in the gadget department of specialty kitchen shops.) Bake 10 minutes in a 400-degree oven. Remove weights or beans and bake shell until lightly browned. Or instead of using weights or beans, prick holes in the shell every half-inch or so with a fork before baking. That prevents the pastry from puffing while it is baking.
- Makes enough pastry for a single 8- or 9-in. pie crust. For a double-crust pie, double the recipe.

Summer Berry Pudding

Anyone who has dined in England will know that "pudding" there is not always the creamy dessert we think of as pudding in this country. I realized that years ago when I made my first English Christmas pudding, which was not like the pudding I knew but a moist cake. On my first trip to London, I learned that the term "pudding" is generally used for any dessert.

This "pudding" is a very popular one on English menus in the summertime when berries are in season. This dessert was one of the highlights of an extended summer vacation I took in England. This is my Americanized version. It always has fresh currants in England, but I decided not to put them in this recipe because they are so rare in most parts of our country. If you do happen to find some, please include them and use a little less of the other berries. I love this dessert on a hot summer day served as is, but a nice dollop of freshly whipped cream makes it really special company fare. For an even simpler version, substitute some good, firm, white, sliced bread (or challah) for the cake.

    1 pt. each raspberries, blueberries, and blackberries
    ³⁄₄ cup sugar
    1 recipe Cake (see below)
    Sweetened freshly whipped cream or plain
        heavy cream (optional)

- Place the berries in a colander and rinse well (not necessary to drain).
- Pour into a large, nonreactive saucepan and sprinkle with sugar.

- Allow to sit at room temperature for at least 30 minutes.
- Place over heat and bring to a boil; boil for 1 minute.
- Remove from heat and allow the berries to cool in their juice.
- Make the Cake according to the following recipe.
- Cut the cake into $1/2$-in.-thick slices.
- Completely line a 1-qt. plain mold or mixing bowl with some slices of the cake.
- Spoon in half of the fruit with the juice.
- Cover with another layer of the cake and spoon in the remaining fruit.
- Cover the top with the remaining cake.
- Place a saucer or small plate directly onto the cake and place a weight (about 2 lb.) on top of the plate.
- Place the pudding in the refrigerator for 24 hours.
- Invert the pudding onto a serving dish.
- Cut into slices to serve.
- If desired, top with cream.
- Serves 4-6.

Cake

2 large eggs, room temperature
$1/2$ cup sugar
$2/3$ cup cake flour, sifted
$1/4$ tsp. salt

- Beat the eggs with an electric mixer until fluffy.
- Add the sugar, a large spoonful at a time, and beat until mixture is very thick and pale yellow, about 10 minutes.
- Gradually and gently fold in the flour and salt.
- Grease and flour an 8-in. square cake pan.
- Pour in the batter.
- Place in the middle of a preheated 350-degree oven and bake for 20-25 minutes or until a tester comes out clean and the top is golden brown.
- Cool on a rack in pan for a few minutes.
- Invert cake onto the rack to cool completely.

Strawberry Trifle

The English have some wonderful desserts. Trifle is certainly one of the best known but is most often poorly made. Make a really good one and it is hard to beat. This is my own version, which I have adapted from many trifles sampled in England. It is such a good company dessert because it must be made hours ahead and chilled. It is adaptable, too, to other fruits or berries. In fact, many English cooks regularly use a mixture of available or seasonal fruits in this tasty sweet dish.

1 recipe Sponge Cake (see below)
1 recipe Boiled Custard (see below)
1 qt. fresh strawberries
½ cup sweet dessert sherry
1 cup good strawberry preserves
Powdered sugar
1 cup whipping cream

Wash strawberries just before using. Always wash them with stems intact, drain, and then remove stems.

- Make the Sponge Cake according to the following recipe.
- While the cake is baking, make the Boiled Custard according to the following recipe.
- Set aside enough strawberries for garnishing the top; slice the remainder.
- Cut a piece from the middle of the cake that exactly fits the top of the dish used for the trifle (a clear 2-qt. dish or bowl). Set this piece of cake aside.
- Break the remaining cake into large chunks and place in the dish.
- Sprinkle with the sherry.
- Spread with the preserves and spoon over the sliced strawberries.
- Pour over the custard.
- Top with the cut-out cake, gently pushing down so the top of the cake is even with the top of the dish.
- Sift over some powdered sugar.
- Whip the cream with 2 tbsp. powdered sugar until stiff.
- With a pastry bag fitted with a 7- to 8-mm star tip, pipe rosettes of whipped cream around edge of top.
- Top each rosette with an inverted, stemmed strawberry.
- Chill until ready to serve. Serve cold.
- Serves 8-10.

Sponge Cake

6 eggs, separated
1 cup + 3 tbsp. granulated sugar
2 tsp. vanilla
¼ tsp. salt
1½ cups sifted cake flour
6 tbsp. butter, melted and cooled

- Let the egg whites sit for at least 1 hour to come to room temperature.
- Beat them with an electric mixer in a dry, grease-free bowl until stiff.
- Gradually add 3 tbsp. sugar and beat until moist and shiny peaks form. (Do not allow to become too dry.) Set aside.
- In a separate bowl, beat the egg yolks with the vanilla and salt.
- Gradually add the remaining sugar.
- Beat until the mixture is very thick and pale yellow—8 to 10 minutes.
- Fold ¼ of the whites into the yolks.
- Sift over ¼ of the flour and fold gently.
- Repeat, adding the butter in 3 portions, until all of the mixture is folded together.
- Grease and flour a jellyroll pan.
- Pour the batter into the pan and bake in the center of a preheated 350-degree oven for 20 to 25 minutes or until it is golden brown and starts to shrink away from sides of pan.
- Cool on a rack.

Boiled Custard

6 egg yolks
¼ cup granulated sugar
Pinch salt
2 cups milk, scalded
1 tsp. vanilla

- In a heavy saucepan, beat the yolks until light and pale yellow.
- Whisk in the remaining ingredients.
- Cook, stirring constantly, over medium-low heat until custard coats a wooden spoon (should take 7 to 8 minutes).
- Cool and chill until ready to use.

Down-Home Berry Cobbler

I'm apparently not alone in appreciating this type of simple but hearty and delicious dessert. I see cobblers more and more in restaurants, including some pretty swanky ones. It is an American tradition to top warm cobbler with a large scoop of vanilla ice cream. I don't think this is any time to break with tradition.

**2 qt. fresh blackberries, raspberries, or blueber-
    ries (or mixture of all three)
4 tbsp. melted butter
2 cups all-purpose flour
2 cups sugar
4 tsp. baking powder
½ tsp. salt
2 cups milk, regular or 2 percent
Vanilla ice cream or frozen yogurt (optional)**

- Wash and stem the berries. Allow to drain thoroughly.
- Pour the butter into a 2-qt. rectangular dish.
- With an electric mixer, beat together the flour, sugar, baking powder, salt, and milk until a smooth batter forms.
- Pour into the buttered dish.
- Distribute the berries evenly over the batter.
- Bake in the center of a preheated 400-degree oven for 35 to 40 minutes or until crust is golden brown.
- Serve warm with ice cream, if desired.
- Serves 8-10.

Instead of washing delicate summer berries in water, which dilutes their flavor, use some red or white wine—a great way to use up leftover wine in any case. Put the berries in a bowl and pour over the wine. Allow the berries to sit for a few minutes. Lift out the berries with a slotted spoon, so grit remains in the bottom of the bowl, and discard the wine.

Easy Berry Summer Pie with Creamy Cheese Filling

This truly easy pie is the perfect dessert when it is simply too hot to bake. It's a light and cooling treat to serve in the middle of a hot summer afternoon or to round out a summer's lunch or supper.

> 2 cups dark chocolate wafer crumbs
> 4 tbsp. melted butter or margarine
> 8 oz. cream cheese, softened
> ½ cup powdered sugar
> 1 envelope unflavored gelatin
> ½ cup fresh orange juice
> 2 tsp. orange zest
> 1 cup sour cream*
> 1 qt. mixed berries (blackberries, blueberries, raspberries)
> ½ cup red currant jelly

- Mix crumbs and butter well and press firmly into a 9-in. pie pan.
- Place in the freezer for at least 1 hour before filling.
- Whip together the cream cheese and sugar with an electric mixer until light and fluffy.
- Soften the gelatin in the orange juice.
- Heat the mixture (in a glass measuring cup in the microwave or in a small saucepan on the stove), just until the gelatin is dissolved. Cool slightly and mix into the cream-cheese mixture along with the orange zest.
- Fold in the sour cream.
- Wash the berries and place on paper towels to dry.
- Melt the jelly in a glass measuring cup or dish in the microwave or in a small saucepan on the stove.
- Remove the crust from the freezer. Spread the filling in the crust.
- Place in the refrigerator for at least 1 hour or until the filling is set and firm. (This much may be done a day in advance.)
- Arrange the berries in an attractive pattern on top of the filling.
- Using a soft-bristle pastry brush, brush on just enough of the warm jelly glaze to coat the berries.

- Chill until ready to serve.
- Makes 1 9-in. pie.

*Yogurt may be substituted for the sour cream.

Fresh Blueberry Crumble

For those occasions when you want to make a dessert but have no time to cook, fall back on whatever fruits or berries are in season. This light summertime treat is a good choice when blueberries are abundant. I particularly like the flavor from the gingersnaps, but vanilla cookies may also be used.

> **2 pt. fresh blueberries, washed, well drained,**
> **and chilled**
> **2 cups vanilla yogurt**
> **¼ cup honey**
> **2 cups coarse gingersnap crumbs**

- Spoon the blueberries into a 1½-2-qt. glass bowl.
- With a fork, gently stir together the yogurt and honey. Divide into 8 large wineglasses. Spoon over the blueberries. Top with the gingersnap crumbs.
- May be assembled 1 hour before serving.
- Serves 8.

Easy Chocolate Tart

What I have enjoyed most about my association with the International Association of Culinary Professionals (IACP) is the fun people I've gotten to know. Beverly Gruber is high on that list. A great cook with a charming personality, Bev is a well-known cooking teacher in Seattle. This dessert is a favorite of her students. Use the best chocolate you can find for this luscious creamy tart.

> **1 recipe Sweet Tart Pastry (see below)**
> **2 eggs**
> **1 cup cream**

¼ tsp. salt
¼ cup sugar
2 tbsp. liqueur (Grand Marnier, Kahlua, Tia
  Maria, depending on desired flavor)
1 tsp. vanilla
8 oz. semisweet chocolate, cut into pieces
Chocolate shavings, for topping

- Make the pastry according to the following recipe.
- Whisk together the eggs, cream, salt, sugar, liqueur, and vanilla. Set aside.
- Put the chocolate in the bottom of the pastry shell.
- Pour the custard mixture over and bake at 375 degrees on the lower oven rack for 30 minutes.
- Transfer to the top rack for 10 minutes.
- Cool. Sprinkle with chocolate shavings for decorative topping.

Sweet Tart Pastry

1½ cups pastry flour (or unbleached flour)
½ tsp. salt
1 tbsp. sugar
1 stick (4 oz.) cold unsalted butter, cut into 8
  pieces
3-5 tbsp. ice water
1 large egg yolk

- Mix together the flour, salt, and sugar.
- Cut in the butter until the mixture resembles coarse meal. This may be done in a food processor with the cutting blade, or use 2 table knives.
- Beat 3 tbsp. water into the egg yolk and quickly mix into the dry mixture.
- Add as much of the remaining water as needed to make a dough moist enough to easily hold together. (It shouldn't be too sticky.)
- Press into a ball and then flatten into a disc; wrap in plastic and chill for at least 2 hours.
- Allow the wrapped dough to sit at room temperature until it is pliable enough to roll out.
- Roll out on a lightly floured surface into a circle about ⅛ in. thick.
- Roll the dough around the rolling pin, center the pin over the top

Always handle, form, and shape pie or tart dough with a light touch, using your fingertips and the heel of your hand. Avoid using your warm palms so as not to warm up the dough and soften the butter or shortening.

The best tool for trimming the edges of pastry is kitchen shears. It is easier to do and there is less tendency to pull and stretch the dough, which is likely when a knife is used.

of a 10- or 11-in. tart pan, and quickly unroll to cover the pan.

- Gently lift the edges and allow the pastry to fall into the pan. (Take care not to stretch or tear it.)
- Press into the pan, trim off the excess dough on the edge, and press the sides into the pan, fluting the top edge, if desired. (Tart pans with fluted sides don't require extra fluting; just press evenly into the sides of the pan.)

Pumpkin Custard Pizzelle Napoleon with a Cherry-Cranberry Sauce

Pam Sturkey certainly knows her way around a pastry kitchen. Even though I'm aware of all the awards she has won for her extraordinary sweets, I still marvel each time she creates a new dessert menu for the restaurants, "Sturkey's" and "Encore," she owns with her husband, Paul. She has earned her fine reputation for understanding flavors and knowing how to assemble beautiful, mouthwatering treats. Try this recipe featuring the traditional crisp Italian cookies instead of pumpkin pie for your next Thanksgiving feast. If this seems like a lot to do in one day, Pam tells me you can make the pizzelle batter as long as a week ahead. Cover it tightly and refrigerate until you are ready to make your cookies. If you don't have a pizzelle iron, you can substitute a thin spice cookie.

> 3 eggs
> ³⁄₄ cup sugar
> ¹⁄₂ cup butter, melted
> 1³⁄₄ cups all-purpose flour
> 2 tsp. baking powder
> ¹⁄₄ tsp. ground cinnamon
> ¹⁄₈ tsp. ground cloves
> ¹⁄₈ tsp. ground ginger
> 1 recipe Pumpkin Custard (see below)
> 1 cup heavy cream, whipped and sweetened to taste
> 1 recipe Cherry-Cranberry Sauce (see below)
> 1 recipe Rich Chocolate Sauce (see index)

- Beat together the eggs and sugar until fluffy and thick.
- Stir in the cooled butter.

- Sift together the dry ingredients and stir into the egg mixture.
- Drop by spoonfuls onto a preheated pizzelle iron. Bake until crisp. Remove and cool. Makes 24 cookies.
- Pour the prepared custard into a shallow dish. Place in a water bath with hot water halfway up the sides of the dish. Bake in a preheated 250-degree oven for 1 hour and 15 minutes. (The custard should be completely set.)
- Cover and chill until ready to serve.
- Use 2 pizzelles per serving. Put 1 on a plate and put 1 scoop custard on top. Top with 1 dollop whipped cream and then the second pizzelle. Spoon some of the fruit sauce around the plate. Finish with a drizzle of chocolate sauce on top of the pizzelle.
- Serves 12.

Pumpkin Custard

1 qt. heavy cream
¾ cup sugar
9 egg yolks
1⅓ cups pumpkin
½ tsp. ground cinnamon
¼ tsp. ground nutmeg
¼ tsp. ground ginger
¼ tsp. ground cloves
Pinch salt

- Heat the cream and sugar together in a double boiler until scalded. Do not boil. Stir occasionally to dissolve the sugar.
- With an electric mixer, beat together the egg yolks, pumpkin, spices, and salt.
- When the cream and sugar mixture is hot, remove it from the heat and slowly ladle it into the pumpkin mixture, stirring to blend.
- Cover and chill overnight.

Cherry-Cranberry Sauce

2 cups frozen sweet cherries
½ cup dried cranberries
½ cup water
⅛ cup sugar
Splash lemon juice

- Stir together all of the ingredients in a nonreactive saucepan.
- Heat on high heat to a boil. Reduce to medium and boil for 5 minutes.
- Remove from the heat and cool.
- Purée about ⅓ of the mixture and stir back into the sauce.
- Chill until ready to use.
- Makes about 2 cups.

Praline Pumpkin Cheesecake Squares

Since we are not pumpkin-pie eaters at my house, I always experiment with other pumpkin desserts for the Thanksgiving meal. This cheesecake seems to please everyone: those who think they can't have their annual feast without ending with some sort of pumpkin dessert as well as those who are not fond of pumpkin pie. Cheesecake squares also preclude a special pan, and the baking time is shorter than that of a traditional cheesecake.

> **1 lb. cream cheese, softened**
> **⅔ cup dark brown sugar**
> **⅔ cup sugar**
> **4 large eggs**
> **1 cup puréed pumpkin***
> **⅛ tsp. salt**
> **2 tbsp. flour**
> **½ tsp. ground ginger**
> **½ tsp. ground cinnamon**
> **¼ tsp. allspice**
> **36 pecan halves, lightly toasted**

- Cut the cheese into cubes and whip in a food processor or with an electric mixer.
- Beat in the sugars.
- Add the eggs and beat until the mixture is very smooth and fluffy.
- Add the pumpkin, salt, flour, and spices; beat just until blended.
- Make the crust according to the following recipe.
- Pour the filling into the cooled crust.

- Return to the 350-degree oven and bake for about 25 minutes or until set and puffed.
- Remove from the oven and spread with the topping.
- Return to the oven and bake 5 minutes longer.
- Cool on a rack.
- Lightly mark off into squares. Top each square with a pecan half.
- Chill until very cold.
- When chilled, cut into squares with a knife dipped into hot water.
- Makes 36.

*This can be made with canned pumpkin or prepared fresh pumpkin. It is relatively simple to cook fresh pumpkin. Wash the outside and cut it in half. Scoop out the seeds and place pumpkin, cut side down, on a well-greased, shallow baking pan. Bake in a 325-degree oven until the shell starts to collapse and the pulp is fork tender. Remove the cooled pumpkin from the shell. Purée, then place in a strainer and allow the excess liquid to drain off before measuring to make your recipe.

Crust

1 cup flour
¼ packed cup dark brown sugar
1 cup finely chopped pecans
1 stick (4 oz.) butter or margarine, melted

- Stir together all of the ingredients.
- Press into the bottom of a 13-by-9-in. rectangular baking pan.
- Bake for 15 minutes in a preheated 350-degree oven.
- Cool on a rack before adding the filling.

Topping

2 cups sour cream
1 tsp. vanilla
6 tbsp. sugar

- With a whisk, gently stir all of the ingredients together.

Toast pecan (or walnut) halves by spreading them in a single layer on a baking sheet. Place in a 350-degree oven for about 10 minutes (depending on size) or until hot through and lightly browned. Allow to cool completely before using.

Poached Pears with Chocolate and Caramel Sauces

Poached pears are certainly one of the best of the "easy yet elegant" desserts. They are so simple and can be poached hours ahead and left in the poaching syrup until ready to serve. I also like to serve them for an everyday light dessert with a nice wedge of blue cheese on the side. For a special dessert when you are in an indulgent mood, try this combination of two absolutely fabulous sauces, one on each side of the pear that you have elegantly peeled, leaving the stem intact. Finish with a rosette of freshly whipped cream, a candied violet, and a fresh or candied mint leaf. They'll love you for this one and it's not difficult to prepare.

6 ripe but firm fresh pears
1 cup water
1½ cups sugar
1 tsp. vanilla
2 tbsp. coarse orange zest
½ cup water
1 recipe Caramel-Orange Sauce (see below)
1 recipe Rich Chocolate Sauce (see below)
Whipped cream, for garnish
6 candied violets and 6 mint leaves, for garnish

To peel pears and apples ahead of time and prevent them from turning dark, submerge them in a small pan of water with the juice of 1 lemon squeezed into it.

- Peel the pears and slice a thin slice from each bottom so they sit up straight.

- Using a corer, remove the core from the bottom, leaving the stem intact on the top.

- Combine 1 cup water and 1 cup sugar in a saucepan and bring to a boil.

- Boil until the sugar is dissolved.

- Add the pears and simmer, partially covered, until fork tender, about 30 minutes. (Do not overcook, allowing pears to become too soft.)

- Remove from the heat.

- Add the vanilla and allow the pears to cool completely in the poaching syrup.

- To make candied orange zest, place the zest in a small saucepan and cover with some water. Bring to a boil. Strain.

- Repeat the process with some fresh water. Strain and set aside.

- Combine $1/2$ cup water and $1/2$ cup sugar in a saucepan and bring to a boil.
- Add the zest and cook for 10 minutes; allow the zest to cool in the syrup.
- Make the sauces according to the following recipes.
- Place a pear upright on each dessert plate. Carefully spoon some warm caramel sauce over one side of each pear and some warm chocolate sauce over the other side.
- Place the whipped cream in a pastry bag fitted with a large (7 to 8 mm) star tip and pipe 1 or 2 rosettes on each plate beside the pear.
- Sprinkle a few strands of the orange zest over the pears.
- Top each pear with 1 violet and 1 mint leaf.
- Serve immediately.
- Serves 6.

Caramel-Orange Sauce

1$1/2$ cups sugar
3 tbsp. Grand Marnier (or other orange liqueur or orange juice)
$1/2$ cup heavy cream

- In a very heavy skillet, heat the sugar over medium heat until it melts and turns a caramel color.
- Stir occasionally with a wooden spoon for even cooking.
- Pour in the orange liqueur.
- The mixture will harden. Heat, stirring occasionally, until it is liquid again.
- Pour in the cream and heat, stirring, until a smooth sauce forms.
- Remove from the heat, but keep warm.

Note: Sugar melts at a high temperature, so take care when handling the caramelized sugar.

Rich Chocolate Sauce

6 oz. good-quality semisweet chocolate, cut into pieces
½ cup heavy cream

- Combine the chocolate and cream in a double boiler. Heat over gentle heat until the chocolate is melted. Do not allow to boil.
- Whisk into a smooth, shiny mixture. Keep warm.

Bananas Foster

I learned to make a lot of great, rich desserts during the years I lived in New Orleans. This one remains a favorite that I enjoy every time I make it for my guests. It is simple yet elegant, and a flambé is a dramatic way to end a festive meal.

You can make this dessert ahead of time up to adding the rum. Then, at dessert time, you are ready for your dramatic presentation. Take a flambé pan on a portable burner or a chafing dish into the dining room. Finish the dish by adding the rum and flaming the bananas in front of your guests. Have the ice cream dished up into serving dishes and stored in the freezer so they can be easily arranged on a tray, and you are ready to serve this lovely dessert at the table. Be sure to dim the lights just before you flambé.

1 stick butter
½ cup dark brown sugar
4 large bananas
¼ cup banana liqueur
½ cup light rum
Vanilla ice cream

- Melt the butter in a flambe pan or a large, shallow skillet. Add the sugar and stir until it melts.
- Cut the bananas in half lengthwise and then into fourths. Add to the butter mixture and cook until coated.
- Add the liqueur and cook until bubbly.
- To flambé, pour all but a large spoonful of the rum into the banana mixture. Hold a lighted match to the spoonful until it flames. Gently lower the spoon into the mixture to ignite the

Chocolate melts at a low temperature. Overheating it while melting causes it to lose its gloss and become "grainy." Always melt it over hot, not boiling water. When using the microwave for melting chocolate, use low power. Cook a few seconds at a time, stopping and checking each time until the chocolate is soft enough to stir into a smooth mixture.

remaining rum, and stir the mixture constantly until the flame dies. (Stirring introduces more air into the mixture and causes the flame to burn longer so that more of the alcohol is burned off.)

• Serve hot over a generous scoop of ice cream per serving.

• Serves 8.

Orange-Raisin Bread Pudding

Bread pudding is another one of the desserts I learned to make in my early days of culinary training in New Orleans. It is the best way I know to use up stale French bread. But do let me encourage you to only use a coarse-textured, dry bread such as French bread for a successful bread pudding. This bread pudding is one I've developed for my cooking students and it has a particularly yummy sauce.

> 1 large loaf day-old French bread, cut into 1-in. cubes
> 4 cups milk, scalded
> 1 cup golden raisins
> 1 tbsp. orange zest
> 1 tbsp. fresh orange juice
> ⅓ cup Grand Marnier, Cointreau, or Triple Sec
> 1¼ cups sugar
> 6 large eggs, lightly beaten
> 1 tbsp. vanilla
> 1 stick (4 oz.) unsalted butter
> 1 cup powdered sugar
> 2 tsp. cornstarch

• Place the bread in a large bowl.

• Pour over the warm milk and let soak for at least 1 hour.

• Mix together the raisins, orange zest, juice, and liqueur in a small saucepan.

• Heat until boiling; remove from the heat and allow to sit for at least 30 minutes.

• Strain through a fine strainer, reserving the liquid.

• Add the raisins and zest to the bread.

- Whisk together the sugar, eggs, and vanilla.
- Pour over the bread and stir lightly to mix.
- Pour into a well-buttered 13-by-9-by-2-in. pan.
- Bake in a preheated 350-degree oven for 30 to 45 minutes.
- In a heavy saucepan, melt the butter.
- Stir in the powdered sugar and cook gently, stirring, until the sugar is dissolved.
- Stir in the reserved liquid from the raisins.
- Remove a little of the sauce and whisk into the cornstarch. Whisk into the sauce and cook, stirring, until lightly thickened.
- Serve the pudding warm with the warm sauce spooned over.
- Serves 8.

Cranberry-Apple Crisp

This is a cold-weather favorite. Use your favorite tart cooking apple or Yellow Delicious apples. Serve this dessert warm with a scoop of ice cream or a large dollop of sweetened whipped cream. For a special flavor touch, add a splash of Grand Marnier to the whipped cream.

6 large firm tart apples, cored and peeled
½ cup fresh orange juice
1 tbsp. grated orange rind
1 cup fresh cranberries
1½ cups sugar
1½ cups unbleached flour
1 cup dark brown sugar
½ cup rolled oats
¼ tsp. salt
1 tsp. ground cinnamon
½ tsp. ground nutmeg
1½ sticks (12 tbsp.) butter or margarine, softened
½ cup chopped walnuts

- Halve the apples and cut into thin slices.
- Toss the apples with the orange juice, orange rind, cranberries, and sugar.

- With a pastry blender or in a food processor with the steel blade, cut together the flour, brown sugar, oats, salt, cinnamon, nutmeg, and butter until the mixture is the texture of coarse crumbs.
- Stir in the nuts.
- Pour the apple mixture into a buttered 13-by-9-in. glass or ceramic baking dish.
- Distribute the topping evenly over the apple mixture.
- Bake in the center of a preheated 350-degree oven for 1 hour or until brown and crisp.
- Cool slightly on a rack. Serve warm.
- Serves 10-12.

Easy Apple Strudel

This is a tasty reminder that frozen phyllo dough can make any of us look like accomplished pastry chefs. Assemble this a few hours ahead, cover well, and chill. Bake just before serving and serve warm.

¼ cup brandy
1 cup golden raisins
6-8 cooking apples, peeled, cored, and thinly
   sliced
1 cup chopped pecans
1 cup sugar
½ tsp. freshly grated nutmeg
10 sheets frozen phyllo dough, thawed
1 stick (4 oz.) unsalted butter or margarine, melted
¾ cup (approximately) fine breadcrumbs
Freshly whipped cream

- Pour the brandy over the raisins and let sit for 1 hour; drain.
- Stir together with the raisins, apples, nuts, sugar, and nutmeg.
- Stack 5 sheets phyllo, brushing each sheet lightly with some butter and sprinkling each lightly with breadcrumbs before topping with the next sheet.
- Mound half of the filling across the narrow end, leaving a 4-in. border on the end and a 2-in. border on the sides.

- Fold over the sides, fold up the end flap, and roll up.
- Brush the outside with butter and cut 3 small slits in the center
- Repeat the procedure with the remaining phyllo and filling to make a second strudel.
- Place the strudels, seam sides down, on a parchment-paper-lined baking sheet.
- Bake in the center of a preheated 350-degree oven for 30 minutes.
- Allow to cool for 15 minutes before slicing.
- Serve warm topped with freshly whipped cream.
- Makes 2 strudels; each strudel serves 6.

Fried Apple Burritos

Many of us keep flour tortillas around as a regular staple these days. They are so versatile. One of my favorite ways to use them is to make this easy and delicious apple dessert. It is a great ending for a Mexican meal or to enjoy on a chilly afternoon with a cup of coffee or tea. Since these already qualify as a special, indulgent treat, I usually simply sprinkle them with powdered sugar while they are still hot, but some vanilla ice cream scooped on while they are piping hot is pretty tasty.

> **3 cups peeled, chopped cooking apples (6-8 apples)**
> **1 tbsp. lime juice**
> **1 tbsp. water**
> **½ tsp. ground cinnamon**
> **½ cup sugar**
> **1 tbsp. flour**
> **8 flour tortillas (8-10 in.)**
> **Vegetable oil, for frying**
> **Powdered sugar**

- In a small, nonreactive saucepan, combine the apples, lime juice, water, and cinnamon.
- Bring to a boil over high heat, reduce to low, and cook about 8-10 minutes or until the apples are fork tender, stirring occasionally.
- Mix together the sugar and flour.

- Stir into the apples and cook for 2 to 3 minutes.
- Remove from the heat.
- Spoon 2 tbsp. apple filling into the center of each flour tortilla.
- Fold in the sides and fold "burrito style."
- Moisten the ends to seal, and fasten with a wooden toothpick.
- Fry in 375-degree oil on both sides until puffed and golden, about 3 minutes total.
- Drain on paper towels and sift over the powdered sugar.
- Serve hot.
- Serves 8.

Caramelized Apple Tart

Here is another indulgent (but worth every calorie!) recipe I brought back from a cooking-class tour in France. This is a must for the fall apple season while the Golden Delicious apples are still crisp and tart. It is simple, too, but you can make it even simpler by using frozen puff-pastry sheets from the grocery-store freezer case.

4-5 large firm Golden Delicious apples
1 recipe Sweet Tart Pastry, before being placed in a pan (see index)
1 stick (4 oz.) unsalted butter or margarine, softened
½ cup + 2 tbsp. sugar
1 tbsp. Calvados (or Cognac)
Fresh lightly sweetened whipped cream (optional)

- Peel and core the apples; halve and cut into thin slices.
- Roll the tart dough into a 10- to 11-in. circle, using a flan ring or tart pan as a pattern.
- Place the dough circle on a large baking sheet with sides* and prick all over with a fork.
- Dot the pastry with 2 tbsp. butter and sprinkle evenly with 2 tbsp. sugar.

Dark pie pan, tart pans, and baking sheets work best because the dark color absorbs the heat and browns the bottom.

- Arrange the apple slices in an attractive, overlapping circular pattern to cover the top of the pastry.
- Blend the remaining butter with 4 tbsp. sugar and distribute evenly over the apples.
- Place in the lower third of a preheated 425-degree oven and bake for 10 minutes.
- Remove and sprinkle evenly with remaining sugar. Return to oven and bake 10 to 15 minutes longer or until golden brown.
- As soon as it is removed from the oven, lightly sprinkle with the Calvados or Cognac.
- Serve warm either plain or with the whipped cream passed around to spoon over the top.
- Serves 8.

*It is important to use a baking pan with sides for this tart, since some of the butter will cook out and should be prevented from spilling into the oven.

Terrific Tiramisu

"Tiramisu" means "pick-me-up," and when I spent the holidays in Tuscany a few years ago, it was on almost every restaurant menu. Every time I ordered it, the shape, texture, and flavor was different. A bit of research yielded this recipe. It differs from the others I tried because the egg yolks are cooked with the sugar and some of the wine in a sauce that is like a zabaglione.

> 8 oz. ladyfingers
> 1½ cups Marsala
> 4 egg yolks
> ¼ cup sugar
> 2 egg whites
> 8 oz. mascarpone cheese, room temperature
> ¼ cup brewed espresso coffee
> 1 cup heavy cream
> 2 tbsp. sugar (optional)
> Grated semisweet chocolate, for garnish

- Dip the ladyfingers into 1 cup Marsala.
- Line the bottom of a 2-qt. bowl or casserole dish with half of them. Reserve the remainder.

- Beat the yolks and ¹/₄ cup sugar in the top of a double boiler until very thick and pale yellow; whisk in remaining Marsala.
- Whisk over gently simmering water until the mixture is thickened.
- Cool by whisking over ice water.
- Beat the egg whites until stiff but still shiny, and fold into the sauce.
- Mix together the mascarpone and coffee.
- Whip the cream until stiff and sweeten with the remaining sugar, if desired.
- Cover the ladyfingers with half of the sauce, then half of the mascarpone, then half of the whipped cream.
- Cover with the remaining ladyfingers, sauce, and mascarpone.
- Finish with the cream.
- Sprinkle the chocolate over the top for garnish and chill for several hours before serving.
- Serves 8-10.

Old-Fashioned Molasses Cookies

And speaking of a "pick-me-up," here is a perfect treat for an afternoon cup of tea. I hadn't really planned to delve into my cookie file for this book, but this is a favorite "sweet treat" and it is so easy to make. All you need is a saucepan and a wooden spoon. Make a big batch of them and store them in a tin or in the freezer. They are great to have for a snack or to serve as a "side cookie" with some ice cream or fresh fruit.

    1½ sticks unsalted butter
    1½ cups sugar
    ¼ cup dark molasses
    1 large egg, lightly beaten
    2 cups all-purpose flour
    2 tsp. baking soda
    ½ tsp. ground cinnamon
    ½ tsp. ground ginger
    ¼ tsp. ground cloves
    ½ tsp. salt

- Melt the butter in a heavy saucepan over low heat; cool.
- Using a wooden spoon, stir 1 cup sugar, the molasses, and the egg into the melted butter.
- Sift together the flour, soda, cinnamon, ginger, cloves, and salt and add to the butter mixture. Mix well.
- Cover and chill for at least ½ hour.
- Shape the dough into 1-in. balls and roll each in the remaining sugar.
- Place on a lightly greased baking sheet about 2 in. apart and bake in 375-degree oven for 8 to 10 minutes.
- Cool on racks.
- Makes about 4 dozen.

Zell's De-light-ful Sponge Cake

Zell Schulman is a good friend who is always generous with her time as well as her recipes. Zell, who is also the author of Something Different for Passover (Gainesville: Triad), brought this elegant cake recipe to share with my radio listeners on a special Passover show she did for us. It is such a delicious sponge cake that I asked her to share it with you. This is a good choice for summer when you want a light cake for serving with fresh fruit.

6 large eggs, separated
8 large egg whites
1 heaping cup sugar
Juice and rind of 2 lemons
⅓ cup matzo cake meal
⅓ cup potato starch

- Put 10 egg whites in a large electric mixer bowl and 6 yolks plus 4 whites in another.
- Beat the whites on high speed until soft peaks begin to form.
- Add the sugar a little at a time, continuing to beat.
- Beat the yolk mixture until thick.
- Add the yolk mixture, lemon juice, and rind to the beaten whites, mixing well on medium low.
- Sift the cake meal and potato starch together.

- Gently fold the sifted mixture into the eggs until the meal disappears.
- Pour into an ungreased 10-in. tube pan.
- Bake for 1 hour in a preheated 325-degree oven.
- Invert the tube pan and allow the cake to cool in the pan about 30 to 45 minutes. Remove from the pan.
- Makes 1 10-in. tube cake.

Moon Cakes

The wonderful flavor of Clara Jacobs' Moon Cakes will remind you of some of those great old-fashioned desserts we've all savored. I've often said I never ate anything at Clara's house I didn't like and these little cakes are certainly included. They'll make a great addition to your holiday goodie tray. Clara cuts these, one after the other, with a small biscuit cutter to make half-moon shapes. (You can also cut them into little squares and they will still taste delicious.)

2 sticks butter
1⅓ cups sugar
1 tsp. vanilla
1 tsp. grated lemon rind
5 eggs, separated
1⅓ cups all-purpose flour
1 tsp. baking powder
¼ cup crushed English walnuts mixed with
    1 tbsp. sugar

- Cream the butter well.
- Add the sugar slowly and mix well.
- Add the vanilla and lemon rind and beat well.
- Add the egg yolks, one at a time, beating well after each addition.
- Sift the flour and baking powder together 3 times.
- Mix the flour mixture into the butter and egg mixture.
- Beat the egg whites and fold into the mixture.
- Pour into a greased and floured 13-by-9-by-2-in. pan.
- Sprinkle the nut and sugar mixture on top of the batter before baking.

- Bake in a preheated 350-degree oven for 30 minutes.
- Cool. Cut with small biscuit cutter or glass. Cut 1 round out first, then the rest will look like half-moons when you cut them.
- Makes about 24.

Cold Orange Soufflé with Almond Macaroons

I was taught by one of my French cooking teachers that a cold soufflé isn't a "true" soufflé, but we made this recipe in one of her classes anyway. It is a perfect ending for a spring or summer dinner party. It certainly looks like a real soufflé, since you build up the sides of the dish with parchment and remove it after the mixture has set. This is also a good basic recipe for almond macaroons. They are great to have on hand for special treats and when you need an easy dessert. Serve them with some sherbet or fresh fruit.

3 large eggs, separated and room temperature
⅔ cup sugar
1 tsp. grated lemon rind
Grated rind and juice of 2 large oranges
Juice of ½ lemon
¼ cup water
1 envelope unflavored gelatin
1½ cups heavy cream
8 Almond Macaroons (see below)
Extra sweetened whipped cream, for garnish
Thin orange slices, for garnish

- In the top of a double boiler, whisk together the egg yolks, sugar, lemon and orange rinds, and orange juice.
- Whisk over slightly simmering water until the mixture is thickened into a creamy custard consistency.
- Whisk over ice water until cooled.
- Mix together the lemon juice and water and soften the gelatin in the mixture.
- Heat over gentle heat (or in the microwave) until the gelatin is dissolved.

- Fold into the cool custard mixture.
- Whip the cream until soft peaks form. (Do not allow to become too stiff.)
- Fold into the custard mixture.
- Beat the egg whites in a clean, dry bowl until stiff but still shiny.
- Fold into the soufflé mixture.
- Spoon $1/3$ of the mixture into a $1^1/2$-qt. (6-cup) soufflé dish.
- Coarsely crumble the macaroons and sprinkle half of them over the mixture.
- Spread over another $1/3$ of the mixture and top with the remaining macaroons.
- Make a paper collar and place it on the dish (see tip).
- Add the remaining soufflé mixture.
- Chill for at least 4 hours.
- Remove the paper clip and untie the string. Using a flexible metal spatula, loosen the paper from the set soufflé and gently peel away the paper.
- To serve, garnish the top with puffs or rosettes of whipped cream and the orange slices.
- Serves 8.

Almond Macaroons

3 egg whites
$1/4$ tsp. cream of tartar
$2^1/4$ cups finely ground blanched almonds
$1^1/4$ cups sugar
2 tsp. flour

- Beat the egg whites with the cream of tartar in a clean, dry bowl until stiff but still shiny.
- Stir together the almonds, sugar, and flour.
- Gently fold into the egg whites.
- Drop by teaspoonfuls about 2 in. apart onto a parchment-paper-lined baking sheet.
- Bake in a preheated 300-degree oven for 20 minutes or until lightly browned.
- Makes about 24.

To make a paper collar for cold or hot soufflés, tear a sheet of parchment paper long enough to wrap around the dish and leave about 6 in. overlap. Place the paper on the counter and fold in half lengthwise. On the folded edge, fold over a 2-in. edge. Place the paper around the dish with the 2-in. fold toward the outside. Fasten at the top with a metal paper clip and tie a piece of kitchen string around the middle to hold it onto the dish.

In order to maintain a proper texture, chilled desserts containing gelatin should be served no more than 24 hours after they are made. After that they tend to become tough and rubbery.

Hot Lemon Soufflé

It just wouldn't be a complete dessert chapter for me without a hot soufflé. It is also important to include it so I can remind you that it really isn't all that difficult to make. And it is always impressive to end a meal with this delicious dish.

If you have never made one of these pretty dishes, go on and give it a try. You may be surprised at how easy it actually is. For a small group, it is the perfect dessert, light and elegant, and your guests will be so impressed.

Tips for a perfect hot soufflé:
—Classic baked dessert soufflés always use at least 2 more egg whites than yolks.
—Always allow the egg whites to come to room temperature. Beat them in a clean, dry bowl, and don't overbeat. They should be very shiny and stand only in soft peaks.
—Any adjustments in time must be made before baking, since the soufflé waits for no one. For instance, make the egg-yolk base ahead, cover, and hold. Beat the egg whites just before baking and fold the two together.
—Soufflés must be baked in a dish with straight sides.
—Start a soufflé in a hot oven (400 degrees) and lower the temperature 25 degrees after the oven door is closed.

2 tbsp. sweet butter or margarine
2 tbsp. flour
¾ cup milk
¾ cup sugar
Zest of 1 lemon
⅓ cup fresh lemon juice
5 egg yolks
Pinch salt
1 tsp. vanilla
8 egg whites, room temperature
½ tsp. cream of tartar
Freshly whipped sweetened cream

- In a heavy saucepan, melt the butter.
- Add the flour and cook over low heat for 2 minutes. (Do not brown.)
- Scald the milk and stir all but 2 tbsp. sugar into the milk.
- Whisk the milk into the flour and butter mixture (the "roux") and cook for 2 to 3 minutes, to make a smooth sauce.
- Add the lemon zest. Remove from the heat.
- Stir in the lemon juice and the egg yolks, one at a time.
- Add the salt.
- Add the vanilla.
- Beat the egg whites with the cream of tartar in a clean, dry bowl.
- Gradually add the 2 tbsp. sugar and beat until soft peaks form.
- Stir about ¼ of the whites into the sauce mixture, then fold in the rest.
- Pour into a 2-qt. soufflé dish that has been buttered, sugared, and fitted with a 2- to 3-in.-high parchment-paper collar (see tip above).

- Place in the center of a 400-degree oven. Close the oven door, turn to 375 degrees, and bake for 25 to 30 minutes or until puffed and golden.
- Remove the collar and serve the soufflé immediately with freshly whipped and sweetened cream.
- Serves 6-8.

Quick and Easy Strawberry Mousse

This instant blender dessert is perfect for a hot summer day and it can be made the last minute before the meal is served. It can be made in a food processor but works best in a blender. It goes together in a flash and is foolproof. Make it just before dinner, and when you are ready for dessert, your mousse will be ready to eat.

10-oz. pkg. frozen strawberries, packed in sugar
¼ cup milk, chilled
2 envelopes unflavored gelatin
¼ cup sugar
1 cup heavy cream, chilled
1½ cups small ice cubes or crushed ice
Fresh strawberries, for garnish

- Defrost the frozen berries and drain, reserving ½ cup juice.
- Heat the juice to a simmer.
- Pour the milk into a blender.
- Sprinkle the gelatin on top of the milk and let sit for 5 minutes to soften.
- Add the sugar.
- Pour in the hot juice and process until the gelatin is dissolved.
- Add the drained berries and process until puréed.
- Remove the center of the blender lid with the motor running and add the cream slowly, processing until all of the cream is incorporated.
- With the motor still running, add the ice cubes, a few at a time, through the center of the lid, processing on high speed until all of the ice is incorporated.
- Pour into a serving dish or individual dessert dishes.

- Chill for 30 minutes or until set.
- Garnish with berries to serve.
- Serves 6.

Spirited Chocolate Truffles

As you would expect, the holiday season is always an exciting time on a cooking show. Even the most unenthusiastic cooks are likely to go into the kitchen to whip up a festive treat. Everyone who calls my show seems to be either searching for some special recipe or, in the spirit of the season, eager to share just the perfect recipe. We have spent a considerable amount of time on the air talking about chocolate. I have never had a better chocolate truffle than this one, which was shared by a generous listener. Yes, of course, it is rich. But it's only once a year, after all. Use the best chocolate you can find for this recipe.

> 1½ **cups heavy cream**
> 1 **lb. good-quality semisweet chocolate, chopped**
>   **into small pieces**
> 6 **tbsp. unsalted butter, cut into 6 pieces**
> ¼ **cup Cognac or a liqueur like Grand Marnier,**
>   **Drambuie, or Tia Maria***
> ½ **cup unsweetened cocoa**
> 1 **cup finely chopped toasted walnuts or pecans**

- In a small, heavy saucepan, scald the cream.
- Remove from the heat and gradually stir in the chocolate until is melted.
- Add the butter, 1 piece at a time, stirring until it is melted and the mixture is smooth. (Return to gentle heat briefly if needed to melt all of the chocolate and butter.)
- Stir in the liqueur.
- Pour the mixture into a bowl. Cover the bowl with plastic wrap, positioning wrap so that it actually touches the top of the chocolate mixture.
- Seal tightly and refrigerate overnight.
- Using a teaspoon, spoon out a portion of the mixture. Grease your hands and roll the spoonful into a 1-in. ball.

- Roll in cocoa. Place on a waxed-paper-lined tray.

- Repeat the procedure once more, only rolling in nuts this time.

- Continue with the remaining mixture, alternating the coatings and placing all balls on the tray.

- Place the tray in the refrigerator. When the truffles are very cold, remove them to a tin or a plastic container with a tight cover.

- Store in the refrigerator. These truffles freeze well.

- Makes about 24.

*If you want to make alcohol-free candy, substitute 1 tbsp. good natural vanilla extract or 1 tbsp. orange juice and 1 tbsp. finely grated orange peel for the liqueur.

Double Chocolate Brownies

I don't think we've ever discussed a chocolate recipe on the show that didn't provoke a lot of interest. This brownie was particularly popular. All you chocolate lovers will see why.

> **2 sticks unsalted butter**
> **4 oz. unsweetened chocolate**
> **4 eggs**
> **2 cups sugar**
> **12 oz. chocolate chips**
> **1 cup chopped pecans**
> **1 tsp. salt**
> **1 cup flour**
> **1 tsp. vanilla**

- Melt the butter with the unsweetened chocolate; cool.

- Beat the eggs and slowly add the sugar. Continue beating until light and thick, then fold into cooled chocolate mixture.

- Fold the chocolate chips, pecans, and salt into the flour. Add to the chocolate mixture, stirring until mixed.

- Add the vanilla.

- Pour into a greased and floured 13-by-9-by-2-in. pan and bake in a preheated 375-degree oven for 40 to 45 minutes.

- Makes 30 brownies.

Christine's Baklava

Christine Chronis writes a column called "Cooking with Christine" for the Mount Desert Islander, the newspaper in the small town in Maine where she and her family go for the summer. As friends and fellow columnists, we have often shared recipes and ideas. She has also helped occasionally with my show. When she shared this fabulous authentic baklava recipe with us, it sent many people to the market to buy phyllo dough. It's somewhat time-consuming but well worth it, and one recipe makes a lot. It keeps well in the refrigerator and may be frozen.

> 1 lb. walnuts, finely ground
> ½ lb. blanched almonds, toasted and finely ground
> 1 tsp. ground cinnamon
> 2 tbsp. sugar
> 1 lb. frozen phyllo dough, thawed
> 1 lb. unsalted butter, melted
> Whole cloves

- Mix the nuts, cinnamon, and sugar. Set aside.
- Lay the phyllo flat and cover with a slightly damp cloth.
- In a buttered 13-by-9-by-2-in. baking pan, stack 10 sheets phyllo, brushing the top of each with butter before stacking.
- Butter the 11th sheet and place in the pan. Cover with a thin layer of the nut mixture.
- Repeat with 10 more buttered sheets.
- Tuck in the sides of the top sheet of phyllo and brush with butter.
- Cut the mixture into small diamond shapes by cutting on the diagonal in one direction and then in the opposite direction.
- Stick a whole clove into the center of each diamond.
- Bake for 1½ hours in a 300-degree oven or until golden and crisp.
- Meanwhile, make the syrup according to the following recipe.
- Remove the baked pastry from the oven and immediately pour over the cooled syrup.
- Serves 12-16.

Syrup

2 cups sugar
1 cup water
1 tsp. lemon juice
½ cup honey
1 whole cinnamon stick (optional)

- Combine the sugar, water, and lemon juice in a small nonreactive saucepan. Bring to a rolling boil. Reduce to simmer and cook for 8 minutes.
- Stir in the honey. Remove from the heat.
- For cinnamon flavor, break a cinnamon stick into pieces and add to the hot syrup. Remove cinnamon pieces when cool and discard.
- Cool syrup completely.

Key Lime Squares

When they are in season and available, you may want to try this with the tiny, tart key limes. I will warn you that they are a lot of work to squeeze. This recipe works fine with the bottled key lime juice, too.

3 oz. blanched almonds
2 sticks unsalted butter or margarine, softened
1 tbsp. powdered sugar
2¼ cups all-purpose flour
5 eggs
2 cups granulated sugar
¾ cup key lime juice
¼ cup powdered sugar

- Chop the almonds in a food processor.
- Add the butter, the 1 tbsp. powdered sugar, and the flour. Blend together thoroughly.
- Press the almond pastry into a greased 13-by-9-by-2-in. baking dish.
- Bake in a preheated 350-degree oven for 15 minutes.
- Remove from the oven (it will be partially baked) and reduce the temperature to 325 degrees.

- Gently stir the eggs, granulated sugar, and lime juice together. (The mixture shouldn't have much foam.)
- Pour the lime mixture over the crust and return to the oven.
- Bake at 325 degrees for 25 to 30 minutes or until the filling is set and firm.
- Cool completely.
- Cut into squares and remove from the pan. Sift over the $^1/_4$ cup powdered sugar to cover the tops.
- Makes 20 squares.

A Collection of Quick and Easy Treats

One of the most popular topics with my radio listeners has been recipes that are easy to make and especially child-pleasing. Over the past years, I have received such a wonderfully colorful array of ingenious, tasty, quick, and simple treats. So I'll end this book with a little treasury of these fun and easy sweet treats for your enjoyment.

Easy Coconut Macaroons
14 oz. flaked coconut
14-oz. can sweetened condensed milk
2 tsp. vanilla extract
1$^1/_2$ tsp. almond extract
Halved candied cherries, for tops

- In a mixing bowl, stir together the coconut, milk, and extracts, just until well blended.
- Drop by teaspoonfuls onto a well-greased baking sheet.
- Top each with a cherry half, cut side down.
- Bake in a preheated 350-degree oven for 8-10 minutes.
- Remove from the baking sheet while hot and cool on racks.
- Makes about 4 dozen.

Skillet Peanut Butter Fudge

2 cups sugar
3 tbsp. butter or margarine
1 cup evaporated milk
1 cup miniature marshmallows
12-oz. jar peanut butter (smooth or crunchy)
1 tsp. vanilla

• In a large skillet, combine the sugar, butter, and milk.

• Bring to a boil over medium heat, and boil rapidly for 5 minutes, stirring often.

• Remove from the heat.

• Add the marshmallows, peanut butter, and vanilla. Stir until the marshmallows are melted.

• Pour into a buttered 8-in. square pan.

• Chill until firm. Cut into squares.

• Makes 2 lb.

Fantastic Microwave Chocolate Fudge

4 cups sugar
14-oz. can evaporated milk
2 sticks butter or margarine, cut into 16 pieces
12 oz. semisweet chocolate pieces
7 oz. marshmallow creme
1 tsp. vanilla
1 cup chopped walnuts or pecans

• In a 4-qt. microwave-proof bowl, combine the sugar, milk, and butter or margarine.

• Place in the microwave and cook on high power for 18 to 20 minutes or until the mixture reaches the soft ball stage.* Remove and stir often while the mixture is cooking. (Watch carefully; do not allow it to boil over.)

• Stir in the chocolate and marshmallow creme until well blended.

• Add the vanilla and nuts.

• Pour into a greased 9-in. square pan.

• Chill and cut into squares.

• Makes 2 lb.

*To test for the "soft ball stage" when making candy, drop about 1/4 tsp.

into a measuring cup of cold water. If the mixture forms a soft ball, it is done. If it simply breaks up in the water, it needs to cook longer.

Yummy Chocolate Squares

12 oz. semisweet chocolate chips
1 cup crunchy peanut butter
4 cups miniature marshmallows

• Melt the chocolate with the peanut butter in a double boiler over just simmering water. Stir until smooth.
• Remove from the heat and stir in the marshmallows. The marshmallows should not melt.
• Spread the mixture into a greased 9-in. square pan.
• Place in the refrigerator and chill for at least 3 hours or until firm.
• Cut into small squares. Wrap each square individually in plastic wrap.
• Store in the refrigerator.
• Makes 36 squares.

Toffee Bars

8 oz. saltine crackers
2 sticks butter or margarine
1 cup brown sugar
12 oz. semisweet chocolate chips
1½ cups nuts

• Line a foil-covered* jellyroll pan with the crackers.
• Melt the butter or margarine in a saucepan.
• Add the sugar and cook, stirring, until dissolved.
• Spread the mixture over the crackers.
• Bake in a 375-degree oven for 5 minutes.
• Remove from the oven and sprinkle the chocolate over the crackers.
• Return to the turned-off oven just until the chips are softened.
• Spread the softened chocolate to cover the crackers.
• Sprinkle with the nuts.
• Refrigerate until the chocolate is set. Cut into bars.
• Makes 4 dozen.

*This is a good time to use nonstick foil.

Praline Grahams

12 double graham crackers
2 sticks butter or margarine
½ cup sugar
¾ cup finely chopped pecans

• Break each graham cracker into 4 rectangles. Place, side by side, in a foil-lined* jellyroll pan.

• Melt the butter or margarine.

• Add the sugar and boil for 4 minutes, stirring, until sugar dissolves.

• Pour the syrup over the crackers.

• Sprinkle with the pecans.

• Bake in a preheated 350-degree oven for 8 to 10 minutes.

• Remove the bars from the pan while hot. Cool.

• Makes 4 dozen.

*This is a good time to use nonstick foil.

Index

Honey-Lime Marinade, 180

J

Jalapeño Poppers, 219
Jezebel Sauce, 217

K

Kentucky Bourbon-Marinated Pork
  Loin, 209
Key Lime Pie, 235

L

Lasagna with Sauce Bolognese, 196
Leek Soup, 100
Lemon Meringue Pie, 241
Lemon-Basil Risotto Cakes, 223
Lemon-Mint Pork Loin, 186
Light Basil Vinaigrette, 154
Light Béchamel Sauce, 151
Light Vinaigrette Dressing, 157
Lime-Cilantro Corn Salsa, 66
Lime-Cilantro Marinade, 164
Lime-Cilantro-Marinated Salmon, 163
Lime-Macadamia Dressing, 85

M

Macaroni and Cheese, 228
Meatloaf, 148
Mediterranean Fish Fillets, 193
Mexican Appetizer Pizzas, 60
Mexican Rice Pilaf, 139
Midnight Marinade, 179
Minestrone alla Genovese, 114
Mixed Bean Salad, 77
Molasses Cookies, 264
Moon Cakes, 266

Mornay Sauce, 34
Muffins, 43, 44
Musakhan, 205
Mushroom Velvet Soup, 109
Mustard and Herb Chicken, 229
Mustard Sauce, 54
Mustard Vinaigrette, 91

O

Omelets, 21
Orange Soufflé with Almond Macaroons,
  267
Orange-Basil Pork Tenderloin, 147
Orange-Raisin Bread Pudding, 258
Oyster and Artichoke Casserole, 192
Oyster and Chicken Gumbo, 131
Oysters Rockefeller, 49

P

Parmesan Rounds, 59
Parsley Noodles, 230
Parsley Soup, 103
Party Fajitas, 184
Pâté, 53
Pâte à Chou, 31
Pâte Brisée, 27
Pea Soup, 106
Peachy Pineapple Salsa, 187
Pears with Chocolate and Caramel
  Sauces, 255
Pecan Pancakes, 45
Pita Bread, 154
Pizza Crust, 145
Pizza Sauce, 61, 144
Poached Eggs, 19
Popovers, 224
Pork and Beef Enchiladas, 212